SCOTTISH SPORTING LEGENDS

Robert Philip is an award-winning sports journalist with 30 years' experience on Fleet Street, including 15 years as the chief sports columnist on the *Daily Telegraph*. He worked with Nick Faldo and Sandy Lyle on their autobiographies.

SCOTTISH SPORTING LEGENDS

Robert Philip

MAINSTREAM
PUBLISHING

EDINBURGH AND LONDON

This edition, 2012

Copyright © Robert Philip, 2011

First published in Great Britain in 2011 by
MAINSTREAM PUBLISHING COMPANY
(EDINBURGH) LTD
7 Albany Street
Edinburgh EH1 3UG

ISBN 9781780575544

All picture section images © Getty Images

A catalogue record for this book is available
from the British Library

Printed in Great Britain by
CPI Group (UK) Ltd, Croydon, CR0 4YY

1 3 5 7 9 10 8 6 4 2

CONTENTS

FOREWORD

In boxing terms, Scotland has always punched way above its weight in sport. For a small nation of around five million souls, we have never been short of sporting legends.

Each of us reveres our own heroes; as a football manager, Jock Stein towered above all others in my opinion. As wise as he was modest, the Big Man luxuriated in the deeds of his Lisbon Lions, while being at pains to minimise his own role in their many great triumphs. Jock could happily talk for hours about his players without ever suggesting that it was his football genius which turned a motley group of individuals drawn exclusively from the west of Scotland into the best team in the world. He was the master tactician but you would never know that from listening to the man.

When I took Aberdeen to the European Cup-Winners' Cup final against Real Madrid in Gothenburg in 1983, I invited Jock – who was then manager of Scotland – to accompany us to Sweden as an 'adviser'. Typically, he offered a fund of advice without ever pushing himself to the front. It was Jock who suggested that I buy the Spanish champions' coach, the great Alfredo Di Stefano, a bottle of expensive malt whisky as a gift. 'Make him feel important,' Jock told me. 'Make him feel that you're thrilled just to be in the final, that you're only there to make up the numbers.'

As a player, I like to think I knew a little bit about the business of scoring goals, which is why Denis Law was another of my idols. In the blue of Scotland or the red of Manchester United, whenever Denis took possession of the ball it was *showtime*! You could feel the ripple of anticipation spread across the terracing.

What a lot of people don't remember is that I almost replaced Denis in the team that beat World Cup winners England 3–2 at Wembley in 1967 when I was named in the squad. Denis was really doubtful with injury but, as we all know, he was declared fit at the last minute and scored the first goal. Given his performance that unforgettable afternoon, which I watched from my seat beneath the twin towers, perhaps it is just as well that he recovered in time to play in the Not-The-World-Cup-Final

7

and that the name A. Ferguson (Dunfermline Athletic) was missing from manager Bobby Brown's teamsheet.

Maybe it was the era into which I was born but I've always admired boxers, people like Sugar Ray Robinson, Rocky Graziano, Roberto Durán – hard, hard fighting men who came out of the ghettos to forge a new life. I have always felt there was something intrinsically Scottish about Muhammad Ali, the greatest sportsman of all time, no question. The word *gallus* might have been invented with him in mind. I met him only once, by which time he was suffering badly from Parkinson's, but it was a great thrill nonetheless. He had an aura about him you could almost touch, a fabulous personality, and if you want to know what part psychology plays in sport, then just look to Muhammad Ali – he was a master of it before anyone else had even thought about it. He and Jock Stein would have got on famously. I can remember going along to Green's Playhouse in Glasgow – which was the biggest cinema in Europe – at about three o'clock in the morning to watch the Rumble in the Jungle live on the big screen.

I was too young to appreciate the many victories of Benny Lynch but I have read everything I can about the fighting bantam from the Gorbals ghetto. As a Glaswegian, I took great pride in his achievements, while mourning his downfall. And what of Ken Buchanan, arguably Britain's greatest-ever fighter? The proudest of Scots, Ken left no one in doubt where he hailed from by fighting in his Buchanan tartan shorts in boxing rings all over the world, including Madison Square Garden.

Golf is another passion – albeit a mightily frustrating one – of mine; like millions of others, I sat up until the early hours of the morning to witness Sandy Lyle win the 1988 Masters at Augusta three years after he had won the Open Championship at Royal St George's. Sandy is the walking lie to the old adage that 'nice guys never win'.

But sport can be mercilessly cruel at times and it is one of golf's great injustices that Colin Montgomerie has never won a major. He's won everything else, mind you, and Monty's leadership of the European team at Celtic Manor in 2010 was the stuff of legend. For once, I was not too aggrieved when Manchester United failed to lift the 'Team of the Year' trophy at the BBC Sports Personality of the Year awards. (After all, we did win it in 1999 . . .)

Books such as this must always be subjective and no doubt some of your personal favourites may be missing from these pages. And so it says much about Scotland's rich history that the names you will not read about include: John Greig and 'Wee' Willie Henderson . . . Alex McLeish and Willie Miller . . . Danny McGrain and David Hay . . . the majestic John White, who was killed by a lightning bolt at the peak of his career, and Martin Buchan . . . Ryder Cup-winning captain Bernard Gallacher and Brian Barnes, who beat the mighty Jack Nicklaus twice in one day in singles play during the 1975 Ryder Cup at Laurel Valley . . . athletes Yvonne Murray and Ian Stewart . . . Jim Watt, a world champion in the boxing ring . . . John Higgins, four times world champion on the snooker table . . . the late Colin McRae, a world champion in motor-rallying – giants all in their respective sports. More than enough, perhaps, for a *Scottish Sporting Legends Volume II*.

And so to borrow the words of Robert Burns, an expert on the curling rink by all accounts, here's tae us, wha's like us?

Sir Alex Ferguson OBE, CBE

1. TOMMY ARMOUR

Golf

Born: Edinburgh, 24 September 1894
Died: Larchmont, NY, 11 September 1968

CAREER:
Major championships (3)
    US Open 1927
    US PGA 1930
    Open Championship 1931
US PGA Tour victories: 25

Tommy Armour was but a lad of 21 when he was blinded in both eyes and sustained serious injuries to the head and left arm during a mustard gas attack at Passchendaele. The young Tank Corps Staff Major was fortunate; around 700,000 were killed on that same battlefield during those woebegone winter months of 1917.

Despite his tender age, Armour was already a highly decorated veteran of the First World War. While still a teenager, he had captured a German tank single-handedly; when the tank commander ignored the invitation to surrender peacefully, given the enclosed confines of the cockpit, Armour was forced to strangle his captive to death: an act of raw courage that earned him a personal audience with George V when the king made a morale-boosting visit to the trenches.

When he was released from hospital with metal plates pinning his skull together and having regained the sight in his right eye (he would remain all but blind in the left), Armour, who had been introduced to golf by his elder brother, Sandy, at the age of four, joined Lothianburn Golf Club near the family home on the outskirts of Edinburgh to rebuild his strength and hasten his convalescence. He also took a wife, Consuelo Carreras, whom he had known since his student days at Edinburgh University, where he studied mathematics after leaving Fettes College.

In 1920, Armour won the French Amateur Championship, following which, like many of his generation who had lived through the horrors of war, he decided that life should be about pursuing pleasures and that the most delicious pleasures were to be found in America.

On board the liner taking him across the Atlantic, Armour fell into the company of Walter Hagen, a kindred spirit in the belief that if a thing – such as drinking and womanising, for example – is worth doing, then it is worth doing to excess. When asked to put together an identikit of the 'perfect golfer' – this being in the time before Tiger – Seve Ballesteros opted for Jack Nicklaus's driving, Nick Faldo's long irons, Lee Trevino's chipping, Ben Hogan's putting, Arnold Palmer's charisma and 'Walter Hagen's ability to play with a large Scotch on the rocks in one hand and a cigarette in the other'. In Tommy Armour he found an enthusiastic pupil both on and off the golf course.

Hagen won eleven 'majors' (four Open Championships, five US PGA titles and two US Opens) in an era before the Masters and had he not worked so hard at having fun – 'Don't hurry, don't worry, you're only here for a short visit so be sure to smell the flowers along the way' – he might have been remembered as the greatest of them all. But time spent on the practice ground was time away from the company of his like-minded Hollywood cronies or the Prince of Wales (the future Edward VIII whom he delighted in calling 'Eddie'), gaining renown as the first professional golfer to earn a million dollars 'and spend two million'.

When Armour fell under Hagen's influence, The Haig was returning from the Open at Deal, where the professionals had been banned from the clubhouse by the snooty members of the day. Hagen responded to the ruling by booking a suite at the Ritz and commuting between London and the Kent coast in a Daimler limousine complete with liveried footman. The car was then parked in front of the clubhouse window through which the crusty members were able to see the millionaire playboy ('I never wanted to be a millionaire, I just wanted to live like one') being ostentatiously served a five-course lunch on the most delicate bone china and vintage wines in the finest crystal.

When the throat cancer that was to kill him was diagnosed in 1965, Hagen lost his voice after his larynx had been removed. He did not, however, lose his spirit. Accompanied by his only son, Walter Jr, Hagen had insisted on stopping off in ten bars on his way to hospital for the operation. 'He was loaded by the time we finally got Dad inside,' recalled the younger Hagen, 'and I'll be damned if he didn't make a pass at the nurse.'

On arrival in New York, Armour flourished under the patronage of his new friend, who not only introduced him to a band of fellow rabble-rousers, including Errol Flynn, Douglas Fairbanks Sr and NY Yankees' home-run king Babe Ruth, but fast-tracked him into the job as secretary at the luxurious Westchester Biltmore Country Club, which was about to open.

Granted US citizenship in 1922 – by which time he had become a redoubtable force on the amateur circuit – Armour turned professional two years later, whereupon he was promptly dubbed 'the Silver Scot' because of his hair colouring – American newspapers have never been able to resist the lure of bestowing nicknames upon the nation's leading sports celebrities. Armour marked his rookie season with victory in the Florida West Coast Open, then claimed his first major by winning the US Open at Oakmont in 1927, a year in which he also recorded four other victories on the US Tour, including the prestigious Canadian Open.

Oakmont was in bestial mood that summer, the rough voraciously devouring errant tee shots, the bunkers rendered virtually unplayable by the driving rain, and one by one the leading challengers – Hagen, Bobby Jones and Gene Sarazen – slipped out of contention. English-born Texan Harry Cooper set a clubhouse total of 301, a remarkable score given the conditions, then sat back to enjoy the mayhem on the closing holes.

When Armour took a seven at the 670-yard twelfth, leaving him to cover the final six holes in one under par to force a play-off, Cooper slipped away to change clothes for the trophy presentation. Already penning the speech of a gracious runner-up in his mind, the seemingly carefree Armour parred the next five holes to arrive on the eighteenth tee requiring a birdie three to force a tie. A 250-yard drive down the middle of the fairway followed by a glorious three-iron to ten feet from the pin and a nerveless putt assured the gallery of an eighteen-hole shoot-out the following afternoon. 'A miracle,' opined the legendary sportswriter Grantland Rice.

Cooper's blithe assumption that it had been time to go and wash his hands in preparation to take possession of the trophy did not sit well with the refined Pennsylvanians, who gave him an icy reception on the first tee of the play-off. 'It was emphatically an Armour gallery,' reported *The Scotsman*. 'Armour was the public's choice. It seemed that Cooper's chesty attitude did not appeal to Pittsburgers. Everybody in that huge crowd was neutral – they didn't care how many strokes Armour won by.' He won by three, as it happens – 76 to 79.

Armour would gather only two further majors: the 1930 US PGA title (then a match-play event) at the Fresh Meadow Country Club in upstate New York, where he beat Sarazen on the last green of their 36-hole final, and, most personally satisfying of all, the 1931 Open Championship at Carnoustie in front of his countrymen and women. By then, however, although he was the most expensive golf tutor in America and author of the game's biggest-selling coaching book, he could not cure himself of the accursed 'yips'.

'The yips are that ghastly time,' he said, 'when with the first movement of the putter, you black out, lose sight of the ball and haven't the remotest idea of what to do with the putter or, indeed on occasion, that you are holding the damn thing at all.'

Despite this fatal flaw – 'once you've had them, you've got them,' he famously observed – Armour remained a consistent winner on the US Tour, while his legend continued to spread. The American public was in thrall to the debonair émigré whose womanising ended in a cripplingly expensive divorce, whose gambling cost him a fortune (which he would win, lose, then win back again) and who was a classically trained violinist to concert standard and a demon at the bridge table.

Future President Richard Nixon was among those who sought out Armour's skills as a guru in an effort to cure an ugly shank. 'Can anyone name the world's greatest atomic scientist?' Armour demanded of Tricky Dicky. 'Well, designing, engineering and constructing an atomic bomb is simple compared to trying to teach someone to stop shanking.'

As famous as he became on the range, Armour was even more renowned for his prowess at the nineteenth hole, where he would down several bourbons and soda, followed by a few gin fizzes, maybe a glass or two of champagne and then a Bromo-Seltzer (a medication to relieve heartburn and acid indigestion) before starting the cycle anew. 'You'd better watch it, Tommy,' Walter Hagen told him as a long day's night headed into the small hours. 'That Bromo-Seltzer is going to kill you.'

When the mood was upon him, Armour could be volatile company. As friend and writer Budington Kelland put it: 'Tommy was temperamental and acid-tongued on occasion. He was possessed of a mouth like a steel trap, a nose like a ski jump and eyes – as deep as Rasputin's – that suggested he would enjoy seeing you suffer a compound fracture of the leg. He was not a man you approached comfortably. He was as temperamental as a soprano with a frog in her throat.'

His adoring following forgave him these little foibles, however, because, despite the acclamation and adulation that came his way, Armour remained steadfastly modest. 'It's nice to be a good golfer and win major championships,' he said, 'but, hell, being the finest golfer in the world never cured anyone of polio.'

When his colourful life finally caught up with Armour 13 days before his 74th birthday in 1968, the obituary in the *New York Times* read: 'His impact on the sport for four decades was rivalled by few and surpassed by none.'

2. JIM BAXTER
Football

Born: Hill of Beath, Fife, 29 September 1939
Died: Glasgow, 14 April 2001

CAREER:
Raith Rovers 1957–60: 62 appearances, 3 goals
Rangers 1960–5 and 1969–70: 254 appearances, 24 goals;
   Scottish League Championship 1960–61, 1962–63, 1963–
   64; Scottish Cup 1961–62, 1962–63, 1963–64; Scottish
   League Cup 1961–62, 1963–64, 1964–65
Sunderland 1965–7: 98 appearances, 12 goals
Nottingham Forest 1967–9: 48 appearances, 3 goals
Scotland 1960–7: 34 appearances, 3 goals

While Liverpool idolised The Beatles in the '60s, a goodly proportion of Glasgow worshipped 'Slim Jim'. If Cristiano Ronaldo is worth £80 million, then you could not buy Baxter today for one penny less.

Like George Best, he was more rock star than footballer: a beauty queen on each arm, a betting slip in every pocket and, most destructively of all, a Bacardi and Coke in every pub. Like Best, Baxter burned the candle at both ends then torched the bit in the middle.

He never trained or practised, he scarcely won a tackle in his entire career, his right foot was placed there purely for symmetry, he never headed the ball, he stood 5 ft 11 in. but weighed only 9 st. 12 lb, and he moved at nothing faster than regal elegance. Yet Jim Baxter was a football god. A swivel of those narrow hips, a dip of that slender shoulder as he drifted in on goal and entire defences would leap out of his way like desperate passengers abandoning a sinking ship.

He scored twice on his first appearance at Wembley in the dark blue of Scotland in 1963 and played keepie-uppie underneath the twin towers four years later when he toyed with Sir Alf Ramsey's world champions. No marvel was beyond his power.

Glasgow may have belonged to Jim Baxter but until his premature death from pancreatic cancer at the age of 61 the lilt forever remained that of the Fife coal-mining community of Hill of Beath, where he worked down the village pit during the week and turned out for Raith Rovers on Saturdays until Rangers paid £17,500 for his blessed genius in 1960.

The combination of drink, gambling, two ill-advised transfers to Sunderland and Nottingham Forest, plus Rangers' snooty refusal to grant him a testimonial – 'Och, I was only there five years [sic],' he insisted with unflinching loyalty – saw Baxter live out his life in modest surroundings on the south side of the city over which he once reigned supreme. If he had been allowed an agent, he would have earned – and no doubt spent – millions.

In 1963, when he played alongside Lev Yashin, Ferenc Puskás and Eusébio in the Rest of the World team that met England at Wembley, Baxter was earning a meagre £35 a week at Rangers, yet he never displayed a shred of bitterness that the riches bestowed upon far less deserving talents were denied him. 'I think Puskás was on two grand at Real Madrid even then. I was a slave during my time at Rangers but the game changed. In my day, the directors had all the power before it passed to the players. But I really was the luckiest guy in the world. I started off with nothing down the pits and went on to have a life money can't buy. I messed up my marriage and my liver but that was inevitable, the way I was going.'

From as far back as he could remember, Baxter's weekends were spent playing his beloved fitba' and bevvyin'; since there was only one full-sized ball in Hill of Beath, everyone joined in. 'Forty-a-side. Until the big boys came out the pub like Frankenstein's monster in their great size-14 wellies. When you get the ball and there's 39 huge miners chasing you, then you've got to have a wee bit of skill to survive.'

Even on a crowded, muddy pitch resembling the battle scene in *El Cid*, Baxter's shimmering brilliance could be seen by all through the gloom. At 17 – by which time he had been one of the big boys in the pub for some years – he signed for Raith Rovers and received £250. 'My mum was the proudest woman in Scotland because I bought her the first washing machine in the whole of Hill o' Beath.'

Still a month shy of his 21st birthday, Baxter joined Rangers and joyously surrendered the last vestiges of self-control. 'After Hill o' Beath, Glasgow was Las Vegas. People might wonder how I went off my head. But one day you're a Raith Rovers player who cannae pull the birds at the Cowdenbeath Palais. Next day you come through to Glasgow and the girls are throwing themselves at you. It was a wee bit o' a change in fortune and I certainly wasn't letting it go by. I was a rascal, all right.'

On many an occasion, Baxter would still be trying to sober up three hours before kick-off, yet despite these well-publicised excesses, which resulted in two liver transplants, he was greeted with affection where'er he roamed. As he lay dying, every new postal delivery reduced him to tears; cards and letters of support arrived from Hong Kong and Australia, from Sean Connery and Billy Connolly, from Rangers fans and Celtic players (Baxter's drinking buddies came from a' the airts), from grandmothers and schoolchildren he had never met. At his funeral in Glasgow Cathedral the then Chancellor Gordon Brown delivered one of the readings.

Beloved by all or not, however, during his original spell at Ibrox Baxter was paid the same modest salary as everyone else. And so at the end of every season he would approach the Rangers captain, who would approach the manager, who would approach the directors with his claim for a wage rise. That was the way things were done. He was not seeking to match Puskás's earnings, merely a 'few quid more than those less gifted. I mean we were all paid equally. Which was a bit like paying Frank Sinatra the same as the Alexander Brothers.'

He almost went to Tottenham as Danny Blanchflower's replacement but Rangers backed out of the deal at the last minute and when Internazionale Milano showed an interest, the Ibrox board refused to part with Glasgow's most glamorous citizen, leaving the Italians to buy European Footballer of the Year Luis Suárez from Barcelona as their second choice. 'Suárez,' sighed Baxter without a hint of conceit. 'He wasn't in the same league as me.'

Only a precious few ever were. Playing in what Craig Brown describes as the 'spiv's role' – Baxter preferred to describe his position as 'attacking nomad' – he wore the number 6 shirt but roamed wherever he chose with the purpose of tormenting the opposition and entertaining the congregation. When the great Gianni Rivera checked into Hampden Park for a World Cup tie against Scotland, Baxter began the festivities by nutmegging the Italian 'golden boy' in the first minute. 'Hey wee man,' he shouted across to Billy Bremner, 'one down, nine tae go.' Bremner stopped keeping count after Baxter nutmegged Rivera for the sixth time.

The Scots expression 'dead gallus' might have been coined especially in Slim Jim's honour. 'I had great inner confidence on the field. As soon as I got the ball I was the guv'nor. It didn't matter who I was playing against, Pelé or any o' them. I could make the ball talk. Some days if I wanted to hit a pass twenty-five yards six and three-quarter inches then I would hit it twenty-five yards six and three-quarter inches.'

Baxter's close friend, Dave Mackay, was a willing crony through many a long night's binge, but whereas the Tottenham captain would work the alcohol out of his system by training harder than anyone else, Slim Jim preferred to sleep it off under the covers. 'Dave warned me that I'd pay the consequences eventually and sure enough I did. Lots of people offered me advice but I loved the booze, it's as simple as that. I just loved getting boozed up.'

Might he have been even better or might his career have extended beyond the age of 29 had he bothered to train? 'Nah, I don't think so. Remember, everything I did on the pitch was off the cuff. Sheer instinct. If I'd been a good boy maybe a' the swashbuckling stuff would have got stifled. I was just a happy-go-lucky guy who would come out the pub, lose four or five hundred pound on the horses, pick a fight with somebody – maybe get battered in the mooth – then win back the five hundred quid the next day. That's how I looked at life . . . it's too precious to waste being sensible.'

Though the Baxter legend began to spread alarm bells throughout England – Don Revie (Leeds United), Matt Busby (Manchester United) and Bill Shankly (Liverpool) were among those who decided they could not afford the sleepless nights although they coveted his genius – in Scotland he was loved as no other, especially after he routed the English at Wembley in '63, scoring the opener with a deft chip over Gordon Banks from a tight angle which floated over the line like a snowflake and the winner from the penalty spot. 'I'd never taken a penalty in my life but Dave Mackay handed me the ball and said, "Here, put this in the net." So I did.'

In '67, Baxter mesmerised England again – Scotland 'annihilating' the recently crowned World Cup winners 3–2 – but the decline was imminent. He finally raised some money by leaving Rangers for Sunderland and then Forest – 'two bad teams' – before returning to the Glasgow club on a free transfer in 1969 and a second marriage that lasted one season. 'I had all sorts of offers when Rangers freed me but it wouldn't have been fair. I wasn't the Baxter of old and I couldn't cheat people. I might have been a bit of a scoundrel in my private life but I'd always done an honest day's work on the pitch, so I retired.'

Though there were no mementos in his flat when he died – 'my sons have all my medals and I think I gave away most of the caps and shirts when I was drunk' – there was a lifetime of memories. Like the golden night in the Prater Stadium in 1964 when Rangers beat Rapid Vienna 2–0 in the European Cup, with Baxter touching new heights even by his standards. He ended the night in hospital, an Austrian defender having snapped his priceless left leg in the last minute. 'Ach, I couldn't blame him really . . . I'd been taking the mickey something terrible.'

Many will tell you he was never quite the same again after that injury but the evidence of Wembley '67 suggests otherwise. 'I went downhill because I left Rangers and went to a bad side, simple as that. I would never have wanted to leave Rangers if I hadn't gambled away all my money. I'd bet on anything. Fifty quid the next man to walk in here is wearing black shoes, that kind o' thing. The bevvy did my liver in and the gambling did my brain in. Was it a waste of talent? In a way it was. But ten years of me was maybe enough. I was lucky enough to be able to play a bit of fitba', but when all's said and done, I was just a human being like everyone else. I was just an ordinary guy.'

An ordinary guy, perhaps, but a far from ordinary footballer, as Puskás recalled when he offered the following tribute on the death of his Fife pal. 'I tried to persuade Real Madrid to buy Jimmy in '63 but it never happened. That was a great pity because Jim Baxter was born to play in the Estadio Bernabéu in the all white strip of Real Madrid.'

3. IAN BLACK
Swimming

Born: Aberdeen, 27 June 1941

CAREER:
British Empire & Commonwealth Games, Cardiff, 1958:
  220 yards butterfly – Gold
  440 yards freestyle – Silver
  4x220 yards freestyle relay – Silver
European Championships, Budapest, 1958:
  400 metres freestyle – Gold
  1,500 metres freestyle – Gold
  200 metres butterfly – Gold

When Ian Black left home in Aberdeen to make his way to London's Grosvenor House Hotel for the 1958 BBC Sports Personality of the Year shindig, he made sure to pack his autograph book and Kodak Brownie camera in the suitcase.

As a 17 year old, he was not about to pass up the opportunity of sharing the glittering ballroom with so many of his sporting heroes; the mighty John Charles, who had led Wales to the quarter-finals of the World Cup in Sweden before losing to Pelé's Brazil . . . tennis player Christine Truman, who had beaten Wimbledon champion Althea Gibson as Britain won the Wightman Cup for the first time in 21 years . . . boxer Henry Cooper, a recent winner over American Zora Folley in a world heavyweight championship eliminator . . . Bobby Charlton, who had survived the Munich air disaster that killed eight of the Busby Babes to become a national treasure . . . and Stirling Moss, winner of four of the season's ten Formula One Grands Prix only to lose the world championship to fellow Briton Mike Hawthorn by a single point – and the runaway sentimental favourite to land the award.

And on the subject of the sympathy vote, what of Bathgate's Eric Brown, who had stood on the eighteenth tee at Royal Lytham that July needing a par-four to win the Open or a five to join Australian Peter Thomson and

Welshman Dave Thomas in a play-off only to drive into a bunker and take a double-bogey six? In strict terms of 'personality', no one in British sport came more packed with the ingredient than 'Bomber' Brown.

It had been a sensational year for Black, himself; winner of a gold and two silver medals in the Commonwealth Games pool at Cardiff, he had returned to Scotland from the European swimming championships in Budapest with three golds – the 400 and 1,500 metres freestyle plus the 200 metres butterfly. But as one after another of the leading Sports Personality contenders was summoned forward to relate their deeds to presenter Peter Dimmock, the star-struck Robert Gordon's College schoolboy was more than content with his role as a humble member of the audience.

As the night drew to a climax, so Dimmock stepped forward to announce the result in reverse order:

In third place . . . Nat Lofthouse. The 'Lion of Vienna' was a vastly popular figure in English football even though he had broken millions of hearts by scoring both goals in Bolton Wanderers' 2–0 victory over a hastily rebuilt Manchester United side in the FA Cup final at Wembley.

In second place . . . Bobby Charlton. With Matt Busby still recovering from the life-threatening injuries he had received on the tarmac at Munich, the Brylcreemed youngster had come to represent the spirit of Old Trafford.

And the BBC Sports Personality of the Year 1958 is . . . Ian Black.

As the trumpeters gamely launched into a lusty if rusty rendition of 'Scotland the Brave', the stunned teenager walked on stage as though in a trance to become the fifth recipient of the famous trophy, previously awarded to middle-distance runners Chris Chataway and Gordon Pirie, cricketer Jim Laker and triumphant 1957 Ryder Cup captain Dai Rees of Wales.

'I can assure you that this is most unexpected,' said the engaging and unfailingly modest Black, who had not given a moment's thought to preparing a victory speech. 'There is nothing I can say that I have not already said except thank you very much, especially to the viewers who voted for me.'

Something about Black's tale had clearly touched the nation. Perhaps the great British sports fans appreciated that swimming was a decidedly unglamorous sporting choice; in the winter, Black trained in Aberdeen public baths in the bleak early-morning hours before school, length after lung-bursting length under the watchful gaze of coach Andy Robb. In the summer, he based himself on Guernsey, where he went through his drills in a tidal saltwater pool carved out of the rocks.

'As a wee laddie from the Highlands who did half his training in the sea, I suppose I was seen as a kind of real life Geordie,' he explained. *Wee Geordie*, for those unfortunate enough not to have seen this 1950s screen classic starring Bill Travers, Stanley Baxter and Alastair Sim, was the romantic saga of a gamekeeper's son who grew into a giant to win the 1956 Melbourne Olympics' hammer-throwing gold medal wearing a kilt.

Resplendent in the trademark MacGregor tartan dressing-gown he favoured at poolside in recognition of the fact that, generations before, an ancestor had changed the family name to Black rather than be associated with the rascally Rob Roy MacGregor, Black exploded onto the scene in Cardiff. He might have won three gold medals in south Wales but for the presence of the great Australian John Konrads, who would set 26 world records in his career. Konrads pipped Black in the 440-yard freestyle, then anchored the Aussies to victory over Scotland in the relay.

Without the Latvian-born Sydneysider to contend with in the European Championships, Black was in unbeatable form and became the hero of all Budapest by interrupting the flow of Soviet Union gold medals. 'Scotland has long been recognised as the home of football,' wrote one local scribe, 'now it is also home to one of the greatest and most sporting swimmers in the world.' In winning the 400 metres freestyle and 200

Murray Rose

It must have been scant consolation to Ian Black, who missed the bronze medal by a hair's breadth, that victory in the 1960 Olympic 400 metres final in Rome went to fellow Scot, Murray Rose.

Born in Nairn in 1939, Rose boarded an emigrant ship bound for Australia with his parents at the conclusion of the Second World War and having swapped the Moray Firth for Bondi Beach, immediately enrolled for swimming lessons at Sydney's Readleaf Pool in Double Bay.

A strict vegetarian known as the 'Seaweed Streak', the teenager refused to live in the Athletes' Village during the 1956 Melbourne Olympics because the chefs could not meet his dietary needs which included Russian sunflower seeds, Egyptian halvah, Greek sesame seeds, millet from northern China, unpolished rice from southern China, goat's milk and a special seaweed jelly created by his mum.

Australians did not understand such affectations but Rose became a national hero when he became the youngest competitor ever to win three gold medals at a single Olympics with victory in the 400 metres freestyle, 1,500 metres freestyle and 4x200 metres freestyle relay.

At the 1960 Games in Rome, Rose retained his 400 metres title but had to settle for silver in the 1,500 metres and a bronze in the relay. His Olympic medal haul would almost certainly have been greater had he not been overlooked for selection for the 1964 Tokyo Olympics. Having recently set world records in the 880 yards and 1,500 metres (the 15th

metres butterfly finals in the space of 20 minutes, the Hungarians regarded Black as a wonder boy of the pool.

Although he enrolled at Aberdeen University to begin the studies that would subsequently earn him a Masters degree, Black continued his lonely training vigil in the hope of winning another medal at the 1960 Olympics in his specialist event, the 400 metres freestyle.

The Rome Games were memorable for so many reasons: Muhammad Ali, then known as Cassius Clay, would win the light-heavyweight gold medal in the ring; the future King Constantine II of Greece struck gold in sailing; Abebe Bikila of Ethiopia won the marathon, running barefoot, to become the first black African Olympic champion; and American Wilma Rudolph, who had suffered polio as a child, won three sprint gold medals. All Scotland was captivated by Black's challenge in the 400 metres freestyle final.

Alas, it was not to be. Victory went to Australian Murray Rose – who had been born in Nairn but moved Down Under at a young age – the silver to Tsuyoshi Yamanaka and Black was controversially denied the bronze after finishing in exactly the same time as Konrads. After protracted discussions, the officials decreed that by the blink of an eye, the Aussie had touched first.

At the age of 19, Black's swimming career was over as he concentrated on university life. After graduating, he taught in Canada, Bahrain and Hong Kong, ultimately returning to his alma mater as headmaster of the Robert Gordon's College junior school before retiring to Ballater in 2004.

'You could say that I had a golden patch in my life,' he recalled in an interview in *The Scotsman*. 'A golden spell or era that lasted about six months from June to December 1958 – everything was packed into that little period. I don't think I had even watched the BBC Sports Personality of the Year awards before. I was quite young and things happened very quickly and everything seemed to happen to me. Also, these were only the beginnings of television. But I was absolutely delighted to win the BBC award, no question. It has always remained, I suppose, my most

world record of his career), Rose was not considered for the Aussie swim team when he refused to travel from California, where he was studying, for the Australian Championships qualifying meet.

Rose, who still takes vigorous exercise in the waters of Bondi Bay every morning, served as one of the eight Olympic Flag-bearers at the Opening Ceremony of the 2000 Games in Melbourne. Having retired from an executive position in sports marketing, he is now a patron of The Rainbow Club, which teaches disabled children to swim.

pleasant memory of taking part in the competitive arena because it meant that, for a period, I was held in affection by the people of the country.'

A replica of the trophy stands alongside the old tartan dressing-gown in Black's cabinet in the Scottish Sports Hall of Fame. 'Sadly all my medals were stolen some years ago, which was a pity, but it's an irrelevance really. The medals themselves are nothing; they are just mementos. Even to this day people come up and say: "You're Ian Black, the swimmer." And this is over half a century later. It really is nice that people remember. "You're Ian Black, the swimmer." That will probably be my epitaph.'

4. JAMES BRAID
Golf

Born: Earlsferry, Fife, 6 February 1870
Died: London, 27 November 1950

CAREER:
Open champion 1901, 1905, 1906, 1908, 1910
British PGA Matchplay champion 1903, 1905, 1907, 1911

Long, long before the brand name was appropriated by Arnold Palmer, Gary Player and Jack Nicklaus, James Braid was a member of the original 'Big Three' of golf in the company of his two great rivals, Jersey islander Harry Vardon and Devonian J.H. Taylor.

Braid was victorious in five Open Championships – leaving him one behind Vardon on the all-time list and level with Taylor, Tom Watson and Peter Thomson – but might have won several more had his eyesight, damaged in an accident with lime while working as a joiner in his youth, not deteriorated in later years. In the decade 1901–10, before his vision grew increasingly blurred, Braid's Open record read: 1st . . . tied 2nd . . . 5th . . . tied 2nd . . . 1st . . . 1st . . . tied 5th . . . 1st . . . tied 2nd . . . 1st.

Unlike his Scottish contemporaries James Foulis, Fred Herd, Willie Smith, Willie Anderson, Laurie Auchterlonie, Alex Smith, Alec Ross and Fred McLeod, all of whom conquered the leading Americans of the day by winning the US Open, the chance to triumph in golf's other major was denied Braid because he could not be persuaded to sail the Atlantic. He suffered badly from motion sickness, finding it best to travel by train whenever possible. On one of the few occasions he steeled himself to cross the Channel, in 1910, he returned with the French Open trophy in his grasp.

An avid golfer from a young age despite his father's protestation that the game was 'nowt but a waste of time', Braid began his career as a caddie at his local course in Elie before moving to London, where he used his skills as a joiner to become a club-maker. As his reputation as an amateur blossomed, he was offered the job as professional at Romford Golf Club in 1895.

Let us look at Braid's five Open successes in closer detail – and for those of the Tiger generation who might snigger knowingly at his winning totals, it is worth remembering that the balls and clubs of a century ago bear little resemblance to the equipment enjoyed by the modern champions. Nor did Braid resemble Tiger Woods in dress; with his flat cap, heavy tweed suit and collar and tie, he looked more like an office worker than an athlete. But an athlete he was.

MUIRFIELD, 1901
309 – James Braid 79, 76, 74, 80
312 – Harry Vardon
315 – J.H. Taylor

Having won six of the seven previous Open Championships, Vardon and Taylor belonged to an exclusive two-man club until Braid submitted his membership application with a Ballesteros-style display of audacious shot-making for three rounds.

Then, with a five-stroke advantage over Vardon at the start of the final round and with the jeweller preparing to engrave the Scot's name on the Claret Jug, Braid was consumed by an unfamiliar air of caution. Whereas for 54 holes he had used his immense length off the tee to attack even the most distant greens, he suddenly seemed overwhelmed by the presence of destiny hovering at his shoulder over every shot.

Standing on the sixteenth tee, Vardon needed to complete the closing holes in level fours to force a play-off in which, given his greater experience, he would have been the runaway favourite. Fortunately for Braid, Vardon dumped his approach into a pot bunker, eventually signed for a six and, ever the gentleman, strode off the eighteenth green to offer warm congratulations to his equally sporting conqueror.

ST ANDREWS, 1905
318 – James Braid 81, 78, 78, 81
323 – J.H. Taylor, Rowland Jones

With more than one hundred and fifty entrants, the Open was extended to cover three days with eighteen holes on the Wednesday and Thursday, followed by thirty-six holes on the Friday (the club pros were expected to be back at work on the Saturday morning to fit members' grips or sell them a pocketful of tees) by which time the field had been reduced to forty-five.

While Braid shot a fine third round 78, so Vardon's challenge faded, his wild drive on the eighteenth finishing on the roof of a four-storey building overlooking the fairway. It left the home-town boy to go into the final afternoon with a seemingly invincible six-stroke lead over Taylor and Frenchman Arnaud Massy, who, two years later, would become the first non-Briton to win the Open when he triumphed at Hoylake.

Our early-day Seve opted for the adventurous route to victory: Braid sliced his second shot on the fifteenth onto the adjoining railway line, which was not out of bounds; his attempted recovery hit a spectator and he was fortunate finally to get down in six. On the sixteenth, his towering drive trickled into a bunker and in trying to reach the green in two he succeeded only in sending his ball back onto the train tracks, albeit further up the line on this occasion. Standing awkwardly on the sleepers, Braid managed to nudge the ball a few feet forward before sending his fourth shot racing through the green. An immaculate chip across the sharply sloping green salvaged another six, and two fives at the seventeenth and eighteenth were sufficient to secure his second Open title.

MUIRFIELD, 1906
300 – James Braid 77, 76, 74, 73
304 – J.H. Taylor
305 – Harry Vardon

The growing popularity of the Open attracted a record entry of 103. The defending champion was given a late start for the first two rounds and the long wait clearly affected his play throughout the first round. On the Thursday morning, Braid took the precaution of playing in a light-hearted foursomes to pass the time before being called to the first tee.

Not for the first time, the 'Big Three' dominated the championship but it was Braid who withstood the pressure in the final round. Vardon began by four-putting the first green before scuppering his chances completely with a six on the second hole. As Taylor's driving and putting also grew increasingly erratic, so Braid played nearly perfect golf to record his third victory.

PRESTWICK, 1908
291 – James Braid 70, 72, 77, 72
299 – Tom Ball
300 – Ted Ray

'Braid Romps to 4th Open Title Setting New Scoring Record' announced one newspaper headline.

Played in idyllic summer weather with nary a sniff of a sea breeze, England's Ernest Gray set a course record 68 in the first round. Braid was more than happy with his opening 70, doubly so when Vardon and Taylor both struggled home in 79 to leave them languishing in the lower reaches of the leaderboard.

The three-time champion appeared poised to challenge Gray's newly minted mark when he reached the turn in 33 in round two but a six at the thirteenth interrupted his flow; even so, he finished the day with a healthy five-shot advantage over Gray and fellow Scot David Kinnell.

Round three was golf the Keystone Kops way: woefully short with his approach to the first green, he began with a five and worse was to follow at the third, where he drove into the deep rough then despatched his second into the fearsome Cardinal Bunker. Clearly ruffled, Braid then went out of bounds not once but twice and was somewhat fortunate to salvage an eight from the wreckage. After three putting the fourth, Braid finally set about restricting the damage with a birdie two on the fifth en route to a 77 and a comfortable six-stroke cushion over Tom Ball and Ted Ray.

Followed by a huge gallery numbering several thousand, Braid completed his final round in faultless manner to win his fourth Claret Jug with a record low score.

ST ANDREWS, 1910
299 – James Braid 76, 73, 74, 76
303 – Sandy Herd
304 – George Duncan

The four-time champion arrived in the Auld Grey Toun to a hero's welcome and he did not disappoint his local supporters, producing another peerless display, although it took him five rounds to do so.

As so often happens on that corner of the East Neuk coast, the opening day began in sunny weather only to give way to a violent thunderstorm that flooded the greens. Braid was on the thirteenth when told that the first round had been abandoned and would begin anew the following day. Fearful that the news might be nothing more than a rumour, Braid completed his round in a quite remarkable 76, matching the best score of the day completed before the storm.

When Braid could do no better than another 76 in the 'official' first round, he found himself three strokes behind early pacemaker George Duncan, a renowned fast starter. As Duncan's challenge duly disintegrated with an error-strewn 83 in the final round, so Braid assumed total control, beating J.H. Taylor's Old Course record by ten shots.

In doing so, he became the first player to win five Open Championships, all achieved within the span of ten years. His eyesight, however, was already failing and his decade of dominance was at an end.

With his game in decline, Braid's passion in later years became course design and he is remembered as the 'inventor of the dog-leg', and as the creator of the King's and Queen's courses at Gleneagles. He also continued serving as the club pro at Walton Heath, Surrey, up until his death at the age of 80, sharing his ancient philosophy with each and every one of his pupils: 'Keep on hitting it straight until the wee ball goes in the hole.'

5. BILLY BREMNER

Football

Born: Stirling, 9 December 1942
Died: Doncaster, 7 December 1997

CAREER:

Leeds United 1959–76: 771 appearances, 115 goals; English League Championship 1968–69, 1973–74; FA Cup 1972; League Cup 1968; Fairs Cup 1968, 1971; Footballer of the Year 1970

Hull City 1976–9: 61 appearances, 6 goals

Doncaster Rovers 1979–81: 5 appearances, 0 goals

Scotland 1965–75: 54 appearances, 3 goals

Little Billy Bremner is the captain of the crew,
For the sake of Leeds United he would break himself in two;
His hair is red and fuzzy and his body's black and blue,
But Leeds go marching on.

from the song 'Glory, Glory, Leeds United'

'If you were to ask every manager in the country to name the one player above all others that they would like to add to their team,' said the great John Charles, hero of Juventus, Leeds United and Wales, 'their hearts would lean towards George Best – but their heads would tell them to sign Billy Bremner.'

As a player, Don Revie was a football romantic: influenced by Hungarian maestro Nándor Hidegkuti, the midfield architect behind Hungary's 6–3 humiliation of England at Wembley in 1953, the elegant and tactically astute Revie reinvented himself as a midfield 'playmaker', inspiring Manchester City to a 3–1 victory over Birmingham City in the 1956 FA Cup final.

But as a manager, Revie was the ultimate pragmatist. When he began the task of transforming Leeds United from Second Division anonymity into one of the most powerful clubs in Europe after taking power in

March 1961, it was around the fiery-haired and fiery-tempered but immensely skilful 18-year-old Bremner that he decided to create his team.

At 5 ft 5 in., Bremner had earlier been rejected by both Arsenal and Chelsea as being too small to survive in English football but Revie was in awe of the teenager whom a *Sunday Times* headline writer would later describe as '10st of Barbed Wire'. There was one problem: as fearless as he was on the pitch, Bremner was a sensitive young soul who was achingly homesick. After one particularly harrowing telephone conversation with his fiancée Vicky in Stirling, Bremner submitted a transfer request whereupon Hibs manager, Hugh Shaw, tabled a bid of £25,000, an astronomical sum at the time for a relatively untried youngster.

Leeds succeeded in scuppering the deal by demanding £30,000 but with Bremner clearly hankering for a return to Scotland – and particularly to Celtic whom he had supported since boyhood – Revie took steps to secure his starlet's happiness. He drove north to Stirling, where he spent many a long hour persuading Vicky that Leeds and Bremner were poised on the threshold of glory and that Easter Road – or Parkhead, for that matter – represented a misguided career move. Revie's charm offensive clearly paid off when the couple duly married and happily settled down to their new life in West Yorkshire.

For a visionary who had been enthralled by the cherry red shirts of Ferenc Puskás's Hungarians and whose first move after being installed as manager at Elland Road had to been to swap the club's traditional blue and gold colours for the all white strip of Real Madrid, Revie's Leeds United did not set out to appeal to football purists when they gained promotion to the First Division in 1964. Although he favoured players with sublime talents such as Bremner, Bobby Collins and Johnny Giles, it could hardly pass unnoticed that Revie also liked his Leeds 'crew' to come equipped with a bit of an edge.

Lest anyone was still in any doubt whatsoever, Bremner's message of intent was writ large on a sign above his peg in the Elland Road dressing-room: KEEP FIGHTING! 'I'm the captain, which is why it hangs above my hook,' he explained. 'And as captain I'm supposed to set an example to the rest of the lads.'

Although Revie was willing to accommodate a physically fragile genius such as Eddie Gray – 'When he plays on snow, he doesn't leave any footprints,' observed the Elland Road boss in a rare foray into poetic licence – Leeds quickly gained a not fully undeserved reputation for cynicism, skulduggery and assorted on-field shenanigans. 'I didn't used to get frightened on the pitch,' recalled Jimmy Greaves, 'but I was always relieved to get off in one piece when the likes of Leeds United were kicking anything that moved.' Bremner was steadfastly unrepentant that others might perceive Leeds as being football hooligans. 'We were determined that none of the so-called elite clubs were going to stand in our way. We didn't go into the First Division to serve as stargazers.'

Neither Bremner nor Revie lost any sleep over what others might think of their methods. 'Leeds tried to win by fair means or foul,' bemoaned former Arsenal skipper Frank McLintock. 'But they were far too good to do things like that and should have won far more than they did. They were, in fact, a magnificent side, a team made in heaven.'

As the manager's enforcer-in-chief on the other side of the touchline, Bremner refused to concede that the Leeds players might have anything for which to apologise. 'I'm no angel,' he confessed, 'but I've never kicked anyone deliberately.'

Bobby Robson, who liked his teams to play with a smile rather than a snarl on their faces, was another grudging admirer of the Revie–Bremner axis. 'Looking back over the outstanding English sides of the past 50 years, then I suppose Leeds have to be ranked alongside the Busby Babes that were partially destroyed at Munich, the later United side of Best, Law and Charlton, Liverpool of the '70s and the double-winning Spurs team of the 1960s.'

Ed McIlvenny

To many Scots, 28 June is a cross between Hogmanay and Burns' Night. For it was on this day in 1950 that mighty England were humiliated/humbled/disgraced (perm any two from three) by the United States in Belo Horizonte during the World Cup finals in Brazil. And Scotland had a role to play, the American team being captained by Ed McIlvenny, the pride of Greenock who had emigrated only 12 months earlier.

Although the US have become a respected force in world football, 61 years ago they were the Burkino Faso of 2011, having lost their last seven internationals by a combined score of 45–2. Despite missing the injured Stanley Matthews, England began the match like the world beaters they fondly believed themselves to be by unleashing nine shots on target in the first half-hour with only goalkeeper Frank Borghi – one save from a Tom Finney header ranking alongside Gordon Banks's legendary denial of Pelé in Guadalajara 20 years later – standing between the Stars and Stripes and a massacre of historic proportions.

Then, in the 37th minute, the Americans finally broke out of their own half to launch an attack; right-half Walter Bahr swung a speculative cross into the England penalty box and as keeper Bert Williams came out to make a routine interception, Joe Gaetjens appeared from nowhere to launch himself at the ball and graze a gentle header into the corner of the net.

Such was the total lack of interest in the World Cup in the US that a solitary newspaper – the St Louis Post-Dispatch – carried a report of the game (and only because the reporter

Neutrals the land over, however, rejoiced that Revie's Leeds turned out to be serial under-achievers: they won two League Championships but finished runners-up on five occasions (three times in last-game-of-the-season climaxes); reached four FA Cup finals but emerged victorious in only one; won the Fairs Cup but lost their only appearance in a European Cup final against Bayern Munich in 1975.

Leeds' unfathomable ability to fall at the last hurdle was epitomised by the 1969–70 season, when they were chasing the unprecedented treble of League title, FA Cup and European Cup. The championship eventually went to Everton, the FA Cup to Chelsea after a particularly violent replay at Old Trafford in which both teams might easily have finished the game with eight players had the referee not been so lenient, and Celtic were thoroughly deserved 3–1 winners at the semi-final stage of the European Cup, Bremner scoring a brilliant long-range goal in the second leg at Hampden Park.

Despite these disappointments, the pocket-sized Bremner established himself as one of the true giants of the game. He was a ferocious tackler yet possessed of all the dribbling wizardry of a world-class winger . . . he could spray pinpoint 50-yard passes across the length and breadth of the pitch and out-jump the most hulking of defenders . . . he was an inspired sweeper when the occasion demanded, with an in-built crystal ball for detecting danger, yet a remarkably regular goal-scorer from his usual midfield beat. The complete footballer, or as Eddie Gray put it: 'Billy played more with his heart than his head. And he had a heart the size of Elland Road. As a midfield player, he was a free spirit who worked on instinct. He was the very soul of the club during the Don Revie era.'

Bremner was no less influential in the dark blue of Scotland, winning fifty-four caps in an international career spanning ten years; years before Mel Gibson bestowed the sobriquet upon William Wallace, he had become recognised as the original Stirling 'Braveheart'. He made his debut in a goalless draw in a friendly against Spain at Hampden Park in 1965 and by the time of Scotland's epic 3–2 defeat of World Cup holders England at Wembley in 1967 had been appointed captain of his country.

The highlight of his reign as chieftain of the 'Tartan Army' came in

---

was on holiday in Brazil at the time) while in England the cricket team's first defeat by the West Indies dominated the headlines. In fact, three papers blithely assumed the result to be a misprint and published the score as a 10–0 victory for the Three Lions.

Although McIlvenny skippered the US in a game remembered as 'the Miracle on Grass', he never became an American citizen. Having starred for an All-Stars team against a visiting Manchester United earlier in the season, he was signed by Matt Busby immediately after the World Cup before he could become a nephew of Uncle Sam.

1974 when he led his nation to the World Cup in West Germany, the first time Scotland had qualified for the finals since 1958. Scotland, as only Scotland could, departed the tournament unbeaten after beating Zaire 2–0 and drawing with Brazil and Yugoslavia 0–0 and 1–1 respectively. The bitter memory of the game against a physically robust Brazil – who surrendered their traditional 'Samba' football to offer a fair impersonation of Leeds United – would haunt Bremner for the rest of his life. Having been kicked up and down the pitch by the once admirable Rivelino, the skipper scorned a glorious chance to put Scotland into the second phase when he missed a 'sitter' from less than a yard and with the goal gaping.

Despite this aberration, Bremner won a host of new admirers for his three displays. Pelé described him as 'the outstanding player of the World Cup', high praise when you consider that Johan Cruyff and Johan Neeskens, Franz Beckenbauer and Gerd Müller, Gianni Rivera and Sandro Mazzola to name but six were also in attendance.

Sepp Herberger, who had masterminded West Germany's defeat of Hungary in the 1954 World Cup final, was another fan. 'Bremner is a truly great player, a firebrand. He is exactly the type of player that I would look for whenever I was selecting a team.'

Bremner was on top of the world as a footballer but if he had been familiar with Noël Coward's words then he might well have flown home humming 'Bad times are just around the corner'.

Having led Leeds to a second League title success, Revie left Elland Road to become manager of England; his successor, to the surprise and suspicion of the United players, was Brian Clough, a long-time and vociferous critic of Revie's win-at-all-costs mentality. Clough announced his arrival in typically forthright and acerbic manner by gathering Leeds' assemblage of international stars around him and informing them that they 'should chuck all your medals in a dustbin because they were won by cheating'. Manager and captain were on a collision course.

A few weeks after taking over, Clough led his team out onto the Wembley pitch – at the shoulder of Bill Shankly of Liverpool, who had returned from retirement for the day – for the 1974 Charity Shield, the supposedly goodwill curtain-raiser to the English season, pitting champions against FA Cup winners. Televised live for the first time, the great occasion was marred when Bremner and Kevin Keegan were sent off for trading punches.

Such was the sense of outrage throughout the game that the Football Association banned both players for 11 games. By the time Bremner had paid his debt to society and was released back into the football community, Clough was gone from Elland Road, sacked after a turbulent forty-four days during which the champions had won just one of six games and become rooted in nineteenth place in the twenty-two-team First Division.

There was further anguish for Bremner in 1975 when he was banned for life by the Scottish Football Association after being thrown out of a Danish nightclub for bawdy behaviour. Branded a member of the 'Copenhagen Five' (in the company of Willie Young, Arthur Graham, Pat McCluskey and Joe Harper), Bremner would never again represent the country he had served so well and for so long, although the sentence was subsequently rescinded.

Within a year of that incident, Bremner's long association with Leeds United was also terminated when he was transferred to Hull City for the token fee of £35,000; thereafter, he joined Doncaster Rovers as player-manager before returning to Leeds as manager in 1985. Elland Road was no longer the place of such happy memories. Impoverished on the pitch and at the bank, once mighty Leeds had fallen upon hard times and were struggling in the old Second Division. Although Bremner succeeded in leading them to an FA Cup semi-final appearance in 1987, when they were beaten 3–2 by eventual winners Coventry, and a promotion play-off the following season, his failure to restore Leeds to the top flight resulted in his sacking.

After another brief spell as manager of Doncaster Rovers, Bremner retired from football to re-emerge as a hilarious after-dinner speaker, charming everyone with his wit, dignity and modesty.

Without warning, two days before his 55th birthday, he was dead from a coronary thrombosis; the heart the size of Elland Road had most cruelly let him down.

6. GORDON BROWN
Rugby Union

Born: Troon, 1 November 1947
Died: Troon, 19 March 2001

CAREER:

Clubs: Marr College and West of Scotland
Scotland 1969–76: 30 caps, 0 points
British Lions: 1971, New Zealand (won 2–1); 1974, South
Africa (won 3–0); 1977, New Zealand (lost 3–1)

One of rugby's unique characteristics is that it allows – nay, make that encourages – you and your opposite number to knock the living daylights out of each other then repair to the bar to compare bumps and bruises over a drink or three.

Such was the global affection in which he was held by sporting friend and foe alike that, whether he had turned out for the West of Scotland against Hawick or for the British Lions against the South African Springboks, a long queue would form for the privilege of buying Gordon Brown a pint.

Two weeks before he died prematurely of cancer at the age of 53, 1,400 guests assembled for a celebratory – and I do mean 'celebratory' – banquet given in honour of 'Broon frae Troon' in London. To those who did not know the man, he might have presented a pitiful sight that evening, his giant's frame reduced to skin and bone, the untidy boyish locks transformed into a shiny pate by the chemotherapy.

When he rose to speak, however, he was the giant personality of old, armed as he was with tales of roguish adventures such as his infamous brush with the fearsome one-eyed Northern Transvaal forward Johan De Bruyn during the '74 Lions' Third Test victory over the Springboks in Port Elizabeth.

Amid one of the many merry melees that peppered the game, De Bruyn's glass eye – with the encouragement of Brown's fist, it has to be said – flew from its socket and sank in the mud. 'So there we are,' recalled the big fella, '30 players plus the ref on our hands and knees scrabbling about in the mire looking for this glass eye. Eventually, someone yells "Eureka!" whereupon De Bruyn grabs it and plonks it straight back in the gaping hole in his face. And when he stands up I can't believe what I'm looking at . . . there's a huge dod of grass sticking out of his eyeball.'

The selfsame glass eye, now residing as the centrepiece of a hand-crafted trophy, is in the possession of Brown's widow, Linda, De Bruyn having flown from Johannesburg to London to attend the gala dinner and bid a sad farewell to his good friend, popularly known as 'the Baby-Faced Assassin'.

Gordon Brown was born to be a sportsman. His father, Jock, was goalkeeper in the Clyde team that won the Scottish Cup in 1939, the same year that he won his first and only cap against Wales before enlisting in the Royal Navy for the duration of the war. After being demobbed, Brown Sr signed for Gillingham before returning to Scotland, helping Hibs to win the League Championship in 1948. As a scratch golfer, he also competed in the 1962 Open Championship won by Arnold Palmer at Royal Troon. After his playing days were over, Jock Brown trained as a physiotherapist, a role in which he would serve Kilmarnock FC and the Scottish Rugby Union.

Jock Brown's brother, Gordon's uncle Jim, also became a professional footballer of international renown. After serving his apprenticeship as a riveter in Troon Shipyard, Jim Brown emigrated to America, where he subsequently joined the New York Giants. In 1930, he was chosen to represent the United States in the inaugural World Cup in Uruguay, scoring the only goal in his adopted country's 6–1 semi-final defeat against Argentina.

His performances in his team's earlier two games – a brace of 3–0 victories against Belgium and Paraguay – did not go unnoticed on this side of the Atlantic and a posse of managers from both England and Scotland were waiting on the docks at Liverpool when he sailed home to discuss terms with the various teams who had expressed interest in signing him. Obviously operating on the principle that time and tide wait for no man, Manchester United's Scott Duncan hired a tugboat and had Brown's signature on a contract before the pair of them descended the gangway. Brown scored seventeen goals in forty games during a two-year stay at Old Trafford, eventually returning to America, where he worked as a coach.

A second uncle, Tom Brown, played keeper for Ipswich Town in a long career on either side of the war, in which he served as a commando, so it was inevitable that young Gordon – all 6 ft 5 in. and 17 st. of him – should be drawn to football before discovering that his true talents lay with the oval ball. As a teenager he followed in his father's wake by filling the goal for Troon Juniors in the infamous Ayrshire League, which makes a Test series against the Springboks look like a Holyrood Palace garden party in comparison.

The 17-year-old Brown realised that for health-and-safety reasons he would be better advised to pick a more pacific pastime after a local derby against Irvine Meadow. As Brown described events: 'We were getting thumped – in every sense – six–nil or something like that. It was about to become seven when one of the Meadow forwards raced clear with only yours truly to beat. I did what any self-respecting goalie would have done and decked him with a full-blooded rugby tackle. I didn't get sent off – the Ayrshire refs always like to let the game flow – so the Meadow supporters among the 2,500 crowd decided to express their disapproval in the time-honoured manner. They gave me pelters, verbally, bottles, coins, whatever came to hand. I had to be given a police escort to the dressing-room at the end of the game. I went straight to Marr College FP and told them I wanted to take up rugby.'

Such was Gordon Brown's impact upon his new chosen sport that at the age of 22, by which time he was an unmovable force in the West of Scotland pack, he won his first cap at lock forward against the 1969 Springboks at Murrayfield, celebrating his international debut with an impressive performance in a 6–3 victory. His only regret was that his big brother, Peter, a teammate at club level, had not played alongside him.

That ambition was realised, or so he blithely thought, come the 1970 Five Nations, when the selectors decided to ring the changes before Scotland's visit to Cardiff Arms Park following an 11–9 defeat against France in the opening game in Edinburgh.

'Great news,' Peter informed his sibling down the phone. 'I'm back in.'

'So who's out?' enquired the unsuspecting Gordon.

'You!'

Fate was not finished with the brothers Brown. Peter Brown tore a calf muscle before half-time and, despite treatment from his dad (now an SRU employee), limped away from the action. 'And guess who came on as replacement?' grinned Gordon at the bittersweet memory. 'Aye, his wee brother.'

Due to a series of injuries and one lengthy ban, Gordon Brown would represent Scotland on only thirty occasions (winning six out of eight contests against our dear neighbours in white), and so it was as a British Lion that he gained renown far and beyond these shores.

In 1971, he was a member of the last Lions touring party to return triumphant from New Zealand, a series in which the two squads read like a who's who of international rugby. The Lions boasted Barry John,

J.P.R Williams, Gerald Davies, John Dawes, Gareth Edwards and Mervyn Davies of Wales, Mike Gibson and Willie John McBride of Ireland, Englishman David Duckham, plus Sandy Carmichael and Ian McLauchlan of Scotland. Against that, the All Blacks could field Sid Going, Colin Meads, Brian Lochore, Ian Kirkpatrick, Bryan Williams and Laurie Mains.

Although he did not feature in the first two Tests, which resulted in a win apiece, Brown replaced Welshman Delme Thomas alongside Willie John at lock for the Third Test in Wellington, which resulted in a resounding 13–3 demolition of the mighty Kiwis and kept his place for the climactic Fourth Test at Eden Park, Auckland, a 14–14 draw securing a 2–1 series victory.

Three years later under Willie John McBride's captaincy, the British Lions rampaged across South Africa, winning twenty-three of their twenty-four tour games, with Brown setting a record for a visiting forward with eight tries.

'In rugby, you get bankers and brickies, doctors and dockers, teachers and tearaways,' recalled Brown of that tour, during which he formed an enduring friendship with Welsh hooker Bobby Windsor. 'Bobby was a hard-as-nails steelworker. When he came to your house, you put away all the cutlery; when he shook hands, you had to make sure you still had your watch and rings. He was the archetypal loveable rogue.'

Before departing for South Africa the Lions gathered in a London hotel, besieged by anti-apartheid demonstrators who were protesting against sporting links with South Africa. Skipper Willie John made one of his famous rousing speeches: 'If there's anyone here with any doubts, go home now. Not a word will be said. But if you don't leave within the next two minutes, then you're here for four months. I've been in South Africa before and there's going to be a lot of physical intimidation, a lot of cheating. So if you're not up for a fight, there's the door.' There was a brief silence until Bobby, who loved fighting more than anything, jumped up and shouted: 'I'm going to bloody well love this, boyo.'

To counter the violence he knew was coming the Lions' way, Willie John invented the notorious yet cunning '99' ploy: at the very first indication that the Springboks were resorting to dubious tactics, the skipper would bellow the battle-cry '99', in response to which each and every Lion would belt the wearer of the nearest green shirt. A crude but undeniably effective deterrent against any bully. When Moaner (and well done to his parents for coming up with that moniker) Van Heerden had a pop at Bobby Windsor, Brown reacted to the '99' call by breaking his right thumb on the South African's jaw.

Although his Scotland career came to an unfortunate end when he missed the entire 1976 Five Nations tournament after being suspended for retaliation as the victim of an unprovoked stamping to the head during a club game, he became a British Lion for the third time later that season. New Zealand was again the destination and although the All Blacks gained a measure of revenge for the defeat of six years earlier with a 3–1 series win, Brown enhanced his reputation as one of the greatest second-row forwards in rugby history.

At his funeral, which brought the streets of Troon to a halt and reduced battle-hardened teammates and opponents to tears, Bobby Windsor spoke with heartfelt emotion when he revealed: 'I rang Gordon most weekends for the last eight months of his life. Every time before I rang off, I told him I loved him. And that's something I've never told any other bloke.'

7. KEN BUCHANAN MBE

Boxing

Born: Edinburgh, 28 June 1945

CAREER:

Lightweight champion of the world September 1970–June
 1972

Fight record: won 61, lost 8, drew 0

Ken Buchanan is a proud man. Proud of his time as lightweight champion of the world, and proud of his appearance at an awards ceremony in New York in 1970 when he was named 'Fighter of the Year', with Smokin' Joe Frazier and Muhammad Ali relegated to second and third places; proud, too, that many regard him as Britain's greatest fighter of the post-war era, a warrior whose left jab snapped out like a laser-beam of destruction, whose cracklingly crisp combinations were delivered as a drum roll of impending doom.

Aye, Ken Buchanan is a proud man, all right. Proud to be remembered as an honoured champion who topped the bill at Madison Square Garden, that pugilistic La Scala where the knowledgeable audience can detect an imposter when he appears on stage, on three of the eight occasions on which he was invited to appear – an unprecedented accolade for a European. And proud to be remembered as a genuine fighting man who would consent to test his courage and expertise only against other genuine fighting men.

It is an injustice on a monumental scale that boxers of far fewer skills and smaller hearts made millions while Buchanan ended his fighting days five months short of his 37th birthday earning £1,500 for the dubious privilege of losing to a third-rate bum who would not have been permitted to hold the bucket into which he spat between rounds during the glory years.

Oh, yes, there may have been many hard times since the summer of '72 when Roberto Durán took away both his breath and his world title with a vicious low blow which arrived after the bell at the end of 13 torrid rounds in the Garden, but Ken Buchanan, who lives in a modest one-bedroom flat in Leith while existing on his government pension, remains a proud and defiant man.

Two expensive and highly publicised divorces, the loss of his Edinburgh hotel and the collapse of various other business interests saw Buchanan, who first retired in 1976 after a successful European title defence against Italian Giancarlo Usai, make an ill-advised return to the ring as a punchbag for a string of nonentities only too eager to use his honourable name to add lustre to their miserable CVs.

Many were quick to jump to the conclusion that Buchanan had joined boxing's legion of lost souls; that he had become the latest in the pitiable line of those who, having surrendered their titles, surrender their savings, their dignity and, ultimately, their will to live.

'I wasn't world champion any more so obviously I was a bit down for a wee while back then,' he admitted. 'But you can't be world champion all your bloody life. It had to come to an end. If it hadn't been Durán who kneed me in the balls, Father Time would have come forward to do it eventually. Obviously, I wish I could have retired as undefeated British and European champion but my personal life was in a wee bit of a mess on and off. Every time I quit the ring, something or someone kicked me in the Roberto Duráns and I had to go back to work. Och, aye, a lot of the guys I lost to at the end couldn't have laced my gloves but I wasn't ashamed or saddened. It was only the people who cared about me on [the other] side of the ropes who were sad. It's nice to have this romanticised image of the champ walking off into the sunset unbloodied. But only if they don't have a pile of ruddy great bills that have to be paid.'

Raised in an asbestos-walled prefab on an impoverished Edinburgh housing estate and the continual target of the local playground gangs, Buchanan was inspired to lace on his first pair of gloves as a nine year old after seeing *The Brown Bomber*, a Hollywood version of the life of Joe Louis. Sixteen years later he became champion of the world in front of a chillingly hostile crowd and the searing heat of the national baseball stadium in the Puerto Rican capital of San Juan, where he dethroned Ismael Laguna ('A far better fighter than Durán, in my opinion') over 15 rounds. They fought in a temperature of 120 degrees, and Buchanan's cornerman and dad, Tom, had to borrow a parasol from a female spectator to offer his son a measure of shade between rounds. 'It was the only time I won a world title and got sunburned at the same time.'

Buchanan was an active champion, beating Italian-Canadian Donato Paduano, Mexican Ruben Navarro and Carlos Hernandez of El Salvador – noted hard men all – within the space of eight months. After Buchanan outpointed Laguna in a rematch in the Garden, one American boxing writer was moved to comment: 'For boxing skills like that you have to go back to Sugar Ray [Robinson].'

Although he became a man possessed every time he climbed through the ropes, Roberto Durán, aka *'Manos de Piedra'* (Hands of Stone) was possessed of no such skills; Buchanan's next challenger was a swaggering bully who led his pet lion cub along the pavements of Panama City on a diamond encrusted lead. A street fighter who had never bothered to acquaint himself with the Queensberry Rules, Durán would happily accept twenty punches to land one explosive blow of his own – whether delivered with his fists, head or elbows he was unfussy.

Entering the ring in Madison Square Garden in his trademark tartan shorts and to the strains of 'Scotland the Brave', Buchanan was the 8–5 on favourite to retain his title but found himself on the back foot from the opening bell in the face of Durán's brutal assault. As ITV ring commentator Reg Gutteridge described Durán's preferred form of attack: 'He reminded me of a bull rhino crashing through the undergrowth. He was a relentless rather than a destructive knockout puncher who always gave the impression that he resented the presence of the referee.'

For once Buchanan, the peerless master of the noble art, was reduced to slugging it out toe-to-toe in the middle of the ring as Durán moved ahead on the scorecards of all three judges. Such was the ferocity of the contest that neither boxer heard the bell signalling the end of the 13th round and continued pummelling one another until Buchanan was sent writhing in agony to the canvas as a result – so claimed his vastly experienced trainer Gil Clancy (who also worked with Ali, Frazier, George Foreman and Oscar De La Hoya) – of a knee to the groin. Referee Johnny LoBianco awarded victory to the Panamanian on a technical knockout even though Buchanan insisted he was willing and able to continue. Although videotape of the incident was to prove that Buchanan had, indeed, been felled by an illegal blow, respected *New York Times* columnist Red Smith insisted the referee had been right in his judgement because 'anything short of pulling a knife is regarded indulgently' in an American ring. Durán did not need a flick-knife to rip a tear in Buchanan's right testicle. 'I peed blood for weeks afterwards.'

The War in the Garden was to remain fixed in the memory of all 18,000 spectators who witnessed a night of sporting theatre. Among the crowd was 20-year-old wannabe actor/boxer Mickey Rourke, who wrote to Buchanan over a decade later, by which time he had become a member of the Hollywood glitterati, to request a signed photograph for the wall of his gym in his Beverly Hills home.

While Durán went on to defend his lightweight crown 12 times before becoming a world champion at welterweight and middleweight, he studiously avoided another confrontation with the Scot. Years later, when asked to name his toughest opponent, Durán snarled: 'Among the lightweights – Buchanan. Brave as the lion, smart as the fox, as fast as the cobra.'

Blithely believing that Durán would be unable to ignore the public clamour for a rematch, Buchanan began the process of re-establishing himself as the leading contender. In January 1973, he dispossessed Jim Watt (who would subsequently become world champion when Durán relinquished the title to move up a division) of his British title over 15 rounds in the St Andrews Sporting Club. Never having been one to shirk entering any of the ring's notorious 'hot spots', Buchanan then travelled to Cagliari in Sardinia to win the European belt by knocking out local hero Antonio Puddu in the sixth round in front of an angry Italian crowd.

In February 1975, he was finally given another world title shot – the WBC version held by 'Guts' Ishimatsu of Japan – in Tokyo. Although well ahead on points two-thirds through the contest, Buchanan was deemed the loser of a fight many at ringside thought he had won with something to spare. The curtain was clearly coming down on what had been a glorious ring career and all Scotland heaved a collective sigh of relief when Buchanan announced his retirement in 1976 following his successful European title defence on a 12th round technical knockout against Usai on his return to Cagliari.

Having lost but three of his previous fifty-four fights, when Buchanan reappeared in the ring in 1978 he was a pale shadow of his former self; he was beaten in five of his last seven fights. 'Of course, it might all have turned out very differently if I hadn't lost to Durán,' he recalled in later years. 'That was a black, black day for me. He robbed me of my world crown, strong words I know but it's as simple as that. He attacked me after the bell and should have been disqualified. I could have gone on, even though the pain was indescribable, but yon ref was having none of it. Ach, it's a long time ago now, but it still hurts. It had been bloody hard work winning the championship from Laguna in San Juan and holding on to it for two years. Don't forget, this was at a time when any one of half a dozen fighters would have been good enough to win a world title today.

'I was privileged to fight in the golden era of boxing. When I was lightweight champion, there were ten world title holders: Joe Frazier . . . Bob Foster . . . Carlos Monzón . . . José Ángel Nápoles . . . Rubén Olivares. Giants, whatever their weights. Now you've got WBA, WBC, IBF, WBO, welterweight, super-welterweight, junior welterweight. Christ, there must be hundreds of boxers out there all calling themselves world champion.'

But Buchanan has never shed a tear on his own behalf, preferring to save his grief for those he feels are in real peril. 'I was lucky, I only lost my world title and Roberto and I can laugh about it now because we've become great mates over the years. Take Muhammad Ali; now there's a truly tragic figure. We shared a dressing-room twice when we were joint top of the bill in New York, so I got to see him right up close like. It broke my heart when I met him again in Edinburgh years later in 1993. I knew him as a bouncy, loveable rogue. When he came over here to sign copies of his book, he was like a zombie. One of the walking dead. His aides kept saying, "He knows you, Ken, you can see it in his eyes." But the poor man hadn't a clue who I was. He never opened his mouth all the time he was in the bookshop in Princes Street.

'He couldn't even pick up a pen. Do you know that all his so-called autographs had been written beforehand by his entourage on wee pieces of paper? As each person in the queue came forward, Ali peeled one off and stuck it inside the front cover. I was there as a special guest but I had to walk out and go home. Christ, I was about greetin'.'

As compassionate as he was courageous, Ken Buchanan is a proud man who has much of which to be proud.

8. SIR MATT BUSBY CBE, KCSG
Football

Born: Bellshill, 26 May 1909
Died: Manchester, 20 January 1994

CAREER (PLAYER):

**Manchester City 1928–36: 226 appearances, 14 goals; FA Cup
1934**

Liverpool 1936–9: 118 appearances, 3 goals

Scotland 1933: 1 appearance, 0 goals

CAREER (MANAGER):

Manchester United 1945–69 and 1970–71: English League
Championship 1951–52, 1955–56, 1956–57, 1964–65,
1966–77; FA Cup 1948, 1963; European Cup 1968

According to the family history passed down through the generations, as
Nellie Busby snuggled her newborn son on her bed in their cramped
pitman's cottage in Orbiston, the doctor grinned at the sight of the babe
kicking his sturdy legs with gusto and offered the prediction: 'A footballer
has come into this house this day.'

And what a footballer he turned out to be, although such were his
towering achievements as manager of Manchester United that Matt
Busby's playing career is invariably overlooked. When he inspired
United's great rivals Manchester City to victory over Portsmouth in the
1934 FA Cup final, a scribe of the day on the *Manchester Guardian* was
moved to write: 'In Matt Busby, City have a player who has no superior
as an attacking half-back.'

Resplendent in a bowler hat and white spats of an evening on the town,
Busby was no less elegant on the pitch, where he was the master of the inspired
interception and 40-yard defence-splitting pass. Despite his burgeoning
reputation to the south, however, Busby represented Scotland only once (a
2–2 draw against Wales in 1933) at a time when Alex Massie of Hearts and
later Aston Villa had laid claim to the international number 4 shirt.

Having enchanted one half of Manchester, Busby became one of the early heroes of the Anfield Kop when Liverpool paid City £8,000 to install him as club captain before, like so many of his generation, his days as a professional footballer were abruptly terminated by Adolf Hitler.

When peace was restored, Liverpool offered the returning Company Sgt Major Alexander Matthew Busby of the Ninth Battalion of the King's Liverpool Regiment the position of assistant manager to George Kay. However, young as he was, the 36-year-old tenderfoot had entrenched ideas about how the game should be played and how a club should be run and did not relish the prospect of being anyone's number two. Thus when Manchester United offered him the keys to the manager's office at Old Trafford, the super-confident Busby produced a list of unprecedented demands encompassing the appointment of coaches and scouts, the buying and selling of players, tactics and training. All this in an era when the board of directors' rule was absolute.

With Old Trafford in urgent need of repair after being bombed during a Luftwaffe raid on a nearby factory where the Rolls-Royce Spitfire engines were assembled (United would share Maine Road when League football was reintroduced for the 1946–47 season), there was little money available for new players. Despite budgetary restraints, however, Busby insisted that £4,000 be found to sign Celtic's dynamic outside-right Jimmy Delaney while enlisting an army of scouts to scour the British Isles for undiscovered – and therefore cheap – talent. As legend has it, every Roman Catholic priest in Ireland was a part-time employee.

Into each and every lad who arrived for a trial was drummed Busby's philosophy: 'Winning matches at all costs is not the test of true achievement; there is no dishonour in defeat as long as you play to the limit of your strength and skill. What matters above all things is that the game should be played in the right spirit, with fair play and no favour, with every man playing as a member of his team and the result accepted without bitterness and conceit. Played at its best between two first-class teams, football is a wonderful spectacle. I love its drama, its smooth playing skills, its carelessly laid rhythms, and the added flavour of contrasting styles. Its great occasions are, for me at any rate, unequalled in the world of sport. I feel a sense of romance, wonder and mystery, a sense of beauty and a sense of poetry. On such occasions, the game has the timeless, magical qualities of legend.'

In addition to building a team that would win with style, Busby harboured another dream: to establish the same 'one for all and all for one' sense of brotherhood that he had shared with his fellow miners at the bleak Lanarkshire pit-face of his youth when he would turn out for

Denny Hibs on a Saturday afternoon. To serve Manchester United – as club captain or tea lady – was to be welcomed into the Busby family.

Within two years, Busby's new family had won the FA Cup and, having finished runners-up four times in the previous five seasons, the First Division championship was finally claimed in 1952, the club's first League title since 1911. United had thrilled spectators throughout the country with their dazzling football but Busby was fully aware that his ageing team had passed its sell-by date long before he watched them being humbled 6–2 by Wolves at Molineux in the October of the new season and then held to a humiliating 1–1 draw by non-League Walthamstow Avenue in a third-round FA Cup tie at Old Trafford.

'If you don't put them in, then you can't know what you've got . . . if they're good enough, they're old enough,' he explained by way of announcing the birth of the Busby Babes, teenagers and fresh-faced 20-somethings all. Captained by the venerable Roger Byrne – at 25 the oldest player by a distance – and built around the peerless Duncan Edwards, who was just 16 years and 185 days when he made his debut against Cardiff City in April 1953, United won the First Division title by 11 points from Blackpool in 1956 with an average age of just 22. 'We didn't think of ourselves as the Busby Babes,' revealed Bobby Charlton. 'We were simply a team of lads, a team of pals.'

With the championship flag fluttering over Old Trafford and the FA Youth Cup captured for the fourth time in what would be five successive seasons, the visionary Busby was impatient to unleash his Babes upon an unsuspecting Europe. The establishment, in the shape of Football League secretary Alan Hardaker, was not best pleased. Hardaker regarded this newfangled European Cup as a direct threat to his domestic empire – 'I don't like dealing with Europe. Too many wops and dagoes,' he told *Sunday Times* football correspondent Brian Glanville – and had cajoled Chelsea into ignoring the inaugural competition won by Real Madrid in 1956.

Busby was not a man to be so bullied. 'Football has become a world game,' he told United chairman Harold Hardman, who was being pestered by Hardaker to snub UEFA's invitation to compete. 'It no longer belongs exclusively to England or Scotland . . . this is where the future lies.' It was a decision that would lead to untold heartache and eventually to his greatest triumph.

The Babes' first European adventure ended at the semi-final stage, when they were beaten 5–3 on aggregate by Real Madrid, but Busby was anything but disappointed. 'It was a contest between two great teams – a mature side and a young side and, of course, experience told. But our time will come.' As League champions for the second successive season,

February 1958 found United in Belgrade to defend a 2–1 quarter-final first-leg advantage against the redoubtable Yugoslav champions Red Star.

A thrilling 3–3 draw secured United's place in the last four for the second successive season before players and officials repaired to the after-match banquet in the Majestic Hotel, where Busby offered a rendition of 'I Belong to Glasgow' and skipper Roger Byrne led the Babes choir in a version of Vera Lynn's wartime classic 'We'll Meet Again'.

Less than 24 hours later, Byrne was dead, as were fellow Babes Tommy Taylor, David Pegg, Billy Whelan, Mark Jones, Eddie Colman and Geoff Bent, killed when their BEA Elizabethan crashed in the snow on the tarmac at Munich Airport after a refuelling stop and two aborted take-off attempts. Duncan Edwards died of his injuries 15 days later in the Rechts der Isar Hospital, in the same ward where Matt Busby twice received the last rites.

Against all medical opinion, Busby recovered and, riddled with guilt that his fascination with Europe had ended in unspeakable disaster, somewhat reluctantly began the process of putting together the Red Devils Mark III (he had always detested the term 'Busby Babes', being of the opinion that it made his fledglings sound weak and naive) around Charlton, Denis Law, a £115,000 signing from Torino, and a teenage winger from Belfast by the name of George Best.

Ten years after Munich, the holy grail was achieved when United defeated Benfica 4–1 in the 1968 European Cup final on an emotion-charged night at Wembley. In the midst of the scenes of jubilation at the end, Charlton and Busby silently clung to one another. 'I didn't say anything to the old man because I didn't need to. I knew exactly what he was thinking and how he was feeling. It was a big thing for the club, but it was a bigger thing for him personally. The lads who were killed in Munich had been his babies. So, yes, it was all very, very emotional.

'There was never a day went by when the old man didn't think about Munich. Those were his kids who died that day. Great, great players like Duncan Edwards, who'd have been captain of England in 1966 if he'd lived. Sir Matt never really got over it. He'd been one of the pioneers of European football and I think he always felt responsible. He was really satisfied when we won the European Cup in '68 – but he'd rather have done it with his beautiful boys. We'd all been infatuated with the European Cup ever since 1956 when we watched Real Madrid beating Reims in the very first final on our old black-and-white televisions. We were just in the process of making our mark in the competition when the tragedy happened, so we weren't able to pursue the dream. The final against Benfica was the biggest game any English club had ever played in, and for those of us who had survived Munich it was a doubly emotional occasion.

'I think the old man had wanted to retire for some time, but he knew we wouldn't let him go until we'd won the European Cup in memory of his "lovely boys", as he always called them. Whenever you think of the accident, you think, "What were we doing in Munich, for God's sake?" It was a very different world back then; people didn't travel the way they do now – planes don't stop to refuel any more – so in football terms, we were pioneers. And I think that's why Sir Matt found it so difficult to cope with his feelings when he finally pulled through. He'd taken us on what he'd regarded as a great adventure – a great adventure from which eight of the lads never came back.'

Nobby Stiles also looks back on Wembley '68 with a touch of sadness. 'If you watch the film of that final, you'll see that as soon as the game was over, we all surrounded Matt. Shay Brennan and myself had been kids at the time of Munich, Bobby Charlton and Bill Foulkes, of course, had actually survived the crash, and the general feeling was we'd done it for Matt and his beloved Babes. As a team, I don't think we ever felt the same spirit again and I don't think Matt did either.

'Few people know that Matt was on the treatment table every day of his life receiving physiotherapy for his injuries. We'll never know what pain he suffered, and maybe he felt his quest was complete when we won the European Cup that the lads who perished might have won a decade earlier. George Best always insisted that was the end of something when it should really have been the beginning; for years I disagreed with him, but I came to understand what he meant by that remark.'

His ambition fulfilled and the recipient of a knighthood in the aftermath of his European Cup triumph, Sir Matt retired a year later as United fell into a period of decline. But until his death from cancer at the age of 84 in 1994, he remained, as former Prime Minister Harold Wilson had put it, 'a symbol of everything that is best in our great national game'.

On 26 May 1999, the 90th anniversary of Busby's birth, another Scottish footballing knight would lead United to their second victory in the competition before adding a third success in 2008 – half a century on from Munich.

9. FINLAY CALDER OBE
Rugby Union

Born: Haddington, 20 August 1957

CAREER:
Clubs: Stewart's Melville FP and Heriot's FP
Scotland 1986–91: 34 caps, 8 points
British Lions: captain, 1989, Australia (won 2–1)

He is such a jolly good fellow – which nobody who has met him can deny – it seems impossible that there are those who would charge Finlay Calder on three counts of high treason.

That at Twickenham on 2 November 1991, when a number of his Scottish teammates donned Wallaby shirts and swagman bush hats to attend the World Cup final and savour England's defeat against Australia, the accused refused to show the same support for our colonial cousins.

Not guilty! As Calder rightly pointed out in his defence, a goodly proportion of the Sassenach contingent had played under him as captain of the British Lions on their tour of Australia two years earlier, on top of which he was close friends with some of the English XV. In all conscience, therefore, he could find no reason in his heart or head to belt out 'Waltzin' Matilda' while dressed up like Rolf Harris.

But surely the man condemned himself through his own mouth by admitting that 'some of my best friends are English'? Given the history of our meetings with the Auld Enemy in the field of sporting battle, what was going though Calder's mind when he agreed to serve as an usher at the wedding of that noted 'hammer of the Scots' Brian Moore?

Not guilty! Despite what he might have us believe, the mischievous Mr Moore is a great admirer of Scotland (except when the Calcutta Cup is on the line, that is) and all things Scottish. On the afternoon following Scotland's Grand Slam victory over the English at Murrayfield in 1990, did he not attend a celebratory lunch at Watsonians RFC where he cheerfully accepted all the ridicule (and drinks) aimed his way? On top of which, Moore specifically asked that Calder don full Highland dress for his wedding, which was held in St Columba's Presbyterian Church of Scotland in London's Knightsbridge.

OK, perhaps Moore is not the blackguard of popular perception but how could any proud Scot describe 'Flower of Scotland' as 'an embarrassing anti-English rant', as Calder has gone on record as suggesting?

Not guilty! Many are they who regard our national anthem as a dirge compared with the stirring sentiments of 'Scotland the Brave'. Calder was mightily impressed when the Irish fans warmly applauded England at Croke Park – scene of a massacre involving British troops in 1920 during the War of Independence – on the afternoon rugby returned to the stadium. At Murrayfield, in contrast, England are routinely jeered. 'I have a dream for Scottish rugby founded upon England's visit to Croke Park when, despite the tragic history, the Irish nation welcomed the English team and supporters as friends. It's time to get back to what people recognise as being Scottish – being fair and friendly.'

So let no one doubt Calder's pride in his nation or his family's efforts in Scotland's cause; his twin, Jim, scored the crucial try in the defeat of France in 1984 at Murrayfield where Scotland registered only their second Grand Slam triumph in history, and Finlay Calder was an inspirational presence six years later when we beat England on the same turf to complete a memorable Calcutta Cup, Triple Crown and Grand Slam treble. No matter what anthem he was singing in his own head, whenever Calder pulled on the dark-blue shirt – and no matter how many chums might be lining up on the other side of the halfway line – he performed like the Furies.

Never more so than that 1990 winner-take-all confrontation with England, who had sauntered into Edinburgh – having crushed France, Ireland and Wales by an aggregate 83 points to 13 – flaunting a confidence bordering on contemptuous arrogance. 'The atmosphere inside Murrayfield was unreal,' recalled England skipper Will Carling. 'I've never known anything like it.'

Within four minutes, Calder took a tap penalty and smashed straight into Mick Skinner and Mike Teague, driving the England maul back 15 yards as the Scottish forwards ploughed joyously into the fray. 'What the hell's going on here?' Carling asked himself as Calder emerged from the mass of bodies sporting a great grin of satisfaction.

'Inspired by Finlay Calder's early heroics, they tore into us as never before,' continued Carling. 'As captain, I'd got it badly, badly wrong. My preparation was crap, to put it bluntly; we were far too complacent while Scotland were absolutely right for it. We totally underestimated them that day because we'd never entertained the possibility of defeat. But we were out-muscled, outmanoeuvred, out-thought and outplayed. The

English lads who had been on the '89 Lions tour with Fin – which I'd missed with a busted leg – didn't really rate some of the Scots who'd been with them in Australia. Oh, we knew they had four or five very good players but a number of others, to be honest, who were not that great. So the level they rose to was incredible; when I got to know David Sole and Finlay a bit better they explained that pulling on a Scotland shirt to play England was like entering a sheep dip of craziness. And what a lovely image that conjures up.

'I can barely remember the after-match dinner because I was in such a state of shock I couldn't even drink myself into oblivion; it was just so weird. Looking across the room at Fin, Soley and the rest of them celebrating – and quite deservedly so – I thought "If I never, ever lose to these bastards again, I'll be happy" – and I never did, as it happens. But I also never got over it. It was at that moment I knew that we had to learn to hate the other countries – I mean hate in a sporting context – as much as they hated us. I wanted to feel as proud playing for England as they so obviously did in playing for Scotland.'

Few before or since have ever felt as proud as Finlay Calder, who did not emerge from the Stewart's Melville back row to make his Scotland debut until the advanced age of 28 by which time brother Jim had already won the last of his 27 caps. Such was his explosive impact upon the international arena, however, that just three years later he was granted the ultimate honour when he was awarded the captaincy of the British Lions.

It would be fair to say that the '89 Lions are not remembered as the most popular visitors ever to pitch up Down Under but Calder had not led his red shirts to Oz in order to pose for photographs beside Sydney Harbour Bridge or Uluru. This was a business trip, not a holiday jaunt, and he was intent on becoming the first British Lions skipper to win a Test series since Willie John McBride's storming campaign in South Africa 15 years before.

When the Lions lost the opening Test 30–12 in Sydney, where the Wallaby forwards held the ascendancy, Calder and coach Ian McGeechan decided that a more physical if less entertaining approach was needed and made wholesale changes for the second international in Brisbane, injecting the pack with a decidedly English flavour. The Lions duly squared the series courtesy of a 19–12 victory but were roundly condemned by the Australian media for what the locals regarded as 'roughhouse' tactics. To purists, it was an ugly 80-minute exhibition of rugby which began with the first scrum of the game descending into a punch-up and was enlivened only by two crucial tries from Gavin Hastings and Jeremy Guscott. It may not have been pretty to watch but

Calder and McGeechan's plan to meet the Aussie pack head-on had been vindicated.

When the two teams returned to Sydney for the decider, a bloodbath was widely anticipated. In contrast, Australia and the Lions combined to provide an enthralling 80 minutes, with the result decided by a rare error from the peerless David Campese, who gifted Welsh winger Ieuan Evans the winning try. Calder's tourists had won the most slender of 19–18 successes. It was the first time in the twentieth century that the British Lions had lost a First Test and gone on to win the series.

In his foreword to Jeff Connor's affectionately crafted *Giants of Scottish Rugby*, Calder wrote: 'Before one Calcutta Cup match against England, Jim Telfer told us, "To represent your country is the highlight of anyone's life but just remember that when you are given the Scotland jersey you are only given a loan of it. It represents everyone who has played for Scotland in the past and will play for Scotland in the future. When your career is over, then you hand that jersey back for future generations."'

As gentle off the pitch as he was fearsome on it, no one took greater pride in that jersey than Finlay Calder.

10. WILLIE CARSON OBE

Horse Racing

Born: Stirling, 16 November 1942

CAREER:
English Classics:
  Derby (4): Troy (1979), Henbit (1980), Nashwan (1989),
    Erhaab (1994)
  1,000 Guineas (2): Salsabil (1990), Shadayid (1991)
  2,000 Guineas (4): High Top (1972), Known Fact (1980),
    Don't Forget Me (1987), Nashwan (1989)
  Oaks (4): Dunfermline (1977), Bireme (1980), Sun Princess
    (1983), Salsabil (1990)
  St Leger (3): Dunfermline (1977), Sun Princess (1983),
    Minster Son (1988)
Irish Classics:
  Derby (2): Troy (1979), Salsabil (1990)
  1,000 Guineas (2): Mehthaaf (1994), Matiya (1996)
  2,000 Guineas (1): Don't Forget Me (1987)
  Oaks (4): Dibidale (1974), Shoot A Line (1980), Swiftfoot
    (1982), Helen Street (1985)
  St Leger (1): Niniski (1979)
British Champion Jockey (5): 1972, 1973, 1978, 1980, 1983
Total wins (Britain): 3,828

The 1994 Derby was like the chariot race in *Ben Hur* without the chariots. 'The worst and roughest race I ever rode in,' observed South African jockey Michael Roberts. 'It was bloody ridiculous.' With a large field of twenty-five runners – eight of whom went under starter's orders at 100–1 and more, including two 500–1 no-hopers – it was something of a miracle that the well-backed Foyer was the only faller amidst the carnage.

By the time the jostling, bumping and general mayhem had subsided, Willie Carson aboard the hot favourite Erhaab found himself ten lengths behind runaway leader Mister Baileys with just two furlongs to run.

Lesser riders and stallions might have been content to canter home, simply relieved to have survived this infamous 'Demolition Derby', instead of which horse and jockey produced the finish of their lives. As Mister Baileys began to fade, so Carson released Erhaab on an electrifying run to shoot clear of the chasing posse like a black streak and pass the post one-and-a-quarter lengths ahead of the field.

Carson had given his noble steed the greatest ride in Derby history and the tributes to his courage and skill poured in. 'I seriously doubt if many other jockeys in living memory would have won on Erhaab,' enthused Alastair Down in the *Sporting Life*. Writing in the *Daily Mail*, the late Ian Wooldridge jokingly suggested that Carson was a suitable case for treatment: 'The man is mad, of course. To slalom through a stampede of wild horses by choice when you are 51 years old and can damned near buy the place is the very definition of insanity.'

Perhaps Carson's was a divine madness, for 13 years earlier, so his fellow jockeys will tell you, he received the last rites after being trampled by six horses during the Yorkshire Stakes at York, where his mount, Silken Knot, slipped and fell while lying third, leaving her rider with a fractured skull. Although American jockey Steve Cauthen described it as the worst fall he had ever seen – 'Willie was lucky to come out alive because the

---

Rubstic

Once upon a time, in 1839 a horse aptly named Lottery won the first Grand National; once upon another time in 1904, Moifaa was shipwrecked off the coast of Ireland en route to Liverpool from New Zealand, swam ashore after being given up for lost by the crew, then strolled to an eight-length victory.

Then came Devon Loch, Aintree's unluckiest loser; Foinavon, the luckiest victor; Red Rum, three times a winner; and Bob Champion and Aldaniti, who both recovered from life-threatening conditions to triumph in 1981. Aye, for 172 years, the Grand National has been spinning fairy tales.

In 1979, one of the strongest fields ever assembled came under starter's orders led by the classy Alverton, the short-priced favourite who had won the Cheltenham Gold Cup two weeks earlier, followed in the betting by Ben Nevis, Rough And Tumble and The Pilgarlic, who would finish 1-2-3 a year later. Among the 34 runners thought to be at Aintree simply to make up the numbers was Rubstic, owned by former Scotland and British Lions rugby player John Douglas and trained by John Leadbetter in the Borders village of Denholm. Although his horse was unknown down south, Leadbetter had been unobtrusively placing a £5 bet every week for eight months leading up to the race, hence the reason Rubstic, the smallest horse in the field, went off at 25–1, 41 points below his opening starting price of 66–1.

Tragedy was waiting at the 22nd fence, the infamous Becher's Brook, where Alverton fell in a tangle of legs. Whether he died of a broken neck or a heart attack in mid-air will

horses galloped right over him' – Carson prefers to look back on events with his trademark cheeky-chappy grin intact.

'I was knocked unconscious so I didn't have a clue what was going on around me. But according to those who were there, then I must have been one lucky fella because the poor filly broke her two front legs and had to be destroyed. Silken Knot was going to win easily, we were cruising along until she must have stumbled into a hole or something; all I heard was this sickening crack! After that, I don't remember anything until I woke up in a hospital bed surrounded by worried faces peering down at me. To me, the worst thing about it all was being suspended from riding for seven months on medical grounds. I was leading the jockeys' championship by 14 winners at the time and no one was going to catch me, so it was goodbye to another title plus a wad of earnings.'

Typically, Carson provides an amusing postscript to his tale of woe when the Queen took an interest in the well-being of her horse's jockey. 'About three weeks after the accident, I received a bill from some flaming doctor I'd never heard of. He turned out to be Her Majesty's personal neurologist, who she'd asked to give me the once-over, so I ended up paying a doctor I wasn't aware I'd ever seen. It was obviously a very serious accident and a lot of experts – medical and racing – reckoned that I'd never be the same again. But as far as I was concerned, it never happened because I was in my own wee twilight world, so why shouldn't I be the same again?'

Carson had grown accustomed to beating the odds both on and off the racecourse; small from birth – even as an adult he would stubbornly remain a quarter of an inch under five feet – he developed a complex about his size at primary school in Stirling. 'I was a war baby, which is probably why I was so small. And being wee, I was picked on because I was an easy target, wasn't I? I was bullied, but I gradually learned the tricks of the trade, how to win people over, how to get out of tricky situations, how to adapt to situations.' Sensing her son's unhappiness,

---

never be known. As jockey Jonjo O'Neill comforted the stricken horse a vet was summoned to put an end to his agony.

By the fourth last fence, only four horses remained in contention: Zongalero, Rough And Tumble, Rubstic and The Pilgarlic. Over the last and into the home straight, it was Rubstic, the only Scottish horse to win the Grand National, who found the reserves of energy to pass the finishing post two lengths ahead of Zongalero, with the exhausted Rough And Tumble third among only seven finishers.

Dismissed by many in light of Alverton's demise, the gallant Rubstic fell only once in his entire career – in the 1980 National – when he started as favourite only to slip and lose his footing at The Chair, the biggest fence on the course.

May Carson fretted as only a mother can. 'He was so tiny I sometimes used to wonder how he was going to manage in life.'

With no Scottish jockeys to act as inspiration and with his knowledge of horses restricted to the local rag-and-bone man's nag – 'Whenever we saw a horse in our street, everyone would rush out with a brush and shovel for the roses' – the possibility of a career in racing had never occurred to Carson. Then, one fateful winter's night in 1954, he filed into the Allanpark Cinema to see *The Rainbow Jacket*, a tale of the turf starring Robert Morley, Bill Owen, Honor Blackman, Sidney James and champion jockey Gordon Richards as himself.

'That was it. Watching that wee fella up on the screen, I suddenly knew that it was a jockey's life for me. I came from anything but the traditional horsey background; my dad was a warehouseman in the local Fyffes banana store. So I took a paper round and spent my entire weekly wage – 10s/6d [52½p] plus tips – on riding lessons at the Cathedral Stables in nearby Dunblane. Funnily enough, years later the mother of the young actor who played the jockey, Georgie Crain – a fella by the name of Fella Edmonds, as it happens – wrote to tell me he'd grown up to be 6 ft 1 in.'

Even when he joined the Yorkshire stable of Gerald Armstrong at Middleham as a sixteen-year-old apprentice in 1959, no one could have foreseen that here was a future winner of seventeen English Classics, five champion jockey's titles, 3,828 wins on the flat in Britain (a total bettered only by Sir Gordon Richards, Lester Piggott and Pat Eddery) and the recipient of an OBE for his outstanding services to horse racing.

'I was never a natural rider, certainly no boy wonder. In fact, I often think that the only natural I ever knew was Lester Piggott. I was a slow developer but I've always believed that was no bad thing. A lot of jockeys who achieved success too early proceeded to blow it. I was quite elderly in comparison to some when I finally hit the big time and I only got there by clawing my way up the ladder rung by rung.'

Carson made his debut in front of the public at Redcar on 18 May 1959, when he finished stone last on Marija 'after being thrown about like a rag doll in the saddle'. It took him over three years to achieve his first victory – 'Aboard Pinkers Pond at Catterick, as if I could ever forget' – but even when he became the first Scot to win the jockeys' championship in 1972, he remained relatively unknown to the country at large.

All that was to change at Epsom in June 1977 when he rode Dunfermline, owned by Her Majesty Queen Elizabeth II, to triumph in the Oaks. 'Seventy-seven was my first year as stable jockey to Major Dick Hern, a job which was regarded as one of the best three jobs in the country. I'd ridden a lot of winners by then but I was still pretty low profile. Winning the Oaks and later the St Leger for the Queen would probably have made headlines in any normal year but it couldn't have come at a better time than slap bang in the middle of all the Silver Jubilee celebrations.

'Major Hern had been telling me for ages exactly how good Dunfermline was but I was a bit sceptical until I rode her for the first and only time before the Oaks in a race at Newmarket, where she duly romped home. She wasn't what you would call a feminine filly, she was like a bloody man, really, but she knew her business and the huge smile on my face was only matched by that on the face of the Queen Mum, who was standing in for her daughter. The Queen couldn't be at Epsom because the Oaks was run in Silver Jubilee week so I expect she was quite busy elsewhere. But I know she was sorry to miss the race because Dunfermline was one of her best ever horses. She sent me a beautiful pair of cufflinks as a "thank you" for presenting her with the Oaks as a Silver Jubilee gift from horse racing.'

Although Carson rates his 1989 Derby winner Nashwan as the greatest horse he rode – 'It was like making love every time I got on him' – it is for his display in the '94 Derby that he will be forever remembered in Turf folklore. 'It certainly has to go down as one of the best races I ever rode in my career. I'd told the world that Erhaab would win and was so confident that I asked my valet to nip down to a local supermarket on the Friday to buy the champagne for everybody in the weighing-room, which has become a Derby tradition. Being a canny Scot, I didn't want to be paying fancy Epsom prices.' Was it the best Derby of them all, as some claim? 'I don't know about that, but it wasn't bad for an old granddad of nearly 52, was it?'

11. JIM CLARK OBE
Motor Racing

Born: Kilmany, Fife, 4 March 1936
Died: Hockenheim, 7 April 1968

CAREER:
Formula One world champion 1963, 1965
F1 Grands Prix (25 wins, 72 races):
  1962: Belgian, British, United States
  1963: Belgian, French, British, Dutch, Italian, Mexican,
      South African
  1964: Belgian, British, Dutch
  1965: Belgian, French, German, British, Dutch, South
   African
  1966: United States
  1967: Dutch, British, United States, Mexican
  1968: South African
Indianapolis 500 winner 1965

Three years before he was killed during the 1994 San Marino Grand Prix at Imola, Ayrton Senna commissioned Mexican artist Hugo Escobedo to craft an oil painting depicting the ultimate 'fantasy' Grand Prix, an impression of the starting grid at Monaco featuring all the greatest drivers in motor-racing history.

This being the era before Michael Schumacher staked his claim to be so recognised, the German is absent from the canvas, but there sits Juan Fangio at the wheel of his 1950 Alfa Romeo 158 . . . alongside the Argentinian, Stirling Moss is seen climbing into his 1960s Vanwall . . . Jackie Stewart, all Sergeant Pepper sideburns, pulls on his helmet in the cockpit of his Matra-Ford . . . Emerson Fittipaldi, the first of the great Brazilians, is there in his early 1970s Lotus . . . Niki Lauda in the classic Ferrari of '75 . . . and Senna himself (well, he was paying for this work of art, after all), squeezed into the all-conquering McLaren-Honda in which he won the 1991 world drivers' championship.

Senna laid down two non-negotiable instructions: Frenchman Alain Prost, with whom he had many an angry confrontation, was to be conspicuous by his absence from this august gathering, and, secondly, that the artist could place the drivers in any formation he chose on the Monaco grid, providing Jim Clark filled pole position. 'After all,' explained the Brazilian in a rare moment of modesty, 'he was the best of the best.'

Even today, four decades and more after his death in an otherwise meaningless Formula Two race at Hockenheim, Jim Clark is still revered as 'the best of the best' by many within F1. In a tragically brief career of 72 Grands Prix, he recorded 25 victories, occupied pole position on 33 occasions, and was the first overseas winner of the Indianapolis 500 in almost half a century. At the time of his crash he had been world champion twice – in 1963 and again in 1965 – and, having only just turned 32, was poised to dominate the sport for years to come.

Born into a wealthy Fife farming family, Clark was raised in the Borders, where, despite parental misgivings, he became the original boy racer. Something mystical overcame a car placed in his tender care. And not just the Jaguar sports car, Sunbeam Talbot touring car and the Ford Cortina rally car which he regularly drove in a variety of competitions. Even the old tractor on the family's Borders farm was said to purr with pleasure whenever Clark took the wheel.

Colin Chapman, owner of the newly formed Lotus team, was also like the cat that got the cream when he signed Clark and gave the 24 year old his first drive in F1 in the 1960 Dutch GP at Zandvoort, where the rookie was lying fourth until forced to retire with transmission failure. Two weeks later Clark claimed his first world championship points by finishing fifth to Australian Jack Brabham in the Belgian GP at Spa Francorchamps, a race blighted by double tragedy.

At the 120-mph Burnenville bend on Lap 20, Clark was flagged down by a steward alerting him to the crashed Cooper-Climax of Londoner Chris Bristow. 'The marshal bent down and grabbed this thing by the side of the road. It looked a like a rag doll. I'll never forget the sight of his mangled body being dragged away. At the end of the race my car was splattered in blood.' Bristow had been decapitated on a barbed wire fence separating the track from an adjoining meadow after his car had slewed off the circuit and mounted an embankment. A few minutes later, Clark's teammate Alan Stacey died of a broken neck on the same bend after being hit in the face by a bird. 'I didn't see Alan's accident or car. If I had, I'm convinced I would have given up motor racing for good that day.'

Clark was to experience further horror and sorrow during the 1961 Italian GP at Monza, where German Wolfgang von Trips moved slightly off line just as Clark pulled alongside to overtake, thereby brushing wheels. Von Trips' Ferrari crashed into the crowd, killing 14 spectators while fatally throwing him clear. Despite being completely innocent, to a shy and sensitive soul such as Jim Clark the death of 15 people was an unbearable torture and it took all of Chapman's avuncular coaxing to prevent him quitting the sport he so loved. Clark determined there and then, however, that he would remain single throughout his driving career. 'I couldn't ask any woman to share this kind of life,' he explained.

By 1963, he was world champion, having won an unprecedented seven of the season's ten Grands Prix. His victory in the driving rain and blinding spray at Spa that spring was the stuff of genius: starting eighth on the grid, by Lap 17 Clark had lapped every driver in the race except New Zealander Bruce McLaren, who was still a good eight miles behind on the old snaking circuit. Little wonder that Fangio and Moss regarded him as a young god, while Soviet cosmonaut Yuri Gagarin said by way of introduction: 'I suppose you will be in awe of me, just as I am in awe of you.'

Not that Clark was ever comfortable with such idolatry. While he was happy to mingle with Prince Rainier and Princess Grace on his annual visit to Monaco – where, curiously, he never won, despite it being his favourite circuit – he was always more comfortable on his regular home visits to Duns, where he was known as 'Jimmy' by the local farming community. Roguishly handsome, wryly amusing and endearingly charming as he was, Clark was a notoriously shy introvert who habitually bit his nails whenever invited to speak or appear in public.

He would have retained the drivers' title in '64 but for an oil leak on the last lap of the last race in Mexico, where he slowed to a crawl on the final bend to take the chequered flag in fifth place. Clark's misfortune allowed Ferrari's John Surtees to become the first man to win world titles on both two and four wheels, having previously claimed seven 350-cc and 500-cc motorcycling crowns.

On New Year's Day 1965, Clark announced his resolution to regain the championship with a storming victory in the South African GP, finishing over 30 seconds ahead of second-placed Surtees. Such was his confidence in his car and his own skills that Clark decided to miss the second race of the season at Monaco to launch a third attempt at winning the Indianapolis 500, an event that had fascinated him since boyhood.

He might have won at the famous 'Brickyard' in '63 but was seriously hampered by the oil spilling from the car of eventual winner Parnelli Jones and had to settle for second place; the following season Clark set the fastest time in practice and led for 14 of his 47 laps before pulling up when the suspension sheared on his Lotus. One year on, Clark was not to be denied: starting in second place on the grid behind four times Borg-

Warner Trophy winner A.J. Foyt, Clark led for 190 of the 200 laps. Although he slowed in the latter stages to preserve fuel, such was his dominance that he cruised to victory by over two minutes to become the Indie's first non-American champion of the post-war era.

Having conquered the United States, Clark returned to F1 well over £1 million richer by today's standards. He won the next five Grands Prix and, although he finished 1965 with tenth place in the Italian GP at Monza and successive retirements in Mexico and the US, by racing to victory in six of the nine events in which he competed, Clark regained the world title ahead of Graham Hill and rookie Jackie Stewart. 'He was so smooth, he was so clean, he drove with such finesse,' said the future Sir Jackie of his idol. 'He never bullied a racing car, he sort of caressed it into doing the things he wanted it to do.'

Clark's Lotus was short of power throughout 1966 but, after retiring in the opening two races of '67, the team roared back with victories in the Dutch, British, US and Mexican Grands Prix. Even so, the title went to the greater consistency of New Zealander Denny Hulme in a Brabham despite Clark producing what many believe to have been the greatest drive in history at Monza.

Starting from his customary place in pole position, Clark was in masterly control when he suffered a puncture and lost an entire lap whilst sitting in the pits. Rejoining the race a lowly 16th, Clark proceeded to set fastest lap after fastest lap in front of the disbelieving Italian spectators, overtaking every car twice to regain the lead from Brabham and Surtees as they headed into the last lap. Alas, his heroics were in vain, Clark running out of fuel (a rare error of judgement on Chapman's part) to freewheel past the chequered flag in third place.

Clark began 1968 in style with a storming victory in the South African GP at Kyalami and a third world championship beckoned until his fateful decision to compete in a Formula Two race in Germany. A generation on, the mystery surrounding Clark's crash at Hockenheim continues to baffle everyone involved in the sport. On the sixth lap and under no pressure, he entered a gentle right-hand bend at over 140 mph, whereupon his Lotus shot off the track. This being in the days before safety barriers at Hockenheim, the car somersaulted into a copse. Although the track was wet from morning rain and the circuit shrouded in mist, driving error was immediately ruled out; Jim Clark did not make mistakes.

Theories abound to this day, the most popular being that shortly before the accident two children had been seen running across the track, causing Clark to perform a fatal swerve. Although a spectator subsequently phoned a German newspaper offering photographs of the incident, no such pictures have ever been published. Lotus team chief Colin Chapman subsequently pieced together every fragment of the wreckage by hand. His conclusion was that Clark died as the result of a puncture to his rear right tyre, 'although this accident need not have been fatal if adequate crash barriers of the type used at Monaco and elsewhere had been installed'.

Ferrari's New Zealand driver Chris Amon spoke for the whole F1 family when he said: 'Beyond the grief, there was also the fear which we all felt. If it could happen to Jim Clark, then what chance did the rest of us have? It felt like we'd lost our leader.'

At the funeral held at Chirnside Old Church in the Scottish Borders three days after his death – a service attended by Jackie Stewart, Graham Hill and Jack Brabham, among many hundreds of mourners – Colin Chapman told the congregation: 'As a man, he meant more to me than any other. He was so thoroughly well brought up, so thoroughly well adjusted. There was so much good in Jimmy. He improved me as a person in so many ways.'

Never one to flaunt his celebrity, his gravestone in the ancient churchyard reads simply: In Loving Memory of Jim Clark OBE. Born 4.3.36, died 7.4.68. Farmer of Edington Mains . . . and World Champion Motor Racing Driver 1963 and 1965.

12. KENNY DALGLISH MBE
Football

Born: Glasgow, 4 March 1951

CAREER (PLAYER):
Celtic 1969–77: 313 appearances, 167 goals; Scottish League Championship 1971–72, 1972–73, 1973–74, 1975–76, 1976–77; Scottish Cup 1972, 1974, 1975, 1977; Scottish League Cup 1975
Liverpool 1977–1989: 515 appearances, 172 goals; English League Championship 1978–79, 1979–80, 1981–82, 1982–83, 1983–84; English League Cup 1981, 1982, 1983, 1984; European Cup 1978, 1981, 1984; European Super-Cup 1978; Footballer of the Year 1979, 1983
Scotland 1971–86: 102 appearances, 30 goals

CAREER (PLAYER-MANAGER):
Liverpool 1985–91: English League Championship 1985–86, 1987–88, 1989–90; FA Cup 1986, 1989; Manager of the Year 1986, 1988, 1990

CAREER (MANAGER):
Blackburn Rovers 1991–5: English Premier League 1995; Manager of the Year 1995
Newcastle United 1997–8
Celtic 2000: Scottish League Cup 2000
Liverpool 2011–12

It was Gordon Strachan who was moved to comment: 'I've always felt there was a scriptwriter up on a cloud somewhere penning Kenny's life story.' If so, then the celestial scribe in question could be forgiven for reaching back into the Hollywood archives for inspiration and entitling the epic 'the Greatest Story Ever Told'.

Worshipped as a god at Paradise, despite his unhappy return as director of football during John Barnes' miserable tenure, twice blessed at Anfield, where he inspired Liverpool to serial glories as both player and manager, and revered at Blackburn Rovers, the club he transformed from Second Division anonymity into Premier League champions with the assistance of steel magnate Jack Walker's treasure chest.

As a player, Dalglish had few equals; beautifully balanced and equipped with a football brain that put him one move ahead of opposing defenders, he could sniff out goals like a champion porker searching for truffles. 'I never saw anyone in this country who could touch him,' enthused his good buddy Graeme Souness. 'I can think of only two players who might go in front of him, Pelé and Cruyff. But he was better than Maradona, Rummenigge or Platini. For three or four years, on his day Kenny was the best player in the world without a shadow of a doubt.'

Nor do you have to be close friends to appreciate the man's genius with a football at his toes or an uncanny ability to find the time and space that would have allowed him a clear run through the Charge of the Light Brigade. 'If Kenny Dalglish had been born in Brazil, he would unquestionably have played for Brazil,' was the opinion of one-time England manager Bobby Robson. Fortunately for Scotland, Super Kenny was raised somewhat closer to Ibrox than Ipanema, winning an unsurpassed 102 caps and scoring 30 goals, a record he shares with Denis Law.

Dalglish's goals – all 369 of them in total for club and country – came in every guise, from the simple tap-in to the exquisite curler he scored against Belgium in the 1982 European Championship qualifier in Brussels. 'When he scores, he has a better smile than Clark Gable,' said Brian Clough. 'Beautiful teeth flashing, arms flung out wide, that's how he celebrates. He isn't that big but he has a huge arse – it comes down below his knees and that's where he gets his strength from.'

Given his subsequent impact at Liverpool, it is curious that no one spotted Dalglish's potential (or his famous backside, for that matter) when he arrived at the club's Melwood training ground for a trial as a 15 year old after scoring twice on his debut for Scotland Schoolboys against Northern Ireland in Belfast. As Anfield centre-forward turned TV pundit Ian St John recalled: 'It was only later that Bill Shankly realised Dalglish had been here as a boy and he went mad. "How did we miss him?" he growled whenever his name was mentioned.'

West Ham's Ron Greenwood was another left ruing 'the one that got away' tale, twice inviting Dalglish to Upton Park for trials only to allow the disappointed teenager to return home without a contract. And so with Rangers also oblivious to the precious talent that stood on the Ibrox terracing of a Saturday afternoon, Dalglish accepted Jock Stein's invitation to join his newly crowned European champions. (On hearing from his dad that Celtic assistant manager Sean Fallon was at the family's front door, Dalglish was compelled to hide away in his bedroom to give himself time to rip down his array of Rangers posters.)

With the Lisbon Lions to act as their inspiration, Dalglish became a member of the Quality Street Gang, the youthful Celtic reserve team containing those such as Danny McGrain, Lou Macari, David Hay, George Connelly and Paul Wilson who drew huge crowds to Parkhead. Although Stein knew he had unearthed a rare nugget, he allowed Dalglish to serve out his apprenticeship in the Second XI before unleashing him upon an unsuspecting football world on 14 May 1971 in a testimonial game for Kilmarnock's long-serving defender Frank Beattie; Celtic won 7–2, with Dalglish scoring six; the young prince had become a king.

Over the next six seasons, Dalglish would amass five championship and four Scottish Cup winner's medals before, almost reluctantly, acknowledging that his native land was too humble a stage for his prodigious skills. When Kevin Keegan quit Liverpool for Hamburg, Bob Paisley had no qualms about paying a British transfer record of £440,000 to parade Dalglish as the departing hero's replacement in the number 7 shirt; like the Lisbon Lions before him, Dalglish wanted to conquer Europe and to do that he had to join the continent's most successful club of the day.

Any doubts the Kop might have harboured as to his ability to replace the seemingly irreplaceable evaporated when he scored within seven minutes of his debut at Middlesbrough and, on his first appearance at Anfield, the opening goal in Liverpool's 2–0 defeat of Newcastle United. By the time of Liverpool's crushing 6–0 victory over Keegan's Hamburg in the second leg of the European Super-Cup, the Kop was awash in banners proclaiming 'Kevin Who?'

Nine months after joining Liverpool, Dalglish achieved his boyhood ambition by scoring the winning goal in the 1978 European Cup final against Bruges at Wembley. In his first two years in England, he scored 55 goals in 111 games and was voted Footballer of the Year.

As the honours accumulated – two further European Cup triumphs in 1981 and 1984, five League Championships, international caps and an MBE – so the accolades poured forth. 'After Kevin Keegan left, no one was quite sure how Bob Paisley would fill the gap but it was a masterstroke to sign Kenny from Celtic,' said teammate David 'Super Sub' Fairclough, scorer of 34 goals in 98 appearances, the majority of which were claimed after coming off the Liverpool bench. 'With his football brain and ability to score goals out of nothing, Dalglish became the main man of the Liverpool sides throughout the late '70s and '80s. The way he could score goals and also create them for other players around him was special. He will always be remembered as the king here at Anfield.'

While former chairman John Smith declared: 'The best player this club has signed this century.' In fact, 25 years after that remark, Dalglish remains Liverpool's best signing by far, even if you add World Cup winner Fernando Torres and England midfielder Steven Gerrard to a mix comprising Keegan, Ian Rush, Alan Hansen, Billy Liddell, Tommy Smith and John Barnes.

But Liverpool were to demand even more of their talisman: when Joe Fagan resigned in the aftermath of the Heysel Stadium riot in 1985, in which 39 Juventus fans lost their lives after being attacked by Liverpool 'supporters' before the European Cup final in Brussels, it was to Dalglish, still only 34 at the time, that the board of directors turned to combine his duties as player with those of manager.

Although Liverpool were banned from Europe for six years (all other English clubs, deemed guilty by association, were handed down a five-year sentence), Dalglish made the transition from teammate to gaffer with consummate ease. In his first season in his dual roles, Liverpool achieved the first League and FA Cup double in their history, Dalglish scoring the championship-winning goal against Chelsea at Stamford Bridge. Having previously won two Footballer of the Year trophies, he duly collected the first of three Manager of the Year awards of his Anfield reign.

Dalglish was no stranger to tragedy: as a young reserve he had been a spectator at the 1971 New Year Old Firm game at Ibrox where 66 people died on Stairway 13 . . . he had witnessed the unfolding horror of Heysel . . . then came Hillsborough, where 93 people were crushed to death before Liverpool's FA Cup semi-final against Nottingham Forest on 15 April 1989. As the figurehead of the club, Dalglish attended as many funerals as humanly possible, visited countless hospital bedsides and comforted scores of grieving relatives amid his managerial duties. One can only imagine his heartbreak.

In February 1991, he stunned the world of football by resigning – citing stress as his reason – the morning after Liverpool had drawn 4–4 in an FA Cup tie against city rivals Everton and at a time when the Reds were mounting a stiff defence of the League Championship. It was time, he said, to put himself and family first. 'The pressure on match days is making my head explode,' he explained. 'This is the first time since I came to the club that I take the interest of Kenny Dalglish over Liverpool Football Club. This is not a sudden decision. The worst I could have done was not to decide. One could argue that this decision hasn't come at a good time but there is no good time in cases like this.'

He returned to the game he loved eight months later – 'The wife wants me out of the house' – when Blackburn Rovers' owner Jack Walker offered him the keys to the safe at Ewood Park. Success again came easily, winning a fourth League title as a manager. He then moved on to Newcastle United whom he led to a Champions League place and the 1998 FA Cup final before being sacked at the start of the following season.

Although there were many at St James' Park who criticised his transfer dealings, ex-club captain and England striker Alan Shearer is not among them. 'I will never have a bad word said about Kenny because as a person he is fantastic. As a manager I think he was fantastic as well. He did not have the best of times at Newcastle but if you ask any of the players who were there when Kenny was manager, they will tell you he was absolutely brilliant. He treated you as a man. He treated you how you wanted to be treated. He was great for us as players.'

Dalglish's man-management skills and powers of persuasion came to Liverpool's rescue in January 2011 when, with the Reds becalmed near the foot of the Premier League, he was the obvious choice of both supporters and players when Roy Hodgson was removed as manager. Originally appointed in a caretaker role by American owners John Henry and Tom Werner, Dalglish subsequently signed a three-year contract when his four months in charge saw Liverpool soar up the League to a sixth-place finish. Although his second spell as the Anfield gaffer would end in ignominy when he was sacked in May 2012 after a disappointing season in which Liverpool finished a distant eighth behind new champions Manchester City, Dalglish's relaxed manner charmed all.

He returned to the fray as a latter-day Shanks, displaying a previously unseen light-hearted manner in his dealings with the media, raising smiles throughout the football family and giving the lie to a reputation held by many of our friends in the south that he is 'a typically dour Scot'. 'He's the biggest mickey-taker I know,' revealed John Barnes. 'Kenny is completely different from his public image. Yes, he is very guarded with those he doesn't know, so I understand why some people might label him dour. But in private, nobody loves a good laugh more than Kenny.'

Despite his record as a comic and a manager, however, it is as a player that Kenny Dalglish will forever be remembered. As George Best put it: 'When I was growing up, my hero was Alfredo Di Stefano of Real Madrid. Kenny, for me, was on a par with Di Stefano. That is the ultimate compliment I can pay him.'

13. SIR ALEX FERGUSON OBE, CBE
Football

Born: Govan, 31 December 1941

CAREER (PLAYER):
Queen's Park 1957–60: 32 appearances, 11 goals
St Johnstone 1960–4: 37 appearances, 19 goals
Dunfermline Athletic 1964–7: 88 appearances, 66 goals
Rangers 1967–9: 57 appearances, 44 goals
Falkirk 1969–73: 106 appearances, 37 goals
Ayr United 1973–4: 24 appearances, 9 goals

CAREER (MANAGER):
East Stirlingshire 1974
St Mirren 1974–8
Aberdeen 1978–86: Scottish League Championship 1979–80, 1983–84, 1984–85; Scottish Cup 1982, 1983, 1984, 1986; Scottish League Cup 1986; European Cup-Winners' Cup 1983; European Super-Cup 1984
Manchester United 1986–: English League Championship 1992–93, 1993–94, 1995–96, 1996–97, 1998–99; 1999–2000, 2000–01, 2002–03, 2006–07, 2007–08, 2008–09, 2010–11; FA Cup 1990, 1994, 1996, 1999, 2004; English League Cup 1992, 2006, 2009, 2010; UEFA Champions League 1999, 2008; European Cup-Winners' Cup 1991; European Super-Cup 1991; World Club Cup 2008; Manager of the Year 1994, 1996, 1997, 1999, 2000, 2003, 2007, 2008, 2009, 2011
Scotland (caretaker) 1985–6

When you have signed Cristiano Ronaldo, Wayne Rooney, Roy Keane, Eric Cantona, Peter Schmeichel, Dimitar Berbatov and Ruud Van Nistelrooy among others, then you might be expected to have forgotten the identity of your very first purchase as manager of humble East Stirling the best part of four decades ago.

'Tom Gourlay,' answers Sir Alex Ferguson without a pause in reply to the question, 'who was playing in goal for Partick Thistle reserves. He cost me seven hundred and fifty pounds and weighed in at about the same.'

Fergie describes his adventure from ramshackle Firs Park to the splendour of Old Trafford – from the Field of Screams to the Theatre of Dreams – as 'a bit of a journey' but just as he delights in his present lifestyle of the rich and famous so he luxuriates in his roots. Hence the reason that the sign which once hung in pride of place above his desk at Manchester United's previous training ground read: 'AHCUMFRAEGUVIN'.

'Sadly, it got lost the day we moved everything from The Cliffs to our new complex at Carrington back in 2000. But, hey, I don't need a sign to remind me where I come from. It's etched on my heart. Reminding everyone I was born in Govan is the one touch of vanity I have. It bestows bragging rights.'

As the most successful manager in the history of British football, a more conceited individual would find much to brag about. For here is a visionary who made St Mirren the most exciting sight in Scotland, Aberdeen the best team in Europe and Manchester United the most popular club in the world; a former shipyard worker who has become one of the most instantly recognisable figures on the planet.

'But I'm still the same boy from Govan I always was,' insists Fergie. 'I suppose some folk might think that I've moved on to another pinnacle in life, if that's the right way to put it, by being invited into all kinds of different social circles and having been awarded a knighthood by the Queen, but none of that changes you as a human being. Why should it? All my old mates from the Harmony Row Youth Club – pals I've known for over 50 years now – still come down to Manchester for a boys' weekend every March to give me pelters. That's what your old friends are for, surely? To remind you of who you truly are. In football, just as in any walk of life, it's easy to have your head turned by money or success but I would like to think my mum and dad would find me completely unaltered by all that's happened to me over the years.'

Alex Sr and Lizzie Ferguson could offer their family little in the way of consumer luxuries but they brought a wealth of old-fashioned virtues into their tenement home standing in the shadows of the cranes on the River Clyde. 'They passed down all their traditional working-class values – discipline, good manners, honesty and decency. To help keep me and my brother Martin out of trouble, they also suggested simple things like joining the Life Boys and later the Boys' Brigade.

'My dad was strict but not overly so; you were never remotely afraid of him or anything like that but you knew there was an invisible line drawn on the lino that shouldn't be overstepped. When he said something, you knew he meant it but he was a very, very fair man. One of his favourite sayings was that "If a thing's worth doing, then it's worth doing well." So when it came to playing football, then he was always a great encouragement. Although, needless to say, if I ever became a bit carried away with myself then I got a clip round the ear to bring me back down to earth. I honestly believe that the greatest blessing in life is to be born into a loving family.'

It is this same sense of 'family' that Sir Alex has instilled at all four clubs he has managed, even the global brand that is Manchester United. 'Any football club – no matter how big or how small – is a family unit of sorts. And despite the size of Manchester United, I'm proud to say there's still something of a family atmosphere about the place. About three-quarters of the Old Trafford and Carrington staff have been with me well over 20 years now.'

But surely there must be a world of difference in managing a family member like affable Tom Gourlay, say, as opposed to the prodigal Wayne Rooney? 'Actually, in essence there's not one jot of difference. It's when you allow yourself to be affected by the star-status thing that your difficulties begin. As a manager, you can only achieve success when the players want to please you and not when you want to please them. It simply won't work that way. Some people fall into the trap of trying to keep players happy all the time and allow powerful personalities in the dressing-room to rule the roost but that's not being a manager; you might as well be the assistant kit man.

'You have to remember two things, whether you're managing East Stirling or Manchester United: number one, you've got to have the players trying their utmost to win for you; and number two, you've got to have control and discipline over them. Anything else and you're fighting against the wind.'

It says much about Sir Alex that José Mourinho – the self-proclaimed 'Special One' who rarely has a good word to say about his rivals – is glowing in his praise. 'He is a great, great manager; he is clever and uses all his power and his prestige. I call him "Boss" because he is the manager's boss. Maybe when I become 60, the kids will call me the same.'

Winner of an astonishing 35 trophies at Pittodrie and Old Trafford, Fergie is often portrayed by those who do not know him as a bad loser whose famous 'hairdryer' tirades and myriad rants are the stuff of legend. 'As a player – whether at Queen's Park or Rangers – I never liked losing and I carried that selfsame attitude into management. I think if I have one quality then it's that I have always been a trier. I tried every day during the brief time I was at East Stirling and I am trying to this day at

Manchester United after 20-odd years. Of course, you can't win every game – Muhammad Ali, my great sporting hero, didn't win every time he entered the ring – but if you try to win them all and show the right desire then you'll win more than you lose. And that's important as a manager because if you lose a couple of games then you can be out of the door.'

God, it is said, loves a trier and someone has certainly smiled upon Sir Alex. When he left East Stirling to descend upon Love Street, St Mirren's average attendance was a meagre 1,908. Even after assembling the most exhilarating team in the land around the youthful talents of Tony Fitzpatrick, Frank McGarvey and Billy Stark, Paisley Buddies were slow to respond at first, forcing Fergie to drive round the streets of the town with his head stuck through the sunroof and a megaphone at his mouth exhorting passing pedestrians to support their local heroes. By the time of his departure to Aberdeen in 1978, St Mirren's average home attendance had risen to a remarkable 11,230.

Nor has Sir Alex ever been one to rest on his laurels. When he guided Aberdeen to the league title in 1980 (the first time the championship flag had not flown over Ibrox or Parkhead since Kilmarnock's victory 15 years previously), many a young manager might have reached for the bubbly and a cigar, sighing, 'Ah, well, that's my job done.' Like Sir Matt Busby and Jock Stein before him, however, Ferguson's ambitions lay far beyond the coastline of Scotland. 'As a youngster, I used to go along to all the big European games at Ibrox to see the likes of Fiorentina, Nice and Standard Liège, great teams and romantic names at the time. Then Eintracht Frankfurt came to Glasgow in 1960, having thrashed Rangers 6–1 in the semi-final first leg and proceeded to hammer the 'Gers 6–3 in the return. I remember thinking to myself, "This German mob are gods." Then Eintracht were slaughtered 7–3 by Real Madrid in the final at Hampden Park, which kind of put the standard of football we were used to watching into perspective. And that's what we tried to aspire to at Aberdeen.'

Fergie's Dons may never have quite reached the heights of Di Stefano, Puskás and Gento, but they did conquer Europe in the grand manner, the young manager attracting covetous glances from Old Trafford, where Manchester United had disposed of a succession of managers in a bid to restore the club to former glories. 'Jock Stein always told me that his biggest regret was turning down United when they asked him to replace Sir Matt Busby in 1971. Jock had actually agreed to leave Celtic but was persuaded to remain in Scotland by his family, a decision he described as the greatest mistake of his life.'

And so after eight years with Aberdeen during which he had rejected job offers from Barcelona, Spurs, Arsenal and Rangers (twice) among others, on 6 November 1986 Fergie flew south to keep his appointment with destiny. When he first cast his eyes over Old Trafford and echoed Sir Bobby Charlton's famous description of the stadium as 'the Theatre of Dreams', Judy Murray was three months pregnant with a son who would be christened Andy, 20-year-old Mike Tyson was 16 days away from becoming the youngest heavyweight champion of the world by bludgeoning Trevor Berbick into submission, and unfashionable Steaua Bucharest were in possession of the European Cup, having beaten Terry Venables' Barcelona on penalties in Seville.

Sir Alex is still at Old Trafford, contentedly filling one of the most demanding jobs in sport after a quarter of a century; a time span, incidentally, during which Real Madrid – the only challengers to Fergie's United as the 'most famous club in world football' – have chewed up coaches the way the Scot chomps Wrigley's spearmint chewing gum.

During Sir Alex's dynasty, over in Madrid they have installed a revolving door for the dizzying round of appointments and redundancies: Leo Beenhakker (twice), John Toshack (twice), Alfredo Di Stefano, José Camacho (twice), Radi Antic, Benito Floro, Vicente Del Bosque (thrice), Jorge Valdano, Arsenio Iglesias, Juup Heynckes, Guus Hiddink, Carlos Queiroz, Mariano Remon, Vanderlei Luxemburgo, Fabio Capello (twice), Bernd Schuster, Juande Ramos, Manuel Pellegrini and José Mourinho plus various 'caretakers'.

No wonder Denis Law can speak without fear of contradiction when he proclaims: 'To the Manchester United fans, Sir Alex is a god.'

And a god who is proud to cumfraeguvin moreover . . .

14. ELENOR GORDON
Swimming

Born: Hamilton, 10 May 1934

CAREER:
Olympic Games:
  Helsinki, 1952: 200 metres breaststroke – Bronze
British Empire & Commonwealth Games:
  Auckland, 1950: 220 yards breaststroke – Gold; 3x110 yards
    medley – Bronze
Vancouver, 1954: 220 yards breaststroke – Gold; 3x110 yards
    medley – Gold

Elenor Gordon could be described as 'the Olympic Champion Who Never Was'.

The 1952 Summer Games in Helsinki were notable for a number of reasons: Hungary's 'Golden Team' of Ferenc Puskás, Sándor Kocsis and Zoltán Czibor swept to victory in the football tournament . . . Czech long-distance runner Emil Zatopek completed a track treble in the 5,000 metres, 10,000 metres and marathon . . . and Britain won a paltry single gold medal in the team show-jumping event when Colonel Harry Llewellyn rode Foxhunter to a clear round.

But was Elenor Gordon the rightful winner of the women's 200 metres breaststroke? As bizarre as it now seems, swimming officials had decreed that the newfangled butterfly was simply a variation of the breaststroke rather than an independent event. Whilst the Hamilton teenager glided through the water in the classic manner, therefore, Hungarian butterfliers Éva Székely and Eva Novak were thrashing away on either side, Székely eventually touching the wall almost six seconds ahead of the third-placed Scot.

'Six months later they separated the breaststroke and butterfly into individual events,' recalled Gordon, who beat the new Olympic champion with ease when next they met in a breaststroke race. 'So, who knows? Maybe I could have won the silver or even the gold.'

Whereas Székely and Novak were products of the hugely successful

Ferencváros Swimming Club in Budapest, where they had a squad of top coaches, fitness trainers and sports scientists at their disposal – not to mention an Olympic-size pool in which to train – and were full-time professionals in all but name, Gordon was the archetypal post-war amateur.

Even having a father who was manager of Hamilton Baths earned Gordon no privileges, the British record holder having to squeeze in her training schedule during the breaks between the 40-minute public swimming sessions before and after school. Whereas the athletes in 2012 had their every whim catered for, four years before her disappointment in Helsinki, when Gordon competed in the 1948 London Olympics, Britain was in the grip of rationing. She was the Games' youngest competitor at the age of 15 years and 82 days.

'We were given food parcels from various parts of the Empire to help us prepare. It included a frozen leg of New Zealand lamb, honey, sugar and butter. We had never seen anything like it. The Americans brought extra supplies to share and the French brought wine, which I'd never tasted before.' The RAF camp at Uxbridge served as the Athletes' Village from where the teams were required to travel by London Underground to the Opening Ceremony presided over by King George VI in Wembley Stadium.

'Even Dutchwoman Fanny Blankers Koen, who won four gold medals on the athletics track, travelled with us on the Tube. We didn't want to get our uniforms dirty, so we carried them in paper bags to change at the stadium. At Wembley there was nowhere to change, as it turned out, so we climbed into the back of an old army lorry to struggle into our white pleated dresses, blazers and white berets. We pulled on stockings, everything – what an experience. What a luxury. I had never seen nylons before, because of the war, and barely knew how to put them on.'

An Olympic semi-finalist in '48, Gordon was granted her own lane amid the splashing revellers in Hamilton Baths when, as a 16 year old, she was selected for the 1950 British Empire & Commonwealth Games in Auckland. The six-week voyage aboard the SS *Tamaroa* from Southampton to New Zealand was an adventure beyond the imagination of any teenager at the time, the highlight being a less than traditional Hogmanay ceilidh in the US naval base at Coco Solo in the Panama Canal, organised by Peter Heatly (now Sir Peter), a serial party animal in his younger days and winner of a diving gold in Auckland.

Gordon's 'training' routine consisted of 20 jogs around the deck of the steamer followed by a session in the *Tamaroa*'s less than luxurious pool, 'A tiny wooden framed canvas tank. A few strokes and you reached the end. By the time we disembarked in Auckland, my turns were brilliant.

The female competitors were strictly chaperoned on board. We were given knitting needles, endless balls of wool and told the deck was strictly off limits after nine o'clock at night. Let's just say that I learned to dance on the *Tamaroa* but I never did learn to knit.'

When the fun ended and the Games began, Gordon streaked to triumph in the 220 yards breaststroke, beating Australian Nancy Lyons by nearly two seconds and bronze medallist Liz Church of England by almost ten seconds. Gordon then combined with fellow teenagers Margaret Girvan and Elizabeth Turner to claim a bronze in the 3x110 yards medley relay.

Next, to Vancouver for the 1954 British Empire & Commonwealth Games which attracted a global audience due to the 'Miracle Mile', the long-awaited showdown between Roger Bannister and Australian John Landy, the world's only two sub-four-minute milers. Bannister emerged triumphant from an epic duel and Elenor Gordon emphasised her dominance in the 220 yards breaststroke with a resounding victory by over four seconds from South African Mary Morgan to retain her Commonwealth title. A second gold was to follow in the relay, when Gordon, Girvan and Margaret McDowell teamed up to bring Scotland victory.

The 1956 Olympics in Melbourne represented another adventure, an eight-stop flight from Glasgow to London, Rome, Cairo, Dubai, Calcutta, Singapore, Jakarta, Darwin and, finally, some 50 hours later, Melbourne. Dick McTaggart won gold for Scotland in the boxing ring but Gordon's run of successes in the pool came to an end when she finished sixth in the 200 metres breaststroke final behind a mini-Armada of Eastern Europeans, the emerging force in world swimming.

Gordon retired after the Melbourne Games to concentrate her energies on being a wife (marrying fellow swimmer Ken McKay) and mother but if ever one athlete epitomised the Olympic creed then it was surely the lass from Hamilton who was robbed of gold in Helsinki:

As the Olympic creed has it: 'The most important thing in the Olympic Games is not to win but to take part, just as the most important thing in life is not the triumph but the struggle. The essential thing is not to have conquered but to have fought well.'

15. HAMPDEN PARK

When Hungary strode out at Hampden Park on 8 December 1954, they did so as the most dazzling team ever assembled. Popularly known as the 'Mighty Magyars' and renowned for a style of play that would later become known as 'Total Football', the previous winter they had become the first foreign country to beat England at Wembley, where they recorded a stunning 6–3 victory. To emphasise their overwhelming superiority, they proceeded to tame the Three Lions 7–1 in the return fixture in Budapest in May 1954.

Two months later, as resounding favourites to win the World Cup in Switzerland, they duly advanced to the final, having been unbeaten in 31 internationals stretching back to 1950; their opponents in Berne were West Germany whom they had thrashed 8–3 in the opening group stage. Two goals ahead after eight minutes, the super confident Hungarians contrived to lose 3–2 in a game remembered in the now unified Germany as the 'Miracle of Berne'. Miracle or complacency, who knows? How can you explain the inexplicable?

But all Scotland acknowledged the identity of the real world champions when 113,146 spectators skived off work and school almost 60 years ago to throng Hampden's sweeping ash terracings and grandstands to pay homage to the magical Magyars in their iconic cherry red shirts. They were to witness a classic: trailing 3–1 at half-time, Scotland produced a stirring second-half performance inspired by Partick Thistle outside-right Johnny MacKenzie, who ran rings round Hungarian left-back Mihály Lantos, and only a last-minute goal by Sándor Kocsis, who would later become the idol of Barcelona, earned the Hungarians a thrilling 4–2 victory.

After the game, which arguably remains Scotland's finest-ever performance, a relieved and mightily impressed Ferenc Puskás said of MacKenzie that he had 'never seen wing play of such a high standard' and described Hampden as 'the most magnificent stadium I have ever seen, it is the life and essence of football'.

Aye, it may have lacked the architectural grandeur of the Bernabéu in Madrid, where Puskás, the 'Galloping Major', would later strut his stuff, or the magnificence of Rio de Janeiro's Maracana, but there was always something special about Hampden Park, football's original theatre of dreams. The new Hampden (aka the National Stadium) is a far safer and cleaner place to watch Darren Ferguson or Rod Stewart, depending upon your taste, but no one who pushed through those clickety-clackety turnstiles of a generation ago will ever forget the experience.

I can recall *The Guardian*'s former football correspondent, David Lacey, studying the surrounding grey sandstone tenements as the slating rain poured forth from a lowering sky before our latest cross-border skirmish with the English and muttering: 'It looks just the same in colour as it does in black and white.' Maybe so, but it was the only stadium in the world that could possibly do justice to the 1960 European Cup final, when Puskás marked his return to Glasgow by scoring four goals (Alfredo Di Stefano assisting with the other three) in Real Madrid's 'ballet in white' 7–3 defeat of an excellent Eintracht Frankfurt side.

The Spanish side would grace the recently rebuilt Hampden in 2002, when they beat Bayer Leverkusen of Germany in the UEFA Champions League final, French maestro Zinedine Zidane scoring the winner with a volley of which even the great Puskás would have been proud. Hampden has always had the ability to bring out the best in those who trod the famous turf.

Rose Reilly

Rose Reilly is not the only Scottish footballer to have been signed by AC Milan; Joe Jordan also graced the San Siro stadium. Nor is she the only Scot to have represented Italy; Denis Law, then playing for Torino, starred for the Italian League against the Scottish League at Hampden in 1961. But she sure as hell is the only Scot ever to have captained Italy to a World Cup triumph, scoring a brilliant goal in the 3–1 victory over the United States in front of a 90,000 crowd in Beijing in 1983.

Forced to 'change sex' and play as Ross Reilly for Stewarton Boys' Club as a young teenager, she attracted a host of scouts – including one sent forth by Jock Stein at Celtic – before her ruse was rumbled. And, so, faced with an SFA ban on women playing professional football in Scotland, Reilly was forced to seek her fortune abroad.

After a brief spell in France with Reims, she joined AC Milan with whom she would win two Italian League Championship medals, thereafter adding another six with a series of clubs including Napoli, Fiorentina, Lecce and Bari, plus two Golden Boot awards as the top scorer in Serie A. In 1978–79 Reilly created another little bit of history when she won the Italian League with Lecce (who played on a Saturday night) and the French title with Reims (on Sunday afternoons).

Despite having been capped ten times by Scotland, she was able to represent Italy in the 1983 Women's World Cup in China because the tournament was not officially recognised by FIFA; she responded by scoring from 40 yards in the final before being voted the 'Best Female Player in the World'.

And then there was the 'Hampden Roar', a blood-curdling war cry that reverberated around the natural bowl of the stadium and which resulted in many a frazzled English goalkeeper becoming a suitable case for treatment in the immediate aftermath of the latest Home International clash with the Auld Enemy.

According to Mount Florida folklore, Oldham Athletic's John Hacking was the first victim of the phenomenon of the Hampden Roar when he never recovered from the events of 1929. With Scotland reduced to ten men throughout the second half, having lost the inspirational Alex Jackson to injury before the interval, the game appeared destined to end in a goalless draw when, in the 89th minute, Aberdeen winger Alec Cheyne shaped to take a corner on the right. As one, 110,512 passionate Scots' voices filled the chill March air, the noise swelling and swelling into a deafening cacophony of sound until, as Cheyne put it: 'You thought your eardrums were about to explode. To us, it was a call to arms; to the English players, it must have sounded as if someone had opened the gates of hell.'

As Cheyne's in-swinging corner curled towards goal – and, so it is said, the Hampden Roar rose in volume until it could be heard several miles away in George Square – the dazed Hacking completely misjudged the flight of the delivery and the ball sailed into the net. Hapless John Hacking would never play for England again.

It is somewhat ironic, therefore, that Scotland's National Stadium was named in honour of – wait for it – a Sassenach: John Hampden was a Westminster MP who was killed during the Battle of Chalgrove in 1643 while fighting for Cromwell's Roundheads against Charles I during the English Civil War.

The original football ground was built in the shadow of Hampden Terrace by Queen's Park's (now the site of Queen's Park Bowling Club) in 1873 and there the Spiders stayed until forced to move in 1884 because of a proposed extension to the nearby railway line; the second Hampden hosted Renton's victory over West Bromwich Albion in the so-called 'Championship of the World' match in 1888 and the first-ever Old Firm

---

In Italy, she became a national icon, regularly appearing in television advertisements and chat shows whilst being inundated with proposals of marriage from besotted fans. When a jewellery shop owner caught sight of her window-shopping through his plate-glass frontage, he dashed out onto the pavement to present *La Reilly* with an expensive watch.

Now 56 and a wife and mother living back home in Stewarton, Reilly spent 22 years in Italian football, gaining 22 international caps for her adopted country before retiring at the age of 40.

Scottish Cup final in 1894. But as football's popularity soared and Queen's Park grew out of their cramped home, so the Spiders sold the stadium to Third Lanark, who renamed their acquisition Cathkin, to finance the building of the third Hampden Park in 1903. Designed by stadium architect Archibald Leitch – who was also responsible for Ibrox, Parkhead, Old Trafford, Highbury, Anfield and Stamford Bridge among many – it was widely regarded as one of the Seven Wonders of the Sporting World.

Hampden Park IV, by contrast, does not take the breath away – nor with the capacity slashed from 147,000 to 52,103 does the 'Roar' strike fear into the hearts of foreign foes – but in terms of facilities it ranks with any football stadium anywhere. Over the years, the stadium has staged speedway, American football, rugby union, boxing, rock concerts and will serve as the venue for the athletics events and the closing ceremony at the 2014 Commonwealth Games. Yet it will forever remain, as Ferenc Puskás observed, 'the life and essence of football'.

16. GAVIN HASTINGS OBE

Rugby Union

Born: Edinburgh, 3 January 1962

CAREER:

Clubs: Cambridge University, Watsonians, London Scottish, University of Auckland

Scotland 1986–95: 61 caps, 667 points

British Lions: 1989, Australia (won 2–1); captain, 1993, New Zealand (lost 2–1)

Evidence suggests that whenever the occasion demanded it, Superman would dispense with that funny red cape and blue Lycra bodysuit in favour of a dark blue rugby shirt with a big white thistle on the chest and the number 15 on the back. Many thousands of witnesses can attest to the fact that 'the Man of Steel' may have been raised in Smallville USA but spent the years 1986–95 hovering around the Murrayfield area of Auld Reekie.

How else can you explain the heroic escapades of the normally mild-mannered Gavin Hastings, who became endowed with superpowers at the first strains of 'Flower of Scotland', enabling him to stop a steam train, run through brick walls and boot a rugby ball high into the stratosphere? Ever since he scored all 18 points in Scotland's 18–17 victory over France on his debut in Edinburgh, Hastings never ignored a plea to come to his nation's rescue in times of need.

For those who require further proof of his derring-do, let us return to 1995 in the Parc des Princes, where Scotland, without a win in Paris for 26 years, were trailing 16–21 with just two minutes remaining. Then Hastings took an outrageous flipped behind-the-back pass from Gregor Townsend and burst clear, although still some 40 lung-bursting yards from the try-line. With all France, it seemed at the time, in frantic pursuit and gaining with every pounding step, the 33-year-old Hastings found hidden reserves to touch down under the posts with the French hordes breathing down the back of his neck. Regaining his breath and his composure and accompanied by 60,000 Gallic hoots and jeers, Hastings stroked the resultant conversion unerringly between the posts to secure a historic 23–21 victory.

But there is more, so much more: capped 61 times – 20 as captain – Hastings scored a record 667 points for Scotland (a mark subsequently beaten by Chris 'the Boot' Paterson in 2008) . . . became the World Cup's top scorer with 227 points until superseded by Jonny Wilkinson in 2007 . . . remains the British Lions' all-time leading points scorer with sixty-six from six Tests . . . was a Five Nations Championship Grand Slam winner in 1990 . . . captained Cambridge to victory against Oxford in a Varsity Match at Twickenham . . . and skippered the first Scotland Schools XV to beat England on English soil.

Not that our Superman's adventures began auspiciously; in his opening act of that first international appearance against the French at Murrayfield in 1986, Hastings contrived to send his kick-off straight into touch. Head drooped, he was trotting back towards the Scottish line in preparation for the scrum on the centre spot when he was roused from his misery by an almighty intake of breath by the crowd; the wily French team had taken a swift lineout and when Big Gav turned round to see what all the fuss was about he found seven grinning Frenchmen bearing down on him. 'Thirty seconds into my debut and I had conceded a try to Pierre Berbizier.' Six penalties later (then a Test record) and a jubilant Hastings, in the company of Watsonians club colleague and younger brother Scott, another debutant that January afternoon, embarked upon the mother of all sibling pub crawls along the length of Rose Street following the after-match banquet.

Scotland ultimately shared the championship with France that year. Despite hammering England 33–6 at Murrayfield (Hastings setting a new Test record with 21 points from the boot) and beating Ireland 10–9 in Dublin, they were undone in Cardiff, where they lost a classic encounter 22–15 – despite a Hastings try and conversion – when Welsh full-back Paul Thorburn kicked the longest penalty ever recorded at a distance of seventy yards eight inches. Scotland had, however, found a worthy successor to Andy Irvine, the Prince of Full-Backs of the 1970s.

Denied a possible Grand Slam by Thorburn's mighty right leg, Hastings achieved that coveted feat four years later in the epic winner-takes-all confrontation against Will Carling's cocky England at Murrayfield, a game in which Hastings yielded the goalkicking responsibilities to stand-off Craig Chalmers, who booted Scotland into a 9–4 half-time lead. 'I was lying down on the turf holding the ball for Craig against the wind and I could hear one wag [wee brother Scott, perhaps?] offer the suggestion that it was the only way I was going to appear on camera.'

But minutes after the interval Hastings the elder burst across the nation's television screens when he collected a pass from scrum-half Gary Armstrong and chipped ahead, the ball obeying his commands by bouncing neatly into the outstretched hands of flying winger Tony Stanger for what proved to be the match-winning score in Scotland's 13–7 victory.

Twelve months later Hastings suffered the greatest disappointment of his career against the Auld Enemy in the 1991 World Cup semi-final at Murrayfield; with the scores level at 6–6 and 18 minutes remaining on the clock, Scotland were awarded a penalty about 20 yards out and almost straight in front of the posts, the kind of attempt that Hastings could have landed with a pint in one hand and a cigar in t'other. Inexplicably, with Australia awaiting Scotland in the final at Twickenham, Superman skewed his kick wide of the uprights; clearly the ball had been fashioned out of Kryptonite rather than leather. If Scotland had gone ahead, then the momentum would undoubtedly have swung their way in such a tight contest; instead, with almost the last kick of the game, Rob Andrew slotted home a drop goal, leaving a tearful Big Gav to apologise to the nation.

There was further misery – and a sense of overwhelming injustice – in the 1994 Calcutta Cup match at Murrayfield, where a Rob Wainwright try, a Gregor Townsend drop goal and two Hastings penalties left Scotland 14–12 ahead and captain Gav preparing his victory speech. Then, in the final climactic ruck, Scotland's Ian Jardine was penalised for the illegal use of a hand. As BBC television freeze-frame photography later proved, Kiwi referee Lindsay McLachlan (and his ancestors could have been nothing but English given that moniker!) had been conned; oh, aye, the ball was flicked free of the pile of bodies by what was undeniably a hand enclosed in a dark blue cuff – at which point the over-hasty whistler made his fateful decision – but that cuff was clearly shown a millisecond later to be attached to the long white sleeve of Rob Andrew.

Seventeen long years may have passed since full-back Jon Callard kicked England to 'victory' but in the hearts and minds of all Scotland, Hastings had led his men to a thoroughly deserved 14–12 triumph. 'Was it Rob Andrew? Nah. Really? I can't believe that,' was the reaction of Will Carling, mischief oozing from every pore, when reminded of England's chicanery. 'But do you know what? I certainly hope it was an England hand – because if it was Rob, then it was an even sweeter day than I remember.'

For his part, Hastings has neither forgiven nor forgotten. 'I will never, ever agree with the referee's decision that day. Not that I want to harp on about it because I don't.' Since we are in the company of the least whingeing personality in world sport, this is Hastings-speak for 'we wuz robbed'. Ever since Carling was left quietly seething when the Scotsman was appointed British Lions captain for the 1993 tour of New Zealand, the two men have never been what you might call soul mates. 'Let me tell you the truth about me and Will Carling' is how Hastings' most popular after-dinner speech begins. (Pause for dramatic effect.) 'I hate the bastard . . . I am joking, of course.'

Having played in all three Tests during the Lions' 2–1 series victory in Australia in 1989 (scoring one try and eight penalties in the process), Hastings was named skipper by coach Ian McGeechan for the series against the All Blacks. The decision left the aforementioned Carling, one of 17 Englishmen in the 30-man squad, decidedly underwhelmed at being named a mere foot soldier under a Scottish captain. 'Without doubt, the pinnacle of my rugby career was to be selected as captain of the British & Irish Lions on their 1993 tour of New Zealand,' recalled Hastings. 'It was something that gave me a marvellous sense of personal fulfilment, but at the same time I was also aware of the enormous honour that the selectors had conferred on me, by recognising that I was the best man to lead the Lions. It was, therefore, an extremely unnerving responsibility and a severe challenge.

'I had the benefit of having been on a previous Lions tour in 1989 and I think I had the even greater benefit of being known to New Zealand and its rugby people. I had been out there in 1987 for the World Cup with Scotland and stayed to play club rugby for Auckland University. I went back with Scotland in 1990 and returned in 1992, this time with a World XV to celebrate the centenary of the New Zealand Rugby Football Union. I think all those factors were extremely important in advancing my claims for the captaincy and I think it was a decision seen as a good one out in New Zealand. I also believe that I had huge support in the British Isles.'

As was his custom, Hastings led from the front, unerringly slotting home six penalties in the First Test in Christchurch to put the Lions 18–17 in front with 60 seconds left to play; but having conceded a highly dubious try accredited to Frank Bunce in the opening minute, Hastings' Lions were left feeling further aggrieved when Grant Fox converted an equally controversial and decisive penalty with the last kick of the game. Never had so many, especially Hastings, given so much for so little reward.

Parity was restored in the Second Test at Wellington, where Captain Marvel converted four crucial penalties to inspire his side to a 20–7 triumph, but the mighty All Blacks secured the series after coming from behind to win 30–13 at Eden Park, Auckland. 'It was a great credit to the

Lions that we came to the third and deciding Test match with the series squared. The highlight of the tour was the Second Test victory in Wellington but it was extremely difficult to raise our game to that level two weeks in a row,' commented Hastings.

'But it was a fascinating experience and I am sure that everyone who went on that tour was richer for it. To me, that is what playing top-level rugby is about. It is not playing in front of your home crowd or 50,000 people at Murrayfield; if you really want to test yourself, then the place to do it is New Zealand because, as far as I am concerned, it is the hardest place I know to play rugby. There are no easy games in New Zealand, the pressure is intense, there is no hiding place and you just have to get on with it.'

Despite the cruel and disappointing outcome, Hastings' place as a giant of the game was secured. 'Gavin is a big man in every sense of the word,' said Ian McGeechan of his captain. 'His greatest asset was to engender confidence in those around him and to lead by example when the opposition had to be taken on. In New Zealand, they considered him simply the best full-back in the world.'

17. STEPHEN HENDRY MBE

Snooker

Born: South Queensferry, 13 January 1969

CAREER:

World Championship: 1990, 1992, 1993, 1994, 1995, 1996,
   1999

UK Championship: 1990, 1991, 1995, 1996, 1997

Masters: 1989, 1990, 1991, 1992, 1993, 1996

Snooker players carry their nicknames before them like battle honours: Joe Davis, who retired undefeated after winning every World Championship staged between 1927 and 1946 (15 consecutive victories interrupted by the Second World War), was renowned as 'the Wizard of Pot'; Ray Reardon glorified in his sobriquet of 'the Prince of Darkness'; Steve Davis was 'the Golden Nugget'; then came 'the Hurricane' (Alex Higgins), 'the Whirlwind' (Jimmy White) and 'the Rocket' (Ronnie O'Sullivan).

Stephen Hendry is simply 'the Great One'. A brasher individual might have been tempted to go all the way and market himself as 'the Greatest' but the most successful player of the modern era has never been one to flaunt his celebrity. 'Anyone can win once. Dozens have proved that. But to win over and over, like a Michael Schumacher or a Tiger Woods, means you have attained a level of greatness. Not that I walk around saying I'm great or anything like that. But the results would back that up' is the closest he comes to Muhammad Ali-style pronouncements. Hendry has always preferred to allow his cue to do any boasting on his behalf.

When he was immortalised in latex by the *Spitting Image* team as a character devoid of personality, Hendry was delighted with his alter ego. 'I think he's great. He's much better looking and he's got fewer zits than me,' he enthused. Whereas some of those politicians, rock stars or athletes lampooned by the puppeteers took grave offence, Hendry cheerfully accepted that his presence among the Queen, Ronald Reagan, Laurence Olivier and the Rolling Stones was intended as a compliment, however mischievously barbed. Indeed, so chuffed was he by the portrayal that when it came time to choose the perfect present for her husband's 40th birthday in 2009, Mandy Hendry turned private eye to bring about a reunion.

After weeks of detective work, she tracked down the puppet to Porthcawl, Wales, where it was in the possession of pub owner Phil Curtis, a collector of sports memorabilia who had bought the rubberised Stephen at a Sotheby's auction nine years earlier. After a round of good-natured bargaining down the phone line, Mandy agreed a suitable transfer fee plus the promise of an Olympic cycling top signed by Sir Chris Hoy.

So there resides the dummy, in its own specially crafted cabinet in the Hendry family home in Auchterarder where it sits expressionless and silent, gazing unseeingly into the distance; the selfsame numbed look, in fact, as adopted by ashen-faced opponents throughout the 1990s when Hendry was in his pomp and every visit to the table carried the threat of yet another century break. Seven World Championships were achieved during that golden decade of dominance and, although the prospect of an eighth title recedes with every passing year, his record of 36 major tournament victories may never be beaten.

When Joe Davis won his fifth World Championship in 1931, the final was played on a table in the back room of his opponent Tom Dennis's pub in Nottingham (Davis winning 25–21 despite Dennis's 'home advantage') where the only spectators were those drinkers who accidentally stumbled across the action on their way to the outside loo. When Alex Higgins triumphed for the second time in 1982, the abiding image remains that of him reducing a king size cigarette to a length of ash with a triple vodka to hand.

Both Davis and Higgins in their entirely different ways were instrumental in popularising their sport but it was Hendry with his towering talent allied to his boy-next-door affability who inspired snooker's global marketing appeal. According to Archbishop Luigi Barbarito, the former papal emissary to Britain: 'Snooker gives you firm hands and helps build up character. It is the ideal recreation for dedicated nuns.'

Hendry would never dream of presenting himself as the Mother Teresa of the green baize but what other sportsman could have attracted a sponsorship deal with Bostik glue? 'It's important for a product like Bostik to have someone with a wholesome image and Stephen fits the bill ideally,' explained the company's sales and marketing executive. 'We have to be aware of the fact that we have solvent-based products that people abuse.'

Born in South Queensferry but raised on the Fife side of the Firth of Forth in Dalgety Bay, the 13-year-old Hendry would watch his boyhood hero, Jimmy White, whenever snooker was on television but was happier outside playing football with his pals in the local park, where he idly dreamed of being a latter-day George Best in the maroon shirt of his beloved Hearts. Come Christmas 1981, however, his parents Irene and Gordon presented him with a tiny three-foot snooker table and overnight their offspring was lost to Tynecastle. 'On Christmas morning my brother and I had a few games with him and beat him easily,' recalled Gordon Hendry. 'We left him to it for an hour or so, and when we played him again he whacked us both. I knew that he was going to be something special.'

Although he had to travel to Dunfermline to practise on a full-size table, Hendry's impact was immediate: a little over a year later, he had become Scottish Under-16 champion, beating Lee Doyle, the son of his soon-to-be manager Ian Doyle, along the way. 'I think I've just played the future world champion,' sighed the vanquished. Hendry's reward was an invitation to compete in the BBC's *Junior Pot Black* event in 1983; to John Parrott went the trophy, but it was the painfully shy young Scot with the Bjorn Borg-like powers of concentration and intensity who won the nation's hearts.

Seven years later he was youngest-ever champion of the world at the age of twenty-one, an 18–12 winner over Jimmy White in an extravaganza of outrageous potting, the entire final being concluded in just over six hours at an average of twelve minutes per frame. It was a triumph tinged with the nagging regret that it was his long-time idol on the losing end and not Steve Davis, the previous king of the baize and a six-time world champion in the 1980s. 'I wanted Davis,' admitted Hendry. 'And there was a bit of the poignant about playing Jimmy since I'd idolised him from boyhood. But I had a job to do.'

Hendry performed that same job again in a 1992 final which touched new heights of skill and drama. Trailing 14–9, Hendry appeared to be heading into the evening session six in arrears when White opened the 24th frame with a trademark whirlwind break of 52 only for his 1990 conqueror to reply with a clearance of 64 to reduce the deficit to four frames.

Hendry was in irresistible mood after the interval, reeling off eight straight frames and clinching his second world title with breaks of 134 and 112. 'I can't feel gutted,' revealed the Londoner. 'Stephen played like a god.' A god with a ruthless streak despite his gentle demeanour. 'Sometimes I feel like a boxer,' explained Hendry. 'When I get a bloke down – even Jimmy – I don't mind hurting him. In fact, I get great pleasure doing it. We are both in the ring and we both know the rules. If you murder a player, he'll be psychologically beaten before he gets on the table the next time.' Twelve months later, White would be humbled 18–5 as Hendry became world champion for the third time.

Hendry–White IV in 1994 was another classic and, in one respect, represented the most remarkable of the Scot's seven world title successes. After beating Surinder Gill 10–1 in the first round, Hendry broke a bone in his left arm after tripping in his Sheffield hotel room, an injury that prevented him from practising for the rest of the tournament. Even so, he overcame Dave Harold (13–2), Nigel Bond (13–8) and Steve Davis (16–9) to qualify for his third successive final against the luckless Whirlwind.

On this occasion it went to the wire, with White seemingly poised to fulfil his lifetime's ambition of winning the World Championship when he took a 37–24 lead in the 35th and deciding frame only to miss a straightforward black off the spot. 'If there's enough pressure, you can miss anything,' as 1980 world champion Cliff Thorburn of Canada so aptly put it. If Hendry felt any pressure or discomfort from his arm, then he displayed nary a trace of either, coolly compiling a break of 58 to secure his fourth Crucible success.

Three further world titles and many millions in prize money on, Hendry may never again be the force of old now that he has become a senior citizen in sporting terms. 'You can't defend against age, you can only come to terms with it,' opined Fred Davis, a three times world champion and a semi-finalist in 1978, aged 64. Since achieving his seventh and last victory in Sheffield in 1999, a new generation of champions led by John Higgins and Ronnie O'Sullivan has emerged.

Hendry's inexorable slide down the world rankings allied to his earlier-than-scheduled departure from many tournaments in his later years on the circuit offered the consolation of being able to spend more leisure time with Mandy and his sons, Blaine and Carter, at their sumptuous home in the Perthshire countryside, not to mention on the nearby courses of Gleneagles where he plays off a handicap of six.

Financially secure for life, he hung up his cue and unclipped his bow tie for the last time in May 2012, when, after defeating reigning champion Higgins in the previous round, he was crushed 13–2 by Stephen Maguire in the quarter-finals of the World Championship at the Crucible, where he once ruled supreme. He retired content in the knowledge that, just like Muhammad Ali, Jack Nicklaus and Pele in their chosen sports, his place as 'the Great One' of snooker is forever secure.

18. SIR CHRIS HOY MBE
Cycling

Born: Edinburgh, 23 March 1976

CAREER:
Olympic Games:
  Sydney 2000: team sprint – Silver
  Athens 2004: 1 km track time trial – Gold
  Beijing 2008: keirin – Gold; sprint – Gold; team sprint – Gold
  London 2012: keirin – Gold; team sprint – Gold
World Championships:
  Berlin 1999: team sprint – Silver
  Manchester 2000: team sprint – Silver
  Antwerp 2001: team sprint – Bronze
  Copenhagen 2002. 1 km time trial – Gold, team sprint – Gold
  Stuttgart 2003: team sprint – Bronze
  Melbourne 2004: 1 km time trial – Gold; team sprint – Bronze
  Los Angeles 2005: team sprint – Gold; 1 km time trial – Bronze
  Bordeaux 2006: 1 km time trial – Gold; team sprint – Silver
  Palma 2007: 1 km time trial – Gold; keirin – Gold; team sprint – Silver
  Manchester 2008: keirin – Gold; sprint – Gold; team sprint – Silver
  Copenhagen 2010: keirin – Gold; team sprint – Bronze
  Apeldoorn, Netherlands 2011: keirin – Silver; team sprint – Bronze; sprint – Bronze
  Melbourne 2012: keirin – Gold; sprint – Bronze

The sporting world tilted briefly on its axis in December 1982. Had six-year-old Christopher Hoy been old enough to watch *Rocky III*, then a ring career might have beckoned; instead of which, his parents took him to see *E.T.* at the local cinema in Edinburgh, where he sat enthralled as Elliot and his extra-terrestrial pal escaped the posse of pursuing police cars aboard a BMX bike after the greatest screen chase of them all.

'I loved that scene with E.T. wrapped up in a blanket while perched in the front basket; it was fantastic,' recalled Hoy, whose victories in the team sprint and keirin events at London 2012 made him Britain's most successful Olympian of all time with six gold medals, one more than rower Sir Steve Redgrave. 'So the following weekend, I went on and on at my dad until he agreed to take me to the local BMX track at Danderhall. All the kids were having such terrific fun that I was hooked and it just spiralled from there.'

Hoy's epic adventure that would also lead to 11 world titles began in the unlikely surroundings of a church-hall jumble sale in Musselburgh, where his mother, Carol, paid a fiver for an old BMX bike. Watched over by his son, David Hoy stripped down the machine, sprayed it black, fixed stickers – as any bairn knows, a bike always goes faster when equipped with some flashy transfers – and new handlebars. 'After all Dad's hard work, I snapped the frame after a month or so doing jumps off planks of wood piled up on bricks. Then I inherited my neighbour's daughter's old bike. Dad gave it the same spray treatment and the same handlebars. I repaid his efforts by bending the frame.'

Young Chris found a better way to say 'thanks' by finishing second in his first competitive outing, at which point his awed gaze fell upon a shining black and gold Raleigh Super Burner in an Edinburgh bike shop carrying an appropriately eye-popping price tag of £99. 'When you've saved up half,' explained Carol Hoy to her wannabe Elliot, 'your dad and I will pay the rest.' Just as he would later prove himself to be in the saddle, the tot was a redoubtable competitor in the fund-raising stakes, as revealed by cycling journalist Richard Moore in his fascinating book *Heroes, Villains and Velodromes*. 'He did it in no time,' explained Carol Hoy. 'He was very clever. If we had people round for dinner, then Christopher would come in to show face, and then he'd talk about his BMX racing, and how well he was doing. Then he'd add, "There's a bike I want but I have to pay half myself," and all his uncles and aunts would feel sympathetic and slip him a fiver.' Her offspring employed a cunning ploy. 'I waited until they'd had a drink or two.'

By the time he grew weary of performing elephant glides, bunny hops and funky chickens, Hoy had become Scotland's number one, the British number two, the European number five and the world number nine in the Under-15 age group. But how does one make the transformation from trick cyclist to champion track cyclist? 'My interest had originally been sparked in 1986 when the Commonwealth Games came to Edinburgh and I caught my first sight of the velodrome on television. It may not have been quite up there with *E.T.* but I remember the excitement of watching Scotland's Eddie Alexander win the ride-off for the bronze medal. I didn't experience an epiphany or anything like that; I certainly didn't think to myself, "One day I'll ride on a track like that and win a gold medal," but it did have a certain appeal, which is why, I suppose, I eventually swapped my BMX for a racing bike.'

Like Hollywood's cute little alien, Hoy was almost left behind by the others on a couple of occasions: as a schoolboy, he was torn between his twin loves of cycling and rowing before he had another difficult decision to make when he discovered that being a dedicated party animal at St Andrews University was not conducive to becoming an Olympic champion. 'At school [George Watson's College, whose celebrated former pupils include David Steel and Malcolm Rifkind from the world of politics, and Gavin Hastings and Olympic Alpine skier Martin Bell from the world of sport], I was also very keen on both rugby and rowing. In my heart, however, I felt it was cycling that offered me the greatest scope for advancement. It was a tricky choice to make at that age because I loved all sports but by the time I reached 16 or 17, I realised that although rugby and rowing [he won a silver medal in the British Junior Championships coxless pairs] were great fun, it was cycling that I was most serious about.'

On to St Andrews University where, as Prince William would later discover, there are temptations to suit every taste. 'I woke up one morning and realised I hadn't sat in a saddle for about six months' – at which juncture he reluctantly quit the Auld Grey Toun after his first year to take a Sports Science degree at Edinburgh University and continue his push for glory in the Commonwealth Games velodrome. 'I still miss the camaraderie of the boathouse and will watch any rowing event when it comes on TV. Having been in a boat – although nowhere near their level, I have to say – it does give you a little bit of an inkling into what Steve Redgrave and Matthew Pinsent had to put themselves through time and time again to achieve everything they did.'

Hoy, too, puts himself through the pain barrier on the nation's behalf every time he completes a training session that leaves him 'feeling like death' for up to half an hour sprawled out on the floor. 'I always find it hard to describe just how intense the pain is to someone who's never experienced the feeling. It's like climbing into a bath full of acid, I suppose. You think the agony is never going to end but gradually it does begin to wear off. You could always slacken off, of course, but you won't win medals of any colour that way. The more it hurts, the faster you go – that's the sprint cyclists' mantra. To me, the great challenge of cycling is not in beating other people but lies in discovering exactly how far I can push myself. As soon as I became Scottish champion, I wanted to be British champion, then European, then world, then the ultimate – Olympic champion. Every time I achieved an ambition, I put the bar on a higher level.'

Three times Tour de France winner Greg Lemond famously said that come the end of each and every stage 'even my eyelashes ache'. So is track cycling a summer breeze by comparison to road racing? 'A few years ago I completed a mountain stage of the Tour de France for charity – at a fairly leisurely pace, I have to say – which gave me a slight idea of the agonies that these guys live through hour after hour, day after day, week after week. Our pain is sharper but we don't suffer for nearly as long. On the track, it's primarily in the legs that you feel it. A sprinter's pain is far more intense because it tends to be concentrated in the legs but what the road racers go through, in terms of both physical and mental suffering, is truly horrendous.'

Having become the first British Olympian for 100 years to win three gold medals at a single Olympic Games when he took the individual sprint, team sprint and keirin titles in Beijing's Laoshan velodrome in 2008, Hoy took a well-earned break from cycling in April 2010 to marry Edinburgh lawyer Sara Kemp in St Giles' Cathedral. But those rivals who were hoping that marriage offered the hint that Hoy might be contemplating retirement were to be sorely disabused.

At London 2012, where his fellow Team GB members overwhelmingly chose Sir Chris to carry the Union flag at the Opening Ceremony, he proved that the competitive fires burned as fiercely as ever at the advanced age of 36. Those giant-redwood thighs took him to two triumphs in the velodrome, but how much longer can he continue plunging his body into that excruciating acid bath? 'The dream scenario,' he revealed after winning his sixth Olympic gold, 'is to use the 2014 Commonwealth Games in Glasgow as my swansong. But it's a big ask, being two more years.'

And what of his liking for a curry washed down with a beer or two? 'You've got to have a balance in your lifestyle. Being happy is the most important thing in life whether you're an architect or an athlete. If you're happy when you're in the saddle, then it will show up in everything you do.' In the ultimate sacrifice for his nation, by the time Hoy led the British team into London's Olympic Stadium, he had not touched alcohol or an Indian takeaway for over five months. 'When it comes to the Olympics, I have always been prepared to do anything to win a gold medal. I never, ever wanted to stand on the podium with a silver medal around my neck thinking, "Maybe if I hadn't gone out that night, maybe if I hadn't had those beers or eaten that lamb madras then I wouldn't have been second."'

And if he had never seen *E.T.*?

'Now that's a question to which there's no answer.'

19. CAROLINE INNES MBE
Athletics

Born: Cupar, Fife, 14 March 1974

CAREER:
Paralympic Games:
  Barcelona 1992: 100 metres – Gold
  Atlanta 1996: 100 metres – Gold
  Sydney 2000: 200 metres – Gold; 400 metres – Gold; 100 metres – Silver
World Championships:
  Assen 1990: 100 metres – Silver; 200 metres – Silver
  Berlin 1994: 100 metres – Bronze; 200 metres – Bronze
  Birmingham 1998: 200 metres – Gold; 400 metres – Gold

'Mind, body, spirit' ran the original Paralympic motto; Caroline Innes has the mind of an egghead, the body of a fashion model and the spirit of a champion. She is also blessed with seriously mischievous blue eyes, a permanent laugh, and a 100-megawatt smile which burns as brightly as will the Paralympic flame over London in 2012. A smile so mesmerising that after a fleeting moment in her company you cease to notice or hear the cruel effects of the cerebral palsy with which she has lived since birth.

A graduate from Dundee University, Caroline, 100 metres gold medallist at Barcelona and Atlanta, and winner of the 200 metres and 400 metres at the Sydney Games of 2000, plus a stash of World Championship medals, speaks for each and every one of her fellow Paralympians when she describes herself as an athlete who happened to be disabled, not a disabled athlete. The distinction is crucial. 'The reason Sydney was so special to everyone – Britons, Cambodians, Palestinians and Israelis, everyone – was because it was the first time we had been made to feel like true Olympians. In '92 and '96, we were distinctly second-class citizens whereas the Aussies treated us with no less respect, no less affection than Cathy Freeman or Ian Thorpe. When we marched into the stadium to the cheers of 100,000 people at the Opening Ceremony, I came out in goosebumps; just thinking about it, I still do. I'll never, ever forget the moment I spotted my mum, fiancé [soon-to-be husband John Baird] and wee brother waving the St Andrew's Cross.'

It is shameful to think that had her local education authority been allowed to dictate Caroline's future 25 years ago then she would never have gone to university and might never have become an Olympian. At the age of 11, a committee formed without the knowledge of her parents, Carol and David, decreed that she should attend a special needs school near her home in Cupar, Fife, rather than the local senior secondary, Bell Baxter High.

'When Mum found out, she said, "over my dead body" – actually, I think she was a lot less polite than that – and demanded that I be treated like any normal child. Up till then, I'd always regarded myself as normal so it was pretty hurtful.' (Memo to aforementioned committee members: Caroline Innes would ultimately leave Bell Baxter High with five Highers.) 'That was definitely a turning point in my life. Because of my speech impediment some people naturally think you're stupid; my BA proved that my body might be a bit dodgy, but there's nothing wrong with my brain.

'Do you know why I liked your articles from Sydney so much?' she once asked me over a riotous assembly in her local watering hole. (Suffused with brilliance, I suggest to a very unladylike chortle.) 'No, you never called me "brave" or said that I "suffer" from CP. I hate those words. I'm not brave, and I certainly don't suffer; John suffers – me!'

Unable to play hockey or netball at school, Caroline took up swimming for exercise, a sport she quickly jettisoned 'because it soon became apparent I was a wee bit deficient in the co-ordination department'. Her affliction also caused her occasional problems on the running track. 'I was never the fastest of starters because my reactions were entirely unpredictable, let's say, so I always found myself with a lot of ground to make up.'

Now a wife and mother to Christy and Connie, Caroline retired from the track at the age of 26 after Sydney to settle into married life and begin a career as a support worker in Dundee, assisting people with learning difficulties. Did university or athletics bring her and John together, you may wonder? 'No [guffaw]. We met in the pub. Incidentally, I have to say that after six or seven glasses of wine my body becomes much more relaxed, so I drink for medicinal purposes [triple-measure guffaw]. Anyway, back to John. His mates all told him, "But she's disabled, do you know what you're taking on?" But he's still around, so I think it's quite serious.'

BOBBY THOMSON: The King of New York celebrates
'The Shot Heard Round the World' to the acclaim of
the jubilant NY Giants baseball fans.

JIM CLARK at the wheel of his Lotus before driving to victory
in the 1966 United States Grand Prix at Watkins Glen.

DENIS LAW: poetry in motion. The Lawman strikes a typical pose against England at Wembley in 1967.

JIM BAXTER: Slim Jim, socks around his ankles, celebrates with Celtic duo Willie Wallace (number 7) and Bobby Lennox after the latter's goal in the 1967 Wembley Wizards victory over the Auld Enemy in the 'World Cup final'.

BILLY McNEILL **leads out the Lisbon Lions on their day of destiny against Internazionale Milano in the 1967 European Cup final.**

KEN BUCHANAN, in trademark tartan shorts, slips a body punch on his way to victory over Hector Matta of Puerto Rico in the Royal Albert Hall in 1973.

DAVID WILKIE stands atop the Olympic podium after his gold medal swim in the 200 metres breaststroke final in Montreal in 1976.

GORDON BROWN, 'the baby-faced assassin', has Auckland in his sights during the 1977 British Lions tour of New Zealand.

ANDY IRVINE launches another Lions attack out of deep defence against Western Province in South Africa in 1980.

ALLAN WELLS (far left) triumphs in the 100 metres at the 1980 Moscow Olympics, despite Margaret Thatcher's efforts to deny him a gold medal.

SANDY LYLE: made to measure. Previous champion Larry Mize helps the 1988 Masters winner slip into the green jacket.

CAROLINE INNES wins the fourth Paralympic gold medal of her career in the 400 metres at the 2000 Games in Sydney.

CHRIS HOY: the golden man of track cycling prepares for the keirin final at the 2011 World Championships in Apeldoorn, Netherlands. On this occasion, he had to settle for the silver medal.

ANDY MURRAY hits a backhand winner during his third-round victory over Croatia's Ivan Ljubicic at the 2011 Wimbledon Championships, which were to end in another bitter disappointment.

It is just as well that Caroline 'likes a drink' because there was a steady succession of champagne celebrations following Sydney, highlighted by a visit to Buckingham Palace to receive her MBE from the Queen. 'She seemed very nice. We chatted about the Paralympics for a few moments then she extended her hand. The handshake is the royal way of saying "now you can bugger off". Seriously, it was fabulous because I thought I'd be coming home to be plain old Caroline Innes again.' (Plain? Hardly – she was voted 'Sexiest British Athlete' by her British teammates in the Paralympic Village. Old and ordinary? She can dominate any occasion with her humour and radiance.) 'After the MBE medal ceremony my parents, John and myself went to an Italian restaurant round the corner from the palace which attracts a lot of sportspeople, for some reason. My photograph is now up on the wall between John McEnroe and Nigel Mansell.'

From Buckingham Palace to Edinburgh's Hilton Hotel for Scotland's Greatest Ever Sportsmen and Women Awards ceremony, where the roll of honour comprised Denis Law (football), Ken Buchanan (boxing), Allan Wells and Liz McColgan (athletics), Willie Carson (horse racing), Andy Irvine (rugby union), Sandy Lyle (golf) and 'little old me – Scotland's Greatest Paralympian. That was a night to remember because everyone made me feel like a real superstar. Denis was lovely, just as nice as you hope a hero will turn out to be, and I never realised how tiny Willie Carson is. I could jump over him.'

The honours flooded in: the Variety Club of Great Britain Disabled Sportsman Award 'made to persons in sport who by word or deed have done so much to assist the course of helping disadvantaged children. Made to Caroline Innes in London in the presence of HRH The Duke of York.'

From the Rt Hon Earl of Airlie KT, GCVO, PC, LLD, Cortachy Castle, Kirriemuir, Angus: 'Dear Miss Innes, I would like to send you my warmest good wishes and congratulations on your award of the MBE. This is richly deserved for all that you have done for services to disabled sport, which is undoubtedly indebted to your hard work and devotion.'

From David Moorcroft of UK Athletics: 'Your MBE is a wonderful recognition of everything you have achieved in athletics. Obviously Sydney was the most recent highlight but the award recognises all your great successes of recent years.'

From Waid Academy School, Anstruther: 'Our thanks to you, Caroline, for being the first Olympic champion to visit the Waid. Once you had left, the overwhelming feeling was that you are an inspirational woman who was a little overawed by all the attention you have received. We found you to be genuine and up for a laugh.'

From Richard Callicott, UK Sport: 'Sir Rodney Walker and I would like to send our best wishes to you. It is the actions of figures such as yourself both past and present that have defined standards to which our top sportsmen and women must aspire. Sydney's Olympians and Paralympians provided some memories which will remain with the British public for some time to come, embodying all that is good in sport while at the same time putting the UK firmly back on the sporting map. Congratulations once again for the lasting legacy your achievements have created.'

Although leading politicians such as William Hague, Kate Hoey and Dr John Reid also took the trouble to pen handwritten letters, it is the messages from families who live with cerebral palsy in which Caroline most delights. 'Dear Caroline, I find myself writing to you to tell you what an inspiration you have been to us. I have a two-year-old daughter called Dana, who one year ago was diagnosed with CP. Things have been difficult all round as we were faced with Dana's condition with no real explanation of what it entailed or of what we could expect. Unfortunately, we were left with quite a negative perspective of what lifestyle Dana would have. Your achievements at the Paralympics, however, have provided us with a great uplift. I'd be most grateful if you have a photo you could send us that we could all look at in times of difficulty to remind us of what Dana could ultimately aspire to.'

And from Liz Moulam, mother of the then seven-year-old Beth, who has been in regular correspondence with Caroline since the events of Sydney: 'Beth was very proud of your MBE. Inspired by you, Beth is now walking everywhere – shopping centre, hospital, school, she is very tired but very, very determined and we're delighted with her progress.' In the same envelope came a personal message which Beth had painstakingly scrawled in pencil. 'To Caroline MBE, so much love. I love your talking. You are my heroine. Love from Beth XXXXXX.'

The two heroines came together a few years ago when Liz Moulam accompanied Beth to a lecture Caroline was giving. 'I wish you'd seen her wee face when we finally met,' Caroline said. 'She's just so lovely. Her mum and dad could understand what Beth was saying but it's quite difficult to a strange ear so she talks to me via her computer. Imagine me being a heroine or someone loving the way I talk? Beth calls me her role model, which is funny, because I always think of Sally Gunnell or Linford Christie as role models.'

Although Caroline is lovingly known as 'motor-mouth' by her nearest and dearest, as a role model and celebrity, she had to master the art of public speaking.

'I used to be absolutely terrified of speaking in front of an audience until someone advised me to pretend that everyone in the room had no clothes on. I must admit, I tend to focus on the best-looking man. I have never, ever wished to be anything other than I am, although I confess to a moment of terror when they invited me to relaunch the Broughty Ferry lifeboat. I told them, "If you want me to hit a boat with a bottle of champagne, we could be there all day." Luckily, I'd only to press a button.'

Having witnessed the lass consume copious amounts of Sauvignon Blanc through a straw over various lunches, I reckon it was very wise of the RNLI not to entrust her with a magnum of bubbly.

20. ANDY IRVINE MBE
Rugby Union

Born: Edinburgh, 16 September 1951

CAREER:
Club: Heriot's FP
Scotland 1972–82: 51 caps, 250 points
British Lions: 1974, South Africa (won 3–0); 1977, New
   Zealand (lost 3–1); 1980, South Africa (lost 3–1)

'Rugby players are either piano shifters or piano players,' commented 1950s French scrum-half Pierre Danos. With a ball in his hands, Andy Irvine was as flamboyant as Liberace, every entrance an adventure. A brilliant virtuoso capable of dazzling brilliance, no full-back has ever knocked out a tune quite like him.

'Le Triomphe de Baroque' ('the triumph of the artistically extravagant') proclaimed *L'Equipe* on the morning of 17 February 1980 to mark Irvine's bravura performance in Edinburgh the previous day. Like all creatures of whimsy, he had fluffed a few notes – a series of penalties, in fact, including a 'gimme' from in front of the posts, which was greeted by resounding jeers from the frustrated Scots fans – and with just 12 minutes remaining, France enjoyed a seemingly insurmountable 14–4 lead.

Cue entrance of the Murrayfield maestro with two typically inventive tries, a brace of penalties and an outrageous conversion from the touchline (Jim Renwick slotted home Irvine's second touchdown while our hero received medical treatment after being injured during the build-up move) to transform looming defeat into an improbable 24–14 triumph. To commemorate the pride of Heriot's RFC's 16-point solo, *L'Equipe* referred to the stadium as Irvinefield.

As a youngster, Irvine had been far too interested in watching schoolboy idols such as Dave Mackay, Gordon Smith and Alec Young at Tynecastle to take more than a passing interest in rugby union; it was only when he left James Gillespie Primary to attend George Heriot's School, where the sport was compulsory, that he was introduced to rugby as a reluctant 13 year old.

In 1967, he was a member of a school party that travelled to Murrayfield to watch New Zealand beat Scotland 14–3 little thinking that when he made his second visit to the ground five years later aged 21, it would be as his country's full-back against the mighty '72 All Blacks. Two penalties from the new cap kept his side within touch of the Kiwis until a Sid Going try in injury time consigned Scotland to a 14–9 defeat. There was disappointment on the terracing and in the grandstands but the buzz that reverberated around the stadium whenever Irvine gained possession suggested the Scottish selectors had unearthed a superstar in waiting.

It was to be a white-knuckle ride, for whilst Irvine had a happy knack of making the inordinately difficult look simple, he was also possessed of an uncanny ability to make the straightforward appear fiendishly complicated, scoring breathtaking tries and landing impossibly angled conversions while fumbling passes and sclaffing easy penalties wide of the posts. 'If you hoisted up a high ball and Andy managed to catch it, then you knew you were in serious trouble,' explained one-time Scotland skipper Peter Brown, who engaged in many a club battle with Irvine's Heriot's in the colours of Gala. 'Fortunately, Andy being Andy, he would drop as many as he caught.'

As swift as a deer and as elusive as a puff of wind, Irvine began his first British Lions tour in 1974 as understudy to Welshman J.P.R. Williams in South Africa. But his form in the midweek 'reserves' convinced Irish coach Syd Millar that a place had to be found for his mercurial skills in the Test XV, albeit on the wing. Irvine would end the tour with 156 points, a record haul for a Lion in the Republic, and a reputation of being one of the most exhilarating attackers in world rugby.

It was a rumbustious introduction to the brotherhood of Lions for the 23-year-old Edinburgh University graduate, with mayhem occurring at regular intervals both on and off the pitch. In an effort to counter the ludicrously biased refereeing they encountered, captain Willie John McBride instigated the notorious '99' call (see page 39). 'There was method to the madness,' explained the skipper. 'You see, there were fights breaking out all over the place and some o' me lads were running 100 yards just to get a kick at a South African – retaliation like. Now that was no use to me. If someone like Gordon Brown, say, was fighting for ten minutes that was ten minutes he wasn't playing rugby. The "99" call ensured everyone had a chance to settle their grievances and be ready to play 30 seconds later. Even a South African referee, so I reasoned, couldn't send off all 15 of us.'

Victory assured – 3–0 in the Test series – and their unbeaten record intact, the Lions held a genteel soirée on the night of the Third Test in their Port Elizabeth hotel. Much furniture was splintered ('Inadvertently,' protested Willie John) and many fire extinguishers were set off ('Accidentally,' pled W.J. McB. in mitigation) before the hotel manager, seeing his beloved lobby disappearing under six feet of water, stormed off in search of the Lions captain.

He would have knocked on McBride's bedroom door except the bedroom in question had been without a door for some days after Willie John, returning from a night on the Port Elizabeth tiles without a key and finding the night porter in unhelpful mode, removed said door – and door frame – 'with a couple of gentle dunts'.

'Mr McBride,' railed the manager, 'your players are wrecking my hotel.'

'Are there many dead?' enquired W.J. McB., puffing contentedly on his pipe and sitting cross-legged and naked but for his Y-fronts on top of the bed.

'I want every one of you locked up. The police are on their way.'

'And tell me,' puffed McBride with a proud smile as the sound of crashing and bashing continued unabated below, 'these police of yours – will there be many of them?'

Boys will be boys, of course, but as one of the mischief-makers-in-chief on that tour, it can be taken as read that, now he is of an age to receive the Government's fuel allowance and a free bus pass, the grown-up Irvine will not condone such shenanigans when he leads the British Lions to Australia as team manager in 2013.

In *Giants of Scottish Rugby*, Irvine told Jeff Connor that of his three Lions tours, 'South Africa in '74 was the most enjoyable because it was the first and I had no idea what it would be like. I had no family responsibilities, I was single and it was almost like one long holiday. I was in a fantastic country with fantastic weather, great hotels, great food, playing the game I love in the sunshine.'

By the 1977 tour of New Zealand, Irvine was a giant of the world game despite the 3–1 series defeat; he scored a Lions-record-equalling 25 points against Hanan Shield Districts with an imperious display, highlighted by a mesmerising solo try in which he ran over half the length of the pitch, sidestepping and swerving past eight baffled All Blacks. He also set a record of five tries against a combined King Country-Waganui side. Little wonder the size of his fan club in New Zealand possibly outnumbers even that of his native Scotland.

Irvine donned the red of the British Lions for the third time in South Africa in 1980, a tour he appeared destined to miss when he was left out of the squad by coach Noel Murphy due to a recurring hamstring injury. Answering an SOS after an injury to Irish full-back Rodney O'Donnell, Irvine joined the party in South Africa halfway through the tour – which the Lions lost 3–1 – and played in the final three Tests, scoring a try in the 17–13 victory in the Fourth Test in Pretoria.

As his ten-year Scotland international career wound to a close, Irvine also had the personal satisfaction of breaking All Blacks full-back Don Clarke's Test points world record of 207 when he kicked four penalties in the 12–6 defeat of Romania at Murrayfield in 1981 to take him on to the 209 mark.

'The way I played, I was always going to make some mistakes, just like the way I play golf; I had a fairly cavalier attitude towards rugby but still believe that the best place from which to attack is from deep in defence.' So sayeth Andy 'Sweet Music' Irvine.

21. DOUGLAS JARDINE
Cricket

Born: Bombay, India, 23 October 1900
Died: Montreux, Switzerland, 18 June 1958

CAREER:
Surrey 1921–33 (141 matches): batting average – 46.83
England 1928–34: Tests – 22; runs scored – 1,296; top score
– 127; batting average – 48.00

Broadcaster Alan McGilvray, 'the voice' of Australian cricket for more than 50 years, went to his grave in 1996 insistent that Douglas Jardine was 'the most notorious Englishman since Jack the Ripper'. Born in Bombay of fiercely patriotic Scottish parents and raised in St Andrews, Jardine would have been doubly amused by this particular Aussie pen-pic.

McGilvray's detestation of Jardine went back over 30 years to the 1932–33 'Bodyline' Ashes series in which the England captain instructed his fast bowlers, particularly the fearsome Harold Larwood, to ignore the stumps and aim short-pitched deliveries at the Australian batsmen in the hope of offering a catch to the posse of fielders lurking like vultures behind the wicket. As a spectacle it was ugly but Jardine was a firm believer that on the cricket pitch the ends justified the means and England duly won the series 4–1 amid bitter recriminations.

Even within the confines of Lord's, where he might have expected unqualified support as England's Test skipper, one Marylebone Cricket Club member of the day was moved to opine: 'Douglas Jardine is insufferable, worse than any German I encountered in the war. I cannot abide the man.'

Almost 80 years after the events that attracted accusations of infamy, Jardine would undoubtedly be knighted as a sporting hero as captain of an England team which sailed back to these shores having regained the Ashes, but many regarded him as simply benighted. Tactical genius or fiendish mastermind (depending upon your point of view) behind

Bodyline, Jardine was vilified Down Under as a ruthless, arrogant snob.

But that is the portrait of a stranger to his daughter, the Reverend Fianach Lawry, an ordained Episcopalian minister, a playful priest who lists *The Vicar of Dibley* among her all-time favourite TV programmes; Fianach (pronounced Fiona) becomes unusually misty-eyed when presented with this image of an ogre. 'Father was shy, reserved, a terribly gentle man with a strict sense of fair play who wouldn't dream of stretching the rules during a family game of Ludo, never mind on the cricket pitch. He had impossibly high standards if you were a child – standards, I have to say, that I failed to meet on numerous occasions. He had a lovely dry sense of humour, however, and used to love reading Rudyard Kipling's *The Jungle Book* to my brother, two sisters and myself before we went to sleep at night. But he had an air of sadness about him right up until his death in 1958. He was never angry about the furore surrounding Bodyline but, yes, he carried this distinct aura of melancholy. More than anything else, father honestly believed that he had done what the MCC had agreed to. He felt that having said one thing, when the going got really difficult the MCC made him the fall-guy.'

There was never a suggestion – not even among his most acid detractors Down Under – that Jardine cheated in any way whatsoever; indeed it could be said that the West Indies refined the Bodyline tactics to devastating effect 50 years later with their four-pronged pace attack. But in an era before helmets and padding it was widely seen as a cynical manoeuvre designed to prevent Donald Bradman, the run-machine who was occasionally vulnerable to fast bowling, from racking up his customary centuries.

On 17 January 1933, an outraged Australian Board of Control fired off a telegram to Lord's stating: 'Bodyline bowling has assumed such proportions as to menace the best interests of the game, making protection of the body by batsmen the main consideration. This is causing intensely bitter feelings between the players as well as injury. In our opinion, it is unsportsmanlike and unless it is stopped at once, it is likely to upset the friendly relations which exist between Australia and England.'

Even before Jardine ordered his fast bowlers, Larwood and Bill Voce, to target bodies rather than the stumps as a shock tactic, the Scots-born, Winchester College and Oxford University educated England captain had incurred colonial wrath by insisting upon wearing his Oxford Harlequin cap on the pitch – a fashion statement regarded as pretentious Down Under – and dismissing the locals as 'an uneducated and unruly mob'. When teammate Patsy Hendren was moved to observe, 'They don't seem to like you very much over here, Mr Jardine,' amid much booing and jeering during the Second Test of the 1928–29 Ashes series in Sydney, the reply was as brusque as it was unambiguous: 'Then it's fucking mutual.'

Such was the vitriol Jardine attracted Down Under during that first visit that when he was appointed captain for the subsequent 1932–33 tour, his former cricket coach at Winchester College, Rockley Wilson, predicted: 'We may well win the Ashes . . . but could lose a dominion in the process.'

Tact and diplomacy were clearly alien concepts to Jardine, as he showed during the bitterly controversial third Bodyline Test at Adelaide, where Larwood seriously injured Australia's captain, Bill Woodfull, with one vicious delivery which landed just below the heart. As the stadium fell quiet, Jardine's imperiously clipped voice rang out: 'Well bowled, Harold.'

Before leaving the dressing-room, Jardine, who saw no point in playing any game unless you played to win, was wont to remind his team that 'an hour of glorious life is worth an age without a name'. 'Yes, he was fiercely competitive,' says Fianach Lawry, 'but there wasn't a malicious bone in his body. Naturally, he taught all us children to play cricket and I was the wicketkeeper at St Margaret's School, Bushy. Father used to come to watch my sister, Mel, and I playing for the first team and I remember one

---

Sir Arthur Conan Doyle (and friends)

While Douglas Jardine, Mike Denness (born, Bellshill; educated Ayr Academy) and Tony Greig (raised in South Africa of a West Lothian father) all captained England, Scotland's most globally celebrated cricketer is undoubtedly Sir Arthur Conan Doyle.

When not knocking out another bestseller, Doyle turned out regularly for the MCC and famously took W.G. Grace's wicket in a match against London County at Crystal Palace in 1900, following which he penned a celebratory poem:

> Once in my heyday of cricket,
> Oh, day I shall ever recall!
> I captured that glorious wicket,
> The greatest, the grandest of all.

Although he averaged only 19.25 with the bat, Doyle's spin bowling could be as difficult to fathom as his plots and in 1899 he took seven wickets for sixty-one runs against Cambridgeshire at Lord's. Such was his fascination with cricket and cricketers, one biographer has suggested that it was Nottinghamshire bowler Frank Shacklock who inspired the surname of Doyle's great literary hero.

An enthusiastic – and highly skilled – golfer (Rudyard Kipling being his regular opponent), boxer (with best friend Harry Houdini serving as his sparring partner), cross-country skier and rugby player, Doyle was also a goalkeeper of some renown. Playing

afternoon when we were both out within five minutes, whereupon he turned on his heel in complete disgust muttering "Jesus". My youngest sister, who was in the junior school, was suitably appalled.'

A stylish if unspectacular batsman, Jardine would captain England against India in 1934, standing down before England's defence of the Ashes later that year when he effectively retired from first-class cricket at the age of 33 with a Test batting average of 48.00. 'Father would occasionally talk about the Bodyline series when we were children,' recalls Fianach, 'but he was a very private man so it wasn't something he discussed at length round the dinner table. As I said, he was very, very shy, which I think was not unconnected with the fact that my grandfather was a judge in Bombay so father was sent over to prep school as a small boy. He spent his holidays with my mother's sister, Aunt Kitty in St Andrews, and only went home to India once a year, a round trip which took about six weeks by boat. I don't suppose that was very easy when you're only five or six years old but, consequently, he was never part of some riotous family assembly and became incredibly self-contained.'

Having departed the Test scene, Jardine was a member of the British Expeditionary Force dropped behind enemy lines in France, from where he was later evacuated suffering from trench foot. 'Father was then sent to the North-West Frontier, to places we had never heard of until the war in Afghanistan, and had, as they say, a lovely war. He used to send the most marvellous letters home which were so fascinating that although he wasn't around for a long time it always felt as though he was there in our midst.'

Jardine was considering retiring to what was Southern Rhodesia, where he owned land outside Salisbury, when he became ill during a trip to Africa in 1958. 'Father caught tick-fever and was sent to the Hospital for

---

under the pseudonym A.C. Smith – possibly because football was considered an ungentlemanly pastime – Doyle was one of the founder members of Portsmouth Association Football Club, the forerunner of the present day Portsmouth FC.

Doyle's love of cricket was shared by J.M. Barrie who, despite standing only 5 ft 3 in. and possessed of an insatiable appetite for alcohol and tobacco, was a keen sportsman. Not good enough to be selected to play for a county, Barrie resolved this issue by starting his own cricket club – the Allahakbarries – comprising some of the most respected writers of the day including Sir Arthur, A.A. Milne, Jerome K. Jerome and P.G. Wodehouse.

All but useless with bat and ball (Doyle apart), the Allahakbarries can be regarded as the original celebrity charity fund-raisers. A heartbroken Barrie disbanded the team in 1913 when two of the four Lllewelyn Davies brothers were killed in action during the First World War, inspiring the 'Lost Boys' characters in the *Peter Pan* adventure.

Tropical Diseases on his return. They discovered he had – among other things – lung cancer, although he'd only been a light pipe smoker. He had terrible trouble breathing so he and mama went to Switzerland to take the clean mountain air but he never came back; his stomach blew up. We took his ashes to a mountain by Loch Rannoch where he had loved shooting and stalking. Although it was July, it was really quite cold and cloudy until the moment came to scatter father's remains when the sky turned blue and a brilliant sun came out.'

Among the many tributes paid to Jardine following his death came this one from Sir Pelham 'Plum' Warner, chairman of the England selectors in 1932: 'If ever there was a cricket match between England and the rest of the world and the fate of England depended upon its result, I would pick Jardine as captain every time.'

Fianach Lawry is of the unshakable belief that 'history has been unfair on father' but added: 'There's no future in being resentful. If you harbour grievances, then you damage yourself. I think he'd be amazed that all these years and Ashes series later, people would still be talking about the events of 1932. The whole thing got completely out of hand. Father had lots of wonderful Australian friends – including [the late former Prime Minister] Bob Menzies, with whom, whenever he came over here, he would always get together. He was very blessed.'

He was also, in the words of Bodyline teammate Bill Bowes: 'The greatest captain England ever had. A great fighter and a grand friend.'

22. JIMMY JOHNSTONE
Football

Born: Viewpark, Lanarkshire, 30 September 1944
Died: Uddingston, Lanarkshire, 13 March 2006

CAREER:

Celtic 1961–75: 515 appearances, 129 goals; Scottish League
  Championship 1965–66, 1966–67, 1967–68, 1968–69,
  1969–70, 1970–71, 1971–72, 1972–73, 1973–74; Scottish
  Cup 1967, 1969, 1971, 1972; Scottish League Cup 1966,
  1967, 1968, 1969, 1970; European Cup 1967
San Jose Earthquakes 1975: 10 appearances, 0 goals
Sheffield United 1975–7: 11 appearances, 2 goals
Dundee 1977: 3 appearances, 0 goals
Shelbourne 1977–8: 9 appearances, 0 goals
Elgin City 1978–9: 18 appearances, 2 goals
Scotland 1964–74: 23 appearances, 2 goals

To describe Jimmy Johnstone as 'a dribbler' is to dismiss Nijinsky as a
hoofer. You think Stanley Matthews, George Best and Garrincha could
trip the light fantastic? Dribbling the 'Jinky' way was to see Gene Kelly
equipped with a football instead of a brolly as a prop; a shimmy, a twist,
a double-shuffle, a somersault and he was off on another meandering
run across three postcodes pursued by a chorus-line of incandescent
defenders.

When he grew bored with dribbling past the opposition, Wee Jinky
would begin to take on his own Celtic teammates. One foggy Saturday in
December against Partick Thistle, so those who were at Parkhead that
afternoon will tell you, he dribbled past all twenty-one players (the
majority of them at least twice), nutmegged the referee, left both sets of
managers, physios and substitutes for dead, rounded six ballboys, fifteen
stewards, twenty-seven programme sellers, five mounted policemen and
was last seen dribbling through the crowds of Christmas shoppers in
Argyle Street.

Five foot five inches of flame-haired wizardry, it is fair to say that the Internazionale Milano players had never seen his like before – or the rest of the Lisbon Lions, for that matter – when they lined up alongside one another in the sweltering underground tunnel connecting the dressing-rooms before the 1967 European Cup final.

'There they were,' remembered Wee Jinky with that trademark grin of mischief. 'Facchetti, Domenghini, Mazzola, Cappellini; all six-footers wi' Ambre Solaire suntans, Colgate smiles and slicked-back hair. Each and every wan o' them looked like yon film star Cesar Romero. They even smelt beautiful. And there's us lot – midgets. Ah've got nae teeth, Bobby Lennox hasn'ae any, and old Ronnie Simpson's got the full monty, nae teeth top an' bottom. The Italians are staring doon at us an' we're grinnin' back up at 'em wi' our great gumsy grins. We must have looked like something out o' the circus.'

Clowns they were not, however, and the memory of the drama which unfolded over the subsequent 90 minutes can still send the heart soaring: Internazionale, twice European Cup winners, twice World Club champions, Italian champions three times in four years and the supreme masters of suffocating defensive tactics, were ripped apart by a team of relative unknowns magically blended together into an irresistible attacking force by Jock Stein. 'Big Jock always said we'd win but I thought we'd get a gubbin', to be honest.'

It was Inter who experienced the gubbin'; the bald statistics show that the mighty Italian champions, who opened the scoring via a Sandro Mazzola penalty after eight minutes before erecting an eleven-man defence, did not win a single corner and forced goalkeeper Simpson (who wrapped his false teeth in his bunnet 'so he'd look nice in the photies if we won') to make but one save; Celtic had two shots off the crossbar, and forty-nine other attempts on goal, thirteen of which were saved by Italian goalkeeper Giuliano Sarti, seventeen were blocked or deflected, and a mere nineteen delivered off-target.

'We kept asking one another, "When are these bastards gonna start playing?" I think that's why there was always so much genuine affection for the Lions. No one really expected us to win. Inter thought they were the best money could buy. The Celtic team – all 11 of us – were born within a 30-mile radius across central Scotland. Now, that'll never happen again, will it? I think we took them by surprise because our free-flowing style was unique. We were like the Dutch speeded up and they'd never played against anything like us.'

It befell the hapless Tarcisio Burgnich – 'Tackling Johnstone was like trying to catch a hornet while wearing boxing gloves' – to trail Jinky across the length and breadth of the field as Celtic, with second-half goals from Tommy Gemmell and Steve Chalmers, held millions of television viewers in thrall with their cavalier capers. 'Although we were a goal down at half-time we should have been three up. I don't think Inter had ever been outclassed before – but we outclassed them from the first minute to last.'

Johnstone's meandering route to Lisbon had begun among the coalmines of Lanarkshire where his every waking moment as a child revolved around football. Usually he played 40-a-side with his school chums. When they were sick, he played by himself; when there was no ball, he fashioned a round shape 'oot o' rags and string. Onything ah could kick.' At 17, he joined Celtic, where he quickly became the most beloved player in the club's history. When Wee Jinky took a pass and set off on a run, his teammates knew governments would fall before they would see the ball again.

'He used to tell me how he wanted the ball presented to him,' explained Johnstone's chief supplier, right-half Bobby Murdoch, another Lion who did not live to see the 40th anniversary of Lisbon in 2007. 'You know, whether he wanted it to his feet, played in front of him, with his back to goal, or whatever. "An' when will I get it back?" I used to say. "Dunno," he'd grin, "when ah'm finished wi' it, ah suppose."' Opposing full-backs did not sleep nights fretting about the horrors that lay in store, kept awake by the prospect of their tiny tormentor dribbling them straight through the gates of the farm for the seriously bewildered.

'Scotland beat us 2–0 one year,' shuddered England's Emlyn Hughes at the memory, 'and I was embarrassed to come off the pitch. Jimmy Johnstone absolutely crucified me. Alf Ramsey came up and said, "You've just played against a world-class player. He can do that to anybody."'

Cruelly, having beaten the bottle as a recovering alcoholic, it was motor neurone disease that would kill him; his playing career and defiant battle against the ravages of the illness led to Johnstone becoming the first living person to have a Fabergé egg named in their honour since the time of Tsar Nicholas II and the Tsarina Alexandra. Among those who saw the film of his career and battle against illness, *Lord of the Wing*, in London was Sarah Fabergé. A granddaughter of the Romanovs' personal jeweller, Carl, Sarah Fabergé was inspired to design 19 limited issue 'Jinky eggs' which, when the gold, silver and jewel-encrusted 'shell' was opened, revealed tiny replicas of his personal trophy collection – the European Cup, nine League Championships, four Scottish Cups and five League Cups.

As someone who 'always liked a drink', as they say in the west of Scotland, wee Jinky's tastes were indulged up to a point by Stein, although the errant number 7 invariably felt he had been electronically tagged every Saturday night. 'Ah used to go into pubs where I thought no one might know me. I mind going into one outside Stirling one time. "A lager shandy," says I. While the barman's still pouring the bluidy thing, the phone goes. "Here, it's for you," he says.' In reply to Johnstone's jaunty 'hello' came the familiar sergeant-major's growl: 'Get your arse out of there right now, wee man.'

'Ah fled. Big Jock had a bigger spy network than the KGB. People talk about his tactical genius, his ability at spotting weaknesses in the opposition an' all that. But his greatest talent was psychology. Footballers are funny animals, as you know. He took all our different temperaments and built the best team in the world. He took charge of all our problems. All he wanted was for you to go out on that park and be at your best for 90 minutes. If you'd committed murder, he'd get you aff wi' it so long as you were right for that game.'

Never did the Big Man and the Wee Man combine to better effect than against Red Star Belgrade in the second round of the 1969 European Cup. 'We were being held 0–0 at half-time in the first leg at Parkhead and as we were going back out for the second half the boss – who knew ah was terrified, absolutely terrified, of flying – whispered in ma ear, "If we win by four clear goals, Jinky, you can stay at home in two weeks' time."'

For 45 minutes, Johnstone played as if blessed by the gods. He scored two goals and manufactured three as Celtic won 5–1. 'The Yugoslav coach pleaded wi' big Jock to let the people of Belgrade see me, but the boss was as good as his word. When the rest o' the team flew oot, ah stayed at hame.'

Johnstone reserved his most memorable performance for a fitting stage, however. Following their triumph in Lisbon, Celtic were invited to provide the opposition for Alfredo Di Stefano's testimonial game in Madrid. 'Real didn't play friendlies. They'd won the European Cup the year before us in '66 and had never been beaten by a foreign side in the Bernabéu.' With Wee Jinky at his most mesmerising, Celtic won 1–0 to the accompanying '*Olé*'s of the 125,000 crowd every time he left another Spanish defender spinning.

At the post-match banquet, Di Stefano asked for a special photograph to be taken of him and his three long-time cohorts, Ferenc Puskás, Francisco Gento and José Santamaria, flanking Wee Jinky in the middle of the quintet. 'It was the great man's way of telling Jimmy "you belong here with us",' said Bobby Lennox, scorer of the winning goal that night. 'That was probably my biggest personal triumph,' admitted Johnstone. 'According to rumours at the time Real offered Celtic a blank cheque to sign me. But if they did, big Jock never said a word to me.'

When not making sporting headlines with his sorcery, Wee Jinky's high-jinks after dark led to frequent appearances on the front page, most famously during Scotland's 1974 World Cup preparations in Largs when he was pushed out to sea at three in the morning by person or persons unknown in a tiny rowing boat equipped with one oar. 'Me and Denis [Law] decided to go fishing,' he told manager Willie Ormond.

'Jimmy couldn't get back in to the shore,' revealed former Rangers full-back Sandy Jardine. 'But he was singing his head off even as he was drifting further and further away. Then two players, who shall remain nameless, started to paddle out to get him and the boat had a hole in it and started to sink.' Some hours later, Johnstone was finally delivered back to shore by the Largs coastguard. 'Ah coulda done with someone like Gazza in those days to take some o' the heat aff me,' laughed the would-be angler.

When motor neurone disease finally killed him on 13 March 2006, Parkhead was immediately festooned in scarves and shirts left in his honour by fans representing every club in Scotland, aye, even including Rangers. Only Wee Jinky could unite both sides of the Old Firm.

23. DENIS LAW
Football

Born: Aberdeen, 24 February 1940

CAREER:
Huddersfield Town 1956–60: 81 appearances, 16 goals
Manchester City 1960–1: 44 appearances, 21 goals
Torino 1961–2: 27 appearances, 10 goals
Manchester United 1962–73: 309 appearances, 171 goals;
    League Championship 1964–65, 1966–67; FA Cup 1963;
    European Footballer of the Year 1964
Manchester City 1973–4: 24 appearances, 9 goals
Scotland 1958–74: 55 appearances, 30 goals

'Denis Law was my idol. To me, he epitomises what it is to be a Scot; he could start a fight in an empty house, he had the courage of a lion – he probably had more fights with the biggest centre-halves in the world than any other player I can remember – and they all knew he could handle himself. He had style, he had skill, he had that something extra which meant that when Denis was on the pitch, you couldn't take your eyes off him.'

Sir Alex Ferguson

The blond thatch may be tinged with grey, the mischievously sparkling eyes a tad dimmer now that he is a grandfather who has passed beyond the age of 70, but in the mind's eye, Denis Law is out there still on the lush Hampden pitch, accepting the acclaim of 135,000 subjects while celebrating his latest goal in the trademark manner, the raised clenched fist clutching the right cuff of his shirtsleeve.

He scored a record 30 goals in 55 matches for Scotland (a mark he shares with Kenny Dalglish, who needed 47 more games to achieve the feat) but was so much more than a simple goal-scorer. The goals came in every shape and colour: searing long-range shots, simple tap-ins, dynamic headers, fluky ricochets, cheeky flicks after mazy solo runs, acrobatic scissor-kicks.

'No other player,' noted Sir Matt Busby, 'scored as many miracle goals as Denis. He was the quickest-thinking player I've ever seen, seconds quicker than anyone else. He had the most tremendous acceleration, could leap enormous heights, and was an impeccable passer of the ball.'

Law may have scored 171 goals in 309 League appearances for Manchester United, 34 in 44 FA Cup ties, 28 in 33 European games, won an FA Cup winner's medal, two League titles, been voted European Footballer of the Year in 1964 and crowned 'the King' by his worshipful followers at Old Trafford's Stretford End but whenever he pulled on the dark blue of Scotland he became a man possessed. As Sir Bobby Charlton remembered the events of their first international confrontation in 1960: 'In the very first minute, I swung in a cross from the left touchline and was promptly knocked flat on my back. The ball was miles away. I thought "You what?" and looked up to see Denis bending over and growling at me like an early-day Rab C. Nesbitt: "See you, Charlton, you blankety Sassenach. S'no Old Trafford now, izzit, eh?" About the only words I could really make out amidst his lengthy diatribe were Scotland and England.'

Law, who was then playing for Manchester City, has never seen fit to apologise to the man who would subsequently become a United colleague: 'Well, there can be no greater compliment than being asked to play for your country. I'm often asked to pick my favourite moment in football – and I was lucky because there were quite a few – but the most important would probably be my first cap as an 18 year old when Matt Busby selected me to play against Wales in 1958.'

Three years earlier, Law had looked anything but a future international in his thick National Health spectacles when reserve-team coach Bill Shankly first laid eyes on Huddersfield Town's latest signing. 'Ah think it's your big brother I wanted, son,' he told the skinny runt of the seven-sibling Law family. Surgery improved his sight, though he always suffered from poor vision and Shankly had to coax him out of the habit of playing with one eye closed.

'Denis looked like a skinned rabbit when he joined us as a 15 year old,' added Shanks. 'But he was like a whippet. And like any pedigree whippet, when he got the hare he shook it to death. He had eyes in the back of his head like Tom Finney, he had guts, and ability, and determination. He possessed the lot.'

Even so, few of Law's fellow Scots had heard of him when Sir Matt plucked him from the obscurity of the English Second Division to make a scoring debut in a 3–0 defeat of Wales. 'Looking back, it's strange to think what an influential role the old man would have on my career.'

There were to be some memorable moments – England 2, Scotland 3 in the 'alternative' Wembley World Cup final of 1967 – and others best forgotten like the humiliating 9–3 mauling six years earlier, but whereas Law has learned to laugh off that particular embarrassment, he still feels the pain of 1962. 'Failing to qualify for the World Cup finals in Chile remains my biggest regret. It's only my opinion but, to me, that was the best Scotland team of all time.'

(For those too young to recall, manager Ian McColl's preferred XI of the day in 2–3–5 formation comprised: Bill Brown; Alex Hamilton, Eric Caldow; Pat Crerand, Billy McNeill, Jim Baxter; Alex Scott, John White, Ian St John, Denis Law, Davie Wilson.)

Having beaten Czechoslovakia 3–2 at Hampden – with two goals from Law, who was hailed by opposing coach Rudolf Vytlacil as 'the world's greatest player' at the final whistle – Scotland had to meet the Czechs again in a play-off in Brussels with a place in the World Cup finals at stake. 'We lost half a team through injury leading up to the game, which was played in the Heysel Stadium. Even so, we were leading 2–1 with eight minutes remaining. What can I tell you? Typically, we lost 4–2 in extra time. Czechoslovakia were a wonderful team bristling with great players like Masopust, Pluskal and Popluhar, so it was consolation of sorts when they went all the way to the final in Chile before losing 3–1 to Brazil.'

Joe Baker

Joe Baker was the greatest centre-forward Scotland never had. Born in Liverpool, where his parents lived for a short spell after his father left the Navy in 1941, Baker was carried to Wishaw as a baby and played for Scotland Schoolboys before joining Hibernian.

Fast, fearless and free-scoring (his four seasons at Easter Road would net him 159 goals), Baker talked like a Scot and thought like a Scot but due to that accident of birth was forced to play for England under the rules of the time. 'Having stood on the terraces at Hampden to cheer Scotland so many times, it was a weird feeling lining up alongside Bobby Charlton in the white shirt of England to play against my own country in 1960,' he recalled.

In 1961, Denis Law and Baker, the first player to represent England whilst playing for a 'foreign' club, joined Torino but it was to be a brief and unhappy stay in Italy. Although both men were an instant success (Baker scoring seven goals in nineteen games, including the winner in the city derby against Juventus), they felt hounded by the paparazzi.

Matters came to a head when the duo, weary of staying cooped up in their apartment, broke club orders by going out on the town, following which they were involved in a car crash which resulted in Baker receiving seven operations before spending forty-two days on a drip-feed. After less than a season in Serie A, Law was sold to Manchester United and Baker to Arsenal for a club record fee of £70,000.

Arsenal's top scorer in 1963, 1965 and 1966, Baker's international career was resurrected by Alf Ramsey, who was piecing together his England formation that would

There was to be another crushing disappointment six years later on 29 May 1968 when, shortly before six in the morning, the door to Denis Law's private room in St Joseph's Hospital in Whalley Range flew back on its hinges. There stood Sister John, all 67 years and 59 inches of her, wreathed in a beatific smile, her nun's habit hidden behind a red-and-white Manchester United rosette the size of a dustbin lid. And so, with the kick-off to the European Cup final against Benfica at Wembley still 14 hours away, began the longest day of Law's life.

'Everyone went a little bit crazy that day. Jesus, even Sister John turned out to be a United fanatic.' Though the King was confined to a hospital bed some 200 miles from the action following a cartilage operation, every minute of that day four decades and more ago still generates waves of pleasure.

'I'd played in the first game against Real Madrid in the semi-final but by then my knee had been knackered for months so I missed the return in Spain when the lads drew 3–3. I suppose I could have come back just for the final but I really wasn't fit. If I'd been forced to pull out on the Saturday prior to the Benfica game, I would have felt like shooting myself. But I had a month to think about it, so by the time Bobby and Bestie were doing the business, I think I had just about accepted the situation. Thankfully, the hospital let me have a few pals round to watch the game on telly. I lay there beneath the sheets in my United tammy and scarf, with a crate of rapidly disappearing McEwan's under the bed.

'It's funny. I never talked to Sister John again in over 25 years until she suddenly asked to see me so I went round to the hospice where she was being looked after. She was 92 and dying from Parkinson's disease but could still remember that night as if it was yesterday.'

And who doesn't? Charlton's rare header, Best's chicanery in extra time, Busby's dignified tears at the end as he stood amid the scenes of celebration a decade after his beloved Babes had been wiped out at Munich. And yet it had so nearly gone horribly wrong. 'The one memory that keeps coming back to haunt me is when Eusébio was clean through with only Stepney to beat two minutes from the end of normal time. I

---

win the World Cup. Although he played spectacularly well and scored the opening goal in the 2–0 defeat of Spain in the Bernabéu Stadium – a match in which Ramsey unveiled his 'wingless wonders' for the first time – Baker was ultimately omitted from England's 22-man World Cup squad. 'It was a great disappointment,' he admitted, 'but not as big a heartache as never being allowed to play for Scotland.'

Baker, who eventually returned 'hame' to play for Hibs and Raith Rovers, died at the age of 63 in 2003 in Wishaw General Hospital after suffering a heart attack during a charity golf event.

thought to myself, "Well, if that was Jimmy Greaves, this ball would be in the back of the net. Bang."

'But I could see Eusébio thinking, "This is going to be tomorrow's headline: Eusébio Wins European Cup For Benfica." And he absolutely battered it, tried to burst the back of the net. And, of course, it wasn't so much that Stepney saved it, but it hit him on the chest. It damn near killed him. I still look back sometimes and wonder, "If that had been Greavsie . . ."'

Law's abiding fascination with two of football's most romantic legends – Manchester United and the European Cup – began in 1957 when, as the spindly 17-year-old jewel in Bill Shankly's promising Huddersfield Town side, he watched Real Madrid whip the Red Devils 5–3 over two legs in a magical semi-final which pitted Kopa, Di Stefano and Gento against Edwards, Taylor and Byrne.

'That was the start of my love affair with the European Cup. I think what struck me most was Real Madrid's kit. All white. There's still nothing quite like it, is there? Then, three years later, Real played in what was the greatest game I've ever seen when they beat Eintracht Frankfurt 7–3 in the final at Hampden Park. I was back home in Aberdeen for a holiday and watched it on television, black and white, of course. That's when I saw my hero for the first time. Remember Di Stefano? Top man, the absolute top man. I actually got to play with both my heroes – Di Stefano and Puskás – at Wembley in '63, when I was picked for the Rest of the World against England. Can you imagine playing on the same team as them, eh?'

Real's strip – an outfit Law almost got to wear when Torino briefly considered selling him to the Spanish club in 1962 – allied to Di Stefano's skills, Puskás's shooting and Gento's sorcery will forever remain etched in Law's memory. 'That was football at its best. Superb. And ever since those days, the European Cup has been the trophy every player wants to win most. Just ask Ryan Giggs or Wayne Rooney or Rio Ferdinand. It's hard to win your own League, but that's only the first hurdle.

'We should have won in '66, the year before Celtic beat Inter Milan in Lisbon to become the first British winners.' But having annihilated Benfica 5–1 on a summer's night when Best was christened El Beatle by 100,000 awestruck spectators in Lisbon's Stadium of Light, United surprisingly surrendered 2–1 on aggregate to Partizan Belgrade in the semi-finals.

'Partizan were awful. I missed a goal in Belgrade that was impossible to miss. The ball came across and I tried to side-foot it home on the volley from a couple of yards out. Somehow it struck me on the inside of the thigh and hit the crossbar. I could have tried it a million times again and never missed.' An impoverished Real Madrid, by then a sad caricature of what they once had been, overcame the Yugoslavians in a mediocre final in Brussels as Law and Busby nursed their increasing resentment back home.

But even after the bitter disappointments of '66 and '68, Law believed his destiny was to claim the prize he had come to treasure above all others. 'I was sure my time had come in '69. We met Milan in the semis and United were the better team, no question. They were not a great side. But we lost 2–0 over there, where we didn't play particularly well. Then we took them back to Old Trafford and murdered them. But it was one of those nights when the ball just wouldn't go in the net. We were one up with 15 minutes to go when I scored a goal which the French referee didn't allow, even though the ball was at least a yard over the line.

'If it had counted, we'd have won the European Cup that year instead of Milan, who walloped Ajax – remember they weren't a major force at that time – 4–1 in the final. The Milan defeat was the start of the break-up of that wonderful United side. I still feel if we'd won the cup in '69, we'd have won it again in '70. It's strange how one goal can change the fortunes of a club. One goal dictated whether United would carry on being a great team or bust up.' A snap of the fingers accompanied the thought. 'One goal and the spirit was gone.'

On that note, we return to the crate of McEwan's – by now empty – beneath the bed in St Joseph's. 'As soon as the final whistle blew at Wembley, David Coleman rang up the hospital with a view to interviewing me live on BBC television. "I'm afraid Denis is far too tired for that kind of thing," Sister John told him. I was as tired as a newt, to be accurate. Bless her, it was probably the only lie she ever told in her life.'

24. ERIC LIDDELL
Athletics

Born: Tianjin, China, 16 January 1902
Died: Weixion, China, 21 February 1945

CAREER:
Athletics: 1924 Olympics (Paris): 400 metres – Gold; 200
   metres – Bronze
Rugby Union: 7 caps, 4 tries

Sunday, 6 July 1924, the Olympic Stadium, Colombes: Harold Abrahams, who will win the gold medal for Great Britain the following afternoon, eases into the semi-finals of the 100 metres with victory over American world record holder Charlie Paddock in his first-round heat.

Sunday, 6 July 1924, the Scots' Kirk, 17 rue Bayard, Paris: six miles away in the centre of the French capital, Eric Liddell delivers the weekly sermon using Isaiah, chapter 40, verse 31 as his inspiration: 'But they that wait upon the Lord shall renew their strength; they shall mount up with wings of eagles; they shall run and be not weary; and they shall walk and not faint.'

Some saw it as the ultimate sacrifice, to Eric Liddell it was the easiest decision of his young life. Although sections of the British press thought he should put King and country before religious ideals, as a devout Christian it was his belief that he should not compete on the Sabbath, even if the price of that conviction might be Olympic glory. Instead of running in the qualifying rounds of the 100 metres sprint, therefore, he chose to preach to the small congregation gathered in the Church of Scotland around the corner from the Champs-Elysées.

In the 1981 multiple Oscar-winning movie *Chariots of Fire*, Liddell was only informed that the heats of the 100 metres were due to be run on a Sunday as he was on the point of boarding the cross-Channel ferry at Dover on his way to the Games; permissible dramatic licence, argued the scriptwriters, because in reality the 'Flying Scot' had known of the Olympic schedule for over six months, hence the reason he opted out of the 100 metres and the sprint relay to enter the 200 metres and 400 metres.

The son of Church of Scotland missionaries working in China, Liddell was born in Tianjin and was 18 years of age before he settled in his native land when he entered Edinburgh University to take a Bachelor of Science degree. A keen rugby player as well as track athlete, his speed on the wing brought him international recognition in the 1922 and 1923 Five Nations Championships.

He made his international debut, coincidentally, in the 3–3 draw against France in the Stade de Colombes, the same stadium in which he would capture the imagination of all mankind as an Olympian two and a half years later, and went on to score four tries in his seven appearances for Scotland. But after beating Abrahams to win the 100 yard sprint at the 1923 AAA Championships in a time of 9.7 seconds (a British record that would stand for 35 years), Liddell announced his retirement from international rugby to concentrate his efforts on Olympic gold on the track.

With his curious running style, head thrown back and thrashing arms, Liddell was no stylist and had to content himself with a bronze medal in the 200 metres in Paris, where he finished third behind American duo Jackson Scholz and Charlie Paddock, with Abrahams a distant sixth. 'In the dust of defeat, as well as the laurels of victory, there is a glory to be found if one has done his best,' he said.

Come the afternoon of the 400 metres final, Liddell, as was his wont, shook hands with each of his rivals, at which point he was approached by the masseur of the United States team, who slipped a scrap of paper into the Scotsman's palm bearing a quotation from the Book of Samuel: 'Those who honour me I will honour.'

Drawn in the outside lane, the least favourable starting position, Liddell set off at a blistering pace, which left most of the opposition trailing hopelessly in his wake by the halfway stage. He eventually broke the tape six metres clear of the field in a world record time of 47.6 seconds, with American Horatio Fitch and England's Guy Butler taking the silver and bronze medals. 'The secret of my success,' he revealed, 'is that I run the first 200 metres as fast as I can. Then, for the second 200 metres, with God's help I run faster. God made me fast and when I run I feel His pleasure.'

After winning the 100, 220 and 440 yard events at the 1925 Scottish Championships in Hampden Park, Liddell, still only 23, all but retired from competition when he returned to China to continue his parents' missionary work as an ordained minister of the Church of Scotland. In 1929, he defeated Otto Peltzer over 400 metres at the North China Championships but, despite the German's pleadings, rejected the prospect of training for the 1932 Olympics in Los Angeles to devote his time and efforts to preaching the gospel.

When the Japanese invaded China in 1937, Liddell, now married, sent his Canadian-born wife, Florence, and three young daughters to the safety of Toronto and carried on his missionary duties until rounded up among a contingent of foreign nationals and sent to an internment camp at Weixion. It was a brutal existence, although some survived better than others; when Liddell discovered that a number of oil executives among the prisoners bribed the guards into secretly supplying them with extra food and medical supplies, he shamed them into sharing these luxuries with the rest of the camp inmates. For the first time in his life, he also engaged in less than religious activity on a Sunday by agreeing to serve as referee in the prisoners' weekly football match.

Whilst camp life broke the will of many, Liddell worked tirelessly to ease others' suffering by tending to the elderly, holding Bible classes, teaching science and arranging games for the children to whom he was affectionately known as 'Uncle Eric'. Before the Beijing Olympics in 2008, the Chinese government revealed that Liddell had been offered his release in 1944 as a result of a deal with Winston Churchill involving an exchange of prisoners; he refused the opportunity, insisting his 'parole' should be given to a pregnant young woman in his stead.

Six months before the atom bombs dropped on Hiroshima and Nagasaki brought an end to the Second World War and the liberation of the camp, Liddell died of a brain tumour in February 1945, his humble grave marked by a small wooden cross, his name recorded in boot polish. Fellow internee Langdon Gilkey would later write: 'The entire camp, especially its youth, was stunned for days, so great was the vacuum that Eric's death had left.'

In 1991, Edinburgh University identified Liddell's burial site and replaced the original cross with a headstone fashioned from Isle of Mull granite and bearing the inscription: 'They shall mount up with wings of eagles; they shall run and not be weary.'

Fifty-six years after Liddell's epic run in Paris, Allan Wells won another track gold for Scotland at the 1980 Moscow Olympics. When asked if he had run the race in honour of Harold Abrahams, the last Briton to win the 100 metres title, Wells replied almost in a whisper, 'No, this one was for Eric Liddell.'

25. THE LISBON LIONS
Football

'If you're ever going to win the European Cup, then this is the day and this is the place. But we don't just want to win this cup, we want to do it playing good football . . . to make neutrals glad we've won it, glad to remember how we did it. We must play as if there were no more games, no more tomorrows.'

Jock Stein, Lisbon, 25 May 1967

The record books show that Celtic did, indeed, win the European Cup on this day and in this place, but what the stark 2–1 scoreline does not reveal is the extent of their superiority over the Italian champions. Stung by the loss of an early penalty – the only threatening shot Inter managed on target throughout the 90 minutes – Celtic proceeded to mount wave upon wave of thunderous attacks; if the game had come with a musical accompaniment, then it would have surely been the 'Ride of the Valkyries'.

Even Internazionale's Argentinian coach Helenio Herrera, the past master of defensive strategy, was moved to admit: 'We can have no complaints. Celtic deserved their victory. We were swept aside by their force. Although we lost, the match was a victory for sport.'

Presenting Jock Stein's Lisbon Lions:

RONNIE SIMPSON (GOALKEEPER)

'Well, that's my arse oot the windae,' the 34-year-old goalkeeper muttered when he heard that Stein had resigned as manager of Hibernian and was on his way through to Glasgow to assume control of Celtic in 1965. The previous season, Simpson had made the same 40-mile trip from Easter Road when Stein, less than impressed by the veteran's displays in the Hibs reserves, had offloaded him to Celtic for the paltry sum of £2,000.

Having played for Great Britain in the 1948 Olympics in London under coach Matt Busby (GB losing the bronze medal play-off to Denmark) while a Queen's Park player, Simpson subsequently moved to

Newcastle United with whom he won the FA Cup at Wembley in 1952 and 1955.

Signed as a stop-gap understudy to John Fallon at Parkhead, Simpson proved Stein's usually infallible judgement wrong for once by forcing his way into the first team and going on to play for Celtic on 123 occasions, becoming a Scottish international in the process. 'The European Cup final was just about my easiest game of the season. I think I only had two goal kicks to take throughout the match.'

Ronnie Simpson died of a heart attack on 19 April 2004.

JIM CRAIG (RIGHT-BACK)

A qualified dentist who, in partnership with Tommy Gemmell on the left, was transformed from resolute defender into one of football's original 'wing-backs' under Stein's all-out attacking philosophy. It was Craig's misfortune to concede the eighth-minute penalty from which Inter took the lead when he was adjudged to have fouled Renato Cappellini, Sandro Mazzola scoring from the spot. The incident served only to sharpen Craig's adventurous instincts and it was following another marauding touchline gallop and precise cut-back that Gemmell crashed the equaliser past the previously unbeatable Giuliano Sarti in the Inter goal.

With the emergence of David Hay and Danny McGrain, Craig's first-team outings became rarer – he did not feature in the 1970 European Cup final side – but was a member of the 1971 and 1972 Scottish Cup-winning teams, which took his domestic trophy haul to a remarkable 14.

Following that final medal, Craig emigrated to South Africa, where he played for Hellenic FC, but returned to the UK after an unhappy six months under apartheid rule.

TOMMY GEMMELL (LEFT-BACK)

The joker in the Celtic dressing-room, Gemmell also found the net in the 1970 European Cup final in the 2–1 defeat against Feyenoord and remains one of only two British players to have scored in two finals (a record he shares with Liverpool's Phil Neal).

A swashbuckling full-back who scored 37 goals in 247 games during his 10-year career at Parkhead, Gemmell recalled his crucial equaliser in Lisbon thus: 'As I was about to shoot, an Inter defender half turned his back on me. If he'd taken another step, then it would have been very difficult for me to get the ball past him. They do say the book of Italian heroes is very thin and he wasn't interested in expanding it.

'If he had succeeded in blocking the ball and Inter had then gone up the pitch and scored at the other end, then I would have got a right bollocking because I shouldn't have been up there when Jim Craig was also up there.'

BOBBY MURDOCH (MIDFIELDER)

On the football battlefields of Europe, Bobby Murdoch served as the calming influence in midfield. He was the escape route his teammates looked to when in trouble, always free to take a pass, opening defences with an inspired through ball, as meticulously accurate as a Swiss watch-maker.

Equipped with a venomous shot that brought him 62 goals in 291 games, a succession of injuries restricted his appearances in the aftermath of Lisbon but Stein revealed his importance to the club when, asked if he thought Celtic could win the European Cup again, he replied: 'Yes, when Bobby Murdoch is fit.'

When Jack Charlton was appointed manager of Middlesbrough in 1973, he made the 29-year-old Murdoch his first signing at Ayresome Park, where he guided his new club to the Second Division title while acting as mentor to his young midfield partner, Graeme Souness.

'As far as I am concerned, Bobby Murdoch was just about the best player I had as manager. I only let him move on because he had run out of challenges,' Stein explained of the unexpected transfer.

Although he became a cult hero at Middlesbrough, Murdoch remained a Celt at heart and was working as a member of the match-day hospitality team when he suffered a stroke and died at the age of 56 in May 2001.

BILLY McNEILL MBE (CENTRAL DEFENDER)

Approaching the age of 25 and having already been with Celtic for seven years without winning a trophy, Billy McNeill was on the verge of submitting a transfer request when Jock Stein arrived at Parkhead as manager.

'Caesar', as he was popularly known, immediately became Stein's on-field presence, a captain who led by example. As Bobby Murdoch said of him: 'Billy set a high standard of conduct for us all. That was the main reason you did not see any long-haired wonders swaggering through the doors at Celtic Park. Billy made us realise that professional football was our business. We did not need to look like a crowd of discotheque drop-outs to attract attention.'

McNeill played over 800 games for Celtic between 1958 and 1975, winning nine League titles, seven Scottish Cup and six League Cup winner's medals before moving into management at Clyde and Aberdeen, where he assembled the basis of the side that Sir Alex Ferguson would lead to European glory.

When Stein left Celtic in 1977, it was inevitable that Caesar would be invited to return to Parkhead as his replacement; in two spells in charge, he guided the club he loved to four League titles, plus three Scottish Cups and one League Cup victory.

JOHN CLARK (CENTRAL DEFENDER)

The most underrated Lisbon Lion – though Jock Stein and his colleagues valued him greatly – John Clark was not given to extravagance on the pitch. Whereas Franz Beckenbauer brought a dash of excitement to the sweeper's role with his perfectly timed forays upfield, Clark went about his task with quiet efficiency, earning himself the nickname of 'the Brush'.

It was said that on the rare occasions he crossed the halfway line he took a map with him but according to Bobby Murdoch: 'John was the quiet man of the Lions but the perfect foil for Caesar at the heart of the defence. He was a player you could depend upon to spot the danger before anyone else. He went unnoticed by the fans on the terraces but to his teammates he was vitally important.'

Clark can recall that afternoon in Lisbon's Stadium of Light with clarity: 'I remember it was a really warm day. The whole setting was ideal, it was just as if a film was being made, we were going to win and everything was just right. There was a fantastic crowd all around the stadium when we came out, the whole arena looked as if it was bedecked in green and white.'

JIMMY JOHNSTONE (OUTSIDE-RIGHT)

Years after Lisbon, when Jimmy Johnstone had long since retired and was a recovering alcoholic, he attended a Friday morning training session at Parkhead, where the successors to Jock Stein's famous Lions were preparing to play Rangers.

Charlie Nicholas, no mean trickster himself with a ball at his feet, recalled what happened next in an awed tone: 'We were having a five-a-side match when Jinky decided to join in. We couldn't get the ball off him for 20 minutes. We all stopped – internationals like Danny McGrain, Paul McStay, Frank McGarvey – and I remember thinking: "This isn't supposed to be happening, we're practising for an Old Firm game." Wee Jimmy was happy as Larry, running rings round us, sitting on the ball, doing everything. I've never seen an exhibition like it.'

To paraphrase our national anthem: when will we see his like again?

WILLIE WALLACE (STRIKER)

Having been Hearts' top scorer for four consecutive seasons before the goals inexplicably dried up, the rumour mill in December 1966 suggested that Willie Wallace was poised to sign for Rangers, the club he had supported from boyhood. It was something of a shock, therefore, when Jock Stein, who liked nothing better than snaffling Rangers' thunder, revealed the striker as his latest £30,000 signing while the Ibrox side were otherwise engaged preparing for a European Cup-Winners' Cup tie in Germany.

On arrival in the east end of Glasgow, Wallace had to share the position with Joe McBride but made the most of his rival's absence through injury by scoring twice in the 3–1 semi-final first-leg victory over Dukla Prague at Parkhead to secure his place in the Lisbon line-up.

Four years after being a member of the European Cup-winning side, Wallace, known as 'Wispy' for his quiet manner of speech, had a serious difference of opinion with Stein; as ever on these occasions behind the doors of Parkhead, there could only be one winner and Wallace was unceremoniously shipped off to Crystal Palace in the company of whimsical winger John 'Yogi' Hughes for a combined fee of £50,000.

He now lives in Australia and although an earlier namesake would find Hollywood fame in Mel Gibson's *Braveheart*, to Celtic fans the world over there is only one William Wallace.

STEVE CHALMERS (STRIKER)

The fourth highest goal-scorer in club history behind Jimmy McGrory, fellow Lion Bobby Lennox and Henrik Larsson, Steve Chalmers hit the target on 228 occasions.

But it was the goal that brought the European Cup to Scotland which earned him his place in Celtic's Hall of Fame. With six minutes remaining and Internazionale doggedly holding out for a replay they scarcely deserved, Chalmers coolly, almost cheekily, redirected a Bobby Murdoch thunderbolt past goalkeeper Sarti to end the Italians' resolute if depressing resistance.

The winning goal, so Chalmers later revealed, owed nothing to good fortune. 'Before we left Parkhead for Lisbon, Jock Stein had us run through this tactic again and again. It was almost as if the Big Man knew it would pay off in this particular game.'

When he retired from football after brief spells with Morton and Partick Thistle, Chalmers devoted his time to his second passion of golf and competed in the Scottish Amateur Championship.

BERTIE AULD (MIDFIELDER)

A wise-cracking Jack-the-lad, Bertie Auld's original six-year stint at Parkhead came to an abrupt end when manager Jimmy McGrory, who felt his talented but wayward winger to be a bad influence in the dressing-room, sold him to Birmingham City in 1961.

It was in the Midlands that, six years before Lisbon, he became the first Scot to play in a European final when he was a member of the City side beaten 4–2 on aggregate by Roma in the Inter-Cities Fairs Cup.

When Stein started piecing together the side that would win nine successive Scottish titles, he paid £12,000 to pluck Auld from the Birmingham City reserves and convert him from traditional winger into Celtic's midfield orchestrator; it was an inspired move.

Still a free spirit, it was Auld who would lead the Lions in their unrehearsed medley of Celtic songs as the two teams lined up in the tunnel before taking the pitch. As European Cup winners in 1964 and 1965, Internazionale might have thought that they had seen and heard it all. But they had never experienced anything like the bold Bertie belting out, 'Sure it's a grand old team to play for . . .'

BOBBY LENNOX MBE (OUTSIDE-LEFT)

Like a number of the Lions – notably Craig, Clark, Wallace and Chalmers – Bobby Lennox found it difficult to impress the Scotland selectors and won only ten international caps. Yet Lennox attracted admirers far and beyond his native shores. 'If Bobby Lennox had been in the same Manchester United and England teams, then I could have played for ever,' commented Sir Bobby Charlton. 'He was one of the best strikers I've ever seen.'

Alfredo Di Stefano was another who would have vastly preferred playing with Lennox rather than against him. 'The Scotsman who always gave Real Madrid the most trouble was Lennox. I chose Celtic as the opponents for my testimonial game in the Bernabéu and although I remember the stadium rising to Jimmy Johnstone, Lennox was Celtic's other great star.'

The last Lion to retire, Lennox collected the final medal of his glittering career as a member of Celtic's 1980 Scottish Cup-winning team, having returned to Parkhead two years earlier following a six-month flirtation with the Houston Hurricanes of the NASL.

26. SANDY LYLE MBE
Golf

Born: Shrewsbury, 9 February 1958

CAREER:
Open champion 1985
Masters champion 1988
European Tour victories: 16
US PGA Tour victories: 4
Senior World Championship 2011
Others: 4
European Tour Order of Merit winner 1979, 1980, 1985
Ryder Cup: 1979, 1981, 1983, 1985 (winners), 1987 (winners)

Imagine how melancholic you would feel if you were the world's most brilliant concert pianist but no one could enjoy your genius because you had locked the lid of the Steinway and misplaced the key?

Twenty-three years ago, Sandy Lyle reigned supreme as the world's greatest golfer, having won the Phoenix Open, Greater Greensboro Open and the US Masters within the space of nine weeks. Later that heady year of '88, the Scot would add the British Masters and the World Match Play Championship titles, then *Bang*! the top slammed down on his career. Occasionally, just occasionally, he was able to unpick the catch, as he showed by winning the Italian Open and the Volvo Masters in '92, but the man who launched that divinely guided seven-iron from the fairway bunker on the eighteenth at Augusta – 'The greatest shot ever to win a major' in the opinion of Seve Ballesteros – to claim the famous green jacket was never the force of old; a player, incidentally, who in the opinion of his great rival Nick Faldo had represented 'the greatest natural talent in the world' when he won the 1985 Open Championship at Royal St George's.

'What went wrong? Who knows? It was as much of a mystery to me as it was to everyone else,' reflected Lyle, who, to the relief and delight of everyone in golf, ended almost 20 years without a tournament victory

129

when he won the Senior World Championship at Mission Hills, China, in March 2011. 'One moment I was a double major winner and playing in the Ryder Cup, then almost overnight I was topping my drives and sending the ball scuttling along the ground like a 24 handicapper. I asked everyone for advice, from Jack Nicklaus and Arnold Palmer to the wackiest golf gurus, but the harder I worked – and I have worked at it for years – the worse I played.'

Although he freely admits he could and should have won more than two majors, Lyle is proud of his achievements in his own understated way. He was the first Briton to win the Open since Tony Jacklin sixteen years earlier . . . the first Briton to win the Masters . . . a member of the 1985 European Ryder Cup team which finally defeated the Americans after so many years of crushing defeats before retaining the trophy with a historic win on US soil two years later . . . and the first European (later followed by Sergio Garcia and Henrik Stenson) to lift the Tournament Players' Championship, the so-called 'fifth major', one of twenty-seven tournaments he won worldwide.

Yet in Jacklin's view, 'Sandy Lyle is the forgotten hero of European golf. His achievements – and what an enormously talented golfer he was – tend to be overlooked. But he was a truly great player. Everything looked so easy.' Big Sandy, surely the nicest, most genuine, least demanding superstar in world sport, has grown accustomed to being cruelly neglected; he is the only member of the one-time 'Big Five' of European golf not to be awarded the Ryder Cup captaincy, an honour enjoyed by Faldo, Ballesteros, Ian Woosnam and Bernhard Langer. And how did a grateful nation repay him after winning the Open in '85? By voting Barry McGuigan, Ian Botham and Steve Cram as their 1-2-3 in the BBC Sports Personality of the Year poll; when he triumphed at Augusta three years later, the great British sporting public rewarded him with third place behind the winner, world snooker champion Steve Davis, and swimmer Adrian Moorhouse. Even the MBE he was granted in 1987 ranks below Colin Montgomerie's OBE, let alone the knighthood bestowed upon Nick Faldo.

Yet this is a golfer Ballesteros described (in the days before Tiger Woods, it has to be said) as 'the greatest God-given talent in history. If everyone in the world was playing their best, Sandy would win – and I'd come second.'

Born south of the border in Shropshire, where his dad, Alex, was the professional at Hawkstone Park, Lyle was something of a Scottish Tiger in his youth, scoring 127 over his first eighteen holes as an eight year old and capturing the club's August monthly medal at the age of eleven (by which time he was already smacking the ball a country mile) with a round of 85, net 64. His prize was a silver teaspoon that sits in pride of place in the glittering trophy cabinet of his rambling home on the banks of Loch Voil in the Trossachs, where he lives with his second wife, Dutch-born Jolande, and children Lonneke and Quentin.

By 1985, Lyle had played in three Ryder Cup contests and won fourteen tournaments at home and abroad, including the European Open, the Kapalua International in Hawaii, the Casio World Open in Japan and the individual title at the 1980 World Cup held in Colombia; the only qualification for true greatness missing from his CV was a major, an omission he was about to put right.

Lyle spent the week of the 114th Open Championship at Royal St George's with his first wife, Christine, and the couple's two-year-old son, Stuart, sharing a house with the Gallacher family, old friend Bernard, his wife Lesley, the nine-year-old Kirsty (who would later find fame as a TV presenter) and seven-year-old Jamie. After an opening round of 68, which left him in a tie for second place, Sandy returned for an evening passed playing Happy Families around the kitchen table. 'I found that a few games of cards with the children was the ideal way to push all thoughts of the Claret Jug to the back of your mind.'

By the time of the final round on the Sunday afternoon, Lyle, lying joint third three strokes behind David Graham of Australia and Bernhard Langer, spent the hours before teeing-off doing what dads – even those on the threshold of greatness – are expected to do at weekends, assembling Lego sets on the floor with young Stuart, 'feeling no nerves, only a strange sense of calm'.

That sense of calm was to be rudely shredded when he came to the eighteenth tee as championship leader guarding a two-shot advantage over Graham, Langer and American Payne Stewart. A slightly wayward drive left Lyle with an awkward six-iron from the light rough into a capricious crosswind from where his approach drifted marginally away from the pin into the notorious ball-swallowing 'Duncan's Hollow' to the left of the green. 'I could scarcely see the ball, which was lying in about eight inches of coarse grass. I played a delicate sand-wedge, hoping to land it on the crest of the green from where it should have trickled down to the flag. But the moment I struck the shot I knew the worst and watched in horror as the ball reached the crest only to roll straight back down into the hollow.'

In a rare show of emotion before a hushed gallery, Lyle famously sank to his knees, buried his face in the grass and slammed his errant club on the ground. Regaining his composure, he rolled his fourth shot to within fifteen inches, sank the putt for a bogey five and repaired to the European Tour bus to watch the television coverage of Graham and Langer, the only players who could force a play-off with birdie threes, tackling the final hole. When neither man could do better than match Lyle's bogey five, the Claret Jug was returned into Scottish hands for the first time since Tommy Armour's victory in 1931.

Home to Wentworth – for a celebratory Indian takeaway with the Gallachers and Howard Clark family – where among the mountain of congratulatory telegrams that arrived over the following days was a missive from Santander in Spain. 'Many ignored your talent but I always knew you are a great champion. Your victory is instrumental for European golf and I could not be any happier. Savour your deserved victory but please be very cautious with commitments that might derive from being British. Bear in mind that you cannot please everybody. Congratulations to all the family, your friend Seve.'

It was a piece of advice that Lyle took to heart and so, a few weeks later, the new Open champion turned down an invitation to compete in the US PGA Championship to fulfil a promise to play in the Glasgow Open. 'Ach, Haggs Castle in front of the Scottish fans who had been supporting me for years or Cherry Hills, Colorado? There was only one choice, wasn't there?'

The drama of the closing minutes at Royal St George's was nothing to compare with the last act of the '88 Masters at Augusta, where Lyle, the leading money-winner on the US Tour that spring, went into the final round holding a two-stroke advantage over a chasing pack containing no fewer than six former winners of the green jacket – Ben Crenshaw, Fuzzy Zoeller, Tom Watson and Craig Stadler, plus Ryder Cup teammates Ballesteros and Langer. As one by one the challengers faltered, Lyle walked onto the 72nd tee needing a birdie three for victory and a par-four to force a play-off against American Mark Calcavecchia, who would win the Open the following year at Royal Troon.

If you are ever caught in a thunderstorm, advised Lee Trevino, reach for a one-iron because even God can't hit a one-iron. It was a club with which Lyle was entirely comfortable, however. 'The single most important drive of my career looked promising in the air but the instant I saw it bounce left I thought, "Bunker."' The television image of the demonic fairway bunker on the 18th fairway at Augusta is deceptive, for while it might look like a single, massive hazard, in reality there are two individual bunkers separated by a narrow grassy spine. Lyle was lucky: instead of plugging in the face of the bunker, his ball was sitting up obediently in the middle of the first trap.

His seven-iron to the flag, however, was still fraught with danger, not least the fact that he could not see the pin from his sandy stance and had to take his line from a cloud over the clubhouse. 'I also knew if I caught the lip, then the ball could easily plop down in the second bunker. Just when I needed it, I achieved perfection, the ball coming off the clubface at exactly the right height, on the right line and what looked to be the right distance.'

As American Tour veteran Chi Chi Rodriguez commented, 'That ol' green jacket can play castanets with your knees,' and Sandy's long-time caddie Dave Musgrove was close enough to hear his boss's knees knocking together as he steered home the 15-foot putt that reinforced his position as golf's undisputed number one.

'It takes a truly great player to win the Open and the Masters – I should know, *si*?' said Ballesteros. 'But what made Sandy stand out wasn't just his brilliance as a golfer but his gentle humour, humility and humanity. Sandy Lyle was a great, great champion with a golf club or a glass of beer in his hand.'

27. BENNY LYNCH

Boxing

Born: Glasgow, 2 April 1913
Died: Glasgow, 6 August 1946

CAREER:
Flyweight champion of the world 1935–38
Fight record: won 81, lost 12, drew 15

It was on the soggy marsh which would become Glasgow Green that the army of Bonnie Prince Charlie camped on their march north before the doomed battle against the Hanoverian redcoat army at Culloden in 1746; here, too, around 180 years later, that Benny Lynch would take the first steps on the path that would lead to his tragic destruction at the age of 33.

To a teenager raised in the abject poverty of a single-end squeezed into the cold heart of the Gorbals during the Great Depression, the boxing booths which went up whenever the travelling fairgrounds rolled onto the Green represented the opportunity of honing his ring-craft while earning a few priceless pennies in the process.

Lynch, who would grow to 5 ft 5 in. but never weigh more than 8 st. until the years of debauchery exacted their terrible toll on his slender body, took on all-comers, whatever their size, whatever their age; his raw courage, heavy punching, speed and cocky defensive skills brought him to the attention of local bookmaker Sammy Wilson, owner of the New Polytechnic Boxing Club at 49 Clyde Place, across the River Clyde from the Broomielaw.

It was a harsh regime but no harsher than the ghetto from which he was determined to punch his escape route, involving six-mile slogs through the Cathkin Braes, twenty rounds and more of strenuous sparring, long hours on the heavy punchbag, followed by a series of painful exercises to build up the muscles in his neck. When not training, Lynch would sit with his hands immersed in a bucket of brine supplied by the neighbourhood fishmonger to toughen the skin on his knuckles.

After turning professional on his 18th birthday, Lynch announced his arrival into the paid ranks in style 12 days later – knocking out Young Bryce in the second round of his flyweight debut in Glasgow. Determined to cash in on his prowess, Lynch fought at every opportunity – in 1933 he fought 17 times – becoming Scottish champion the following year courtesy of a bloody points victory over 15 rounds against title holder Jim Campbell.

Victories over the flyweight champions of Italy, France and Spain (the highly rated Carlo Cavagnoli, Valentin Angelmann and Pedrito Ruiz respectively) earned him a non-title fight against world champion Jackie Brown, the twelve-round draw in Glasgow's Kelvin Hall only feeding the clamour for the two men to meet again with the Mancunian's world, European and British titles at stake.

Six months later, on 9 September 1935, an early-day Tartan Army numbering several hundred made the train journey south to witness the long-awaited showdown in the King's Hall, Belle Vue. World champion for three years, Brown had met and conquered the hardest men in the business but in Lynch he was confronted by an opponent on a mission – that most dangerous of beings, a boxer without fear.

It was all over in under five minutes, Lynch sending Brown crashing to the canvas eight times before the referee rescued the fallen champion by stopping the contest as the Scottish contingent in the arena acclaimed their new world-title holder. Over a quarter of a million people lined the streets from the Central Station to cheer Lynch's victory procession to his home on the south side; Glasgow had a new king and everyone, so it seemed, wanted an audience. It was this very outpouring of affection for Lynch that would help kill him.

The modern sporting celebrity is instantly recognisable to millions via their regular appearances on TV cookery programmes, ballroom dance competitions and – just occasionally – in actual sports events; to Glaswegians of the 1930s, Lynch was suffused in an aura of mystery. Who was this little man with the hands of steel? Thus, when word spread throughout the city that their world champion was slaking his thirst in the Exchange Bar in the High Street, The Scotia in Stockwell Street or Sloans off Argyle Street, they arrived in droves to rub shoulders with their hero, never realising that every drink was luring him nearer alcoholism and premature death.

Despite Lynch's renown amongst his own folk, the Americans did not immediately rush to recognise the Scot as world champion, preferring the claims of Small Montana, a darling of New York's Madison Square Garden crowd. But once the battle-hardened Filipino had been overcome in a 15-round 'war' at the Empire Pool, Wembley, in 1936, the 24-year-old Lynch was universally acclaimed as the undisputed champion of the world.

A British title fight against Liverpool's Peter Kane in October 1937 attracted a 40,000 crowd to Shawfield Stadium, where, in the 13th round, Lynch knocked out the man who would ultimately succeed him as world champion. It was a savage performance: Kane, who had been unbeaten in forty-one previous pro bouts, was sent to the canvas five times before the referee stopped the one-sided carnage. For the time being, Benny Lynch could still beat even the most redoubtable of flyweight opponents but he was swiftly losing the heavyweight fight with the bottle. Lynch had begun drinking as a relief from the pain of migraine attacks; then he drank because he enjoyed being the centre of attraction in the city's watering holes; latterly, he drank because he could not stop.

Although officially listed as a world title defence, just five months later Lynch weighed in at 119 lb 7 oz – over half a stone above the flyweight limit – for the return against Kane in Liverpool FC's Anfield Stadium, escaping with his pride intact after a draw over fifteen rounds. On 29 June 1938, his 33-month reign as world champion came to an end when he was stripped of his title when he failed to make the weight before his defence against American Jackie Jurich.

Ironically, Lynch won the fight with ease – it had been postponed twice while the bloated champion strove to shed the pounds – scoring six knockdowns before the twelfth-round finish. His body and spirit ravaged, Lynch stopped fighting the scales and moved up a weight division to bantamweight, losing to American Kayo Morgan and suffering the only knockout of his career against the unheralded Aurel Toma of Romania. Having failed to land a single blow against Toma, Lynch's licence was revoked by the British Boxing Board of Control.

The subsequent decline was swift but far from painless: still only 25, the once-proud world champion was forced to return to the boxing booths whence he had originally come and pawn his various trophies to satisfy his craving for whisky. His marriage failed, he was left homeless when his mother died and took to sleeping rough and begging on the pavements of the Gorbals where misguided well-wishers would give him money to be squandered on booze rather than bread.

Benny Lynch died in the Southern General Hospital of malnutrition on 6 August 1946, following which all Glasgow, so it seemed, turned out to watch his funeral cortège make its way from the Gorbals to Lambhill Cemetery in the north side of the city.

'I always felt I was fighting for Scotland,' Lynch told a friend before his ruination, 'and my true happiness lies in the fact that I did not let Scotland down.'

28. LIZ McCOLGAN (LYNCH) MBE
Athletics

Born: Dundee, 24 March 1964

CAREER:
Olympic Games:
  Seoul 1988: 10,000 metres – Silver
World Championships:
  Tokyo 1991: 10,000 metres – Gold
Commonwealth Games:
  Edinburgh 1986: 10,000 metres – Gold
  Auckland 1990: 10,000 metres – Gold; 3,000 metres – Bronze
Others:
  1991 New York Marathon – 1st; 1992 Tokyo Marathon – 1st;
  1996 London Marathon – 1st

As far back as she can remember, Liz McColgan has been running for her life; to flee the gangs which roamed the violent streets of the Whitfield council estate in Dundee on which she was raised and to escape the jute factory where, at the age of 16, she was required to clock on at 5.30 each morning to tear herself free from the strangling bonds of poverty and ignorance which would condemn many of her young school friends to a life of state benefits and unmarried motherhood.

At the peak of her renown, McColgan was understandably remorseless in her pursuit of riches, willing to race anywhere, any time, if the price was right, which was why she never stopped running until she had put a million miles between herself and the Whitfield of the 1970s. No son or daughter of hers was going to spend their childhood amidst the boarded-up windows, obscene graffiti, burned-out cars and knife-carrying drug pushers that was home to the young Liz Lynch.

Much has changed in the intervening years: the decent residents of Whitfield overcame the thugs to transform the area into one of which they can be justly proud, while McColgan lives in palatial splendour with her five children (the eldest of whom, 21-year-old Eilish, ran in the women's 3,000 metres steeplechase at London 2012) in the countryside near Carnoustie, the rewards of her determination, defiance and willingness to push mind and body to the outer limits and beyond.

Whilst all too many of her fellow athletes pumped their bodies full of illegal substances to make them run swifter, throw further, jump higher, McColgan's only drugs were money and burning ambition; here is a battler who ran three miles just eleven days after the birth of her first baby and who could browbeat promoters into submission, famously squeezing £10,000 out of Andy Norman to race in Sheffield while Linford Christie settled for £7,000. She even managed to bank £30,000 from two races while on honeymoon in America with husband Peter in 1987.

Knowing of no other way to make a comfortable home for her family, McColgan ran as though her very life depended upon it; when she led from the front to defeat one of the finest women's long-distance fields ever assembled in the 10,000 metres at the 1991 World Championships in Tokyo (leaving Derartu Tulu of Ethiopia, South African Elana Meyer and long-time rival Ingrid Kristiansen of Norway in her lung-bursting wake), BBC commentator Brendan Foster described it as 'the greatest performance by a male or female British athlete in the history of long-distance running'.

That same year McColgan raced to victory in the New York Marathon – her first attempt at the distance – and trounced Nick Faldo, Paul Gascoigne and Nigel Mansell to win the BBC Sports Personality of the Year award. She also appeared on *This Is Your Life* despite trying to tell Michael Aspel 'I'm not old enough . . . I'm not good enough.'

All Scotland had known that she was more than good enough ever since 1986, when the 22-year-old Liz Lynch brightened up the gloom of the Commonwealth Games in Edinburgh, where she won the nation's only track gold with a stirring victory in the 10,000 metres at Meadowbank Stadium; it was a typical 'McColgan' performance, leading from gun to tape with her trademark Woody Woodpecker top-knot bob-bob-bobbing along with every stride.

Two years later, McColgan looked poised to add the Olympic gold medal to her Commonwealth title in Seoul, where she relentlessly ground down the opposition one by one until only Olga Bondarenko of the Soviet Union remained a threat. Lap after lap, McColgan pounded the track, increasing the pace, slowing it down, injecting a burst of acceleration, trying everything to shake off the red-vested stalker following in her slip-stream. Then, with 200 metres remaining, Bondarenko unleashed a devastating sprint finish to which the exhausted McColgan could offer no response.

Still, so everyone consoled her, time was on her side. She was young with at least two more Olympic Games in front of her; no one could be so unlucky again. Unbeknownst to all, however, bad luck in its various guises was to trail McColgan as doggedly as Bondarenko.

None of that could have been foreseen in 1991 when Foster, himself one of Britain's finest distance runners before swapping spikes for microphone, was left close to tears by her efforts in the stifling humidity of Tokyo. That McColgan was competing in the World Championships less than nine months after giving birth to her first daughter, Eilish, surprised many; that she could burn off the big three – Kristiansen, Tulu and Meyer – with her brutally relentless pace in the debilitating heat, was an act of sporting heroism.

No less heroic was her performance at the Barcelona Olympics in '92; any sense of disappointment that the country might have felt at watching an untypically lifeless McColgan struggle home a disappointing fifth in the 10,000 metres final was dispelled three weeks later when it was discovered that she had been suffering from anaemia for some weeks. That complaint cured, then came numerous operations on her knees, toes and lower back in Britain and the United States, followed by spells of recuperation and countless lonely training runs around the Angus countryside – a bore even on a spring or summer day when there is no competitive race at the end of it all; a bitter, uncomfortable chore on a freezing Scottish morning – punctuated by the occasional appearance in an out-of-the-way event.

'How badly did I miss racing? As badly as I would miss my head if it had·been chopped off. Being the type of person I am, very competitive in everything [whether, say family members, it is running, football, table tennis or darts], it's the actual racing that made me tick. To suddenly have that taken away from you, to have to watch the Commonwealth Games and European Championships on television, was very, very hard to cope with. I'd say I actually changed as a person during the worst months. But then you see the light at the end of the tunnel and suddenly you forget all about the bad times.'

After deciding her days as a 10,000 metres runner were over, McColgan won the 1996 London Marathon – coming from over two minutes behind at the halfway stage with a meticulously timed burst to beat Kenya's Joyce Chepchumba by over two minutes – and was one of the favourites for gold at the 1996 Atlanta Olympics. Two days before the event, alas, she was bitten by an unidentified insect in the Athletes' Village and with the poison coursing through her system, trailed over the finishing line in a distant 16th place.

How much ill fortune can one athlete suffer? Oh, the fates were not finished with McColgan just yet. As defending champion at the '97 London Marathon, she entered The Mall a stride ahead of Chepchumba only to be beaten into the runner-up position by one agonising second.

Told by an American surgeon she would never run again after an umpteenth operation on her wounded knee, McColgan, typically, stuck up two fingers to expert medical opinion and is running still in charity events. 'I never believed him. You get to know your own body and I knew I would run again. How does that song go? Always look on the bright side of life . . .'

It must have been difficult for the nine-year-old Liz Lynch to see any bright side when she was first confronted by a gang of teenage boys bent on violence in the Whitfield estate on a dark night all those winters ago. Fighting back the only way she would ever know how, wee Liz ran for her life.

29. BOBBY McGREGOR MBE
Swimming

Born: Helensburgh, 3 April 1944

CAREER:

Olympic Games:
  Tokyo 1964: 100 metres freestyle – Silver
European Championships:
  Utrecht 1966: 100 metres freestyle – Gold
British Empire & Commonwealth Games:
  Perth, Australia 1962: 110 yards freestyle – Silver
  Kingston, Jamaica 1966: 110 yards freestyle – Silver
World Record Holder: 110 yards freestyle, 1964–6

It was Martina Navratilova who best defined the difference between involvement in sport and commitment to your sport. 'Think of ham and eggs,' the tennis diva explained. 'The chicken is involved, the pig is committed.'

In the nicest possible way, from a young age Bobby McGregor was a right little swine in the swimming pool, fiercely committed to becoming the best in the world; as the son of David McGregor, who had represented Great Britain at water polo in the 1936 Berlin Olympics before becoming master of Falkirk Public Baths, young Bobby was the original water babe.

From the age of nine, he began training at seven o'clock in the morning (while his classmates were still demolishing their breakfast cereal), completing countless, lonely lengths of the tiny 25-yard pool while his dad patrolled alongside armed with an old-fashioned, hand-held stop-watch. Summer sunshine, winter snow he was there, putting in mile after mile with only his father's voice echoing back off the tiled walls for company. By the age of ten, he was the Falkirk Primary Schools champion; at fifteen he became Scottish junior freestyle champion over 100 yards; and less than a year later he swam for his country for the first time in a triangular international against Wales and Northern Ireland at the Empire Pool, Cardiff. 'I know he's an outstanding junior, but I want him to become an outstanding senior,' said his father, an always gentle but encouraging presence. 'I've not been driving him yet because he's maturing at his own pace and I don't believe in rushing young swimmers.'

McGregor's spartan lifestyle continued even after he left Falkirk High School to commence the studies that would lead to an Honours degree in architecture at Strathclyde University: up at 6 a.m. for an early-morning dip prior to catching the train to Glasgow, followed by another two-hour stint in the pool before the family sat down to their evening meal. Occasionally, he allowed himself a night off to go to the pictures or to take a girlfriend out to dinner, but those were special treats, strictly rationed to Christmas or birthdays. 'Sometimes it's terrible,' he revealed at the time. 'Then you think of all the hard, dreary work that you've put in and you realise that you cannot throw it all away. Something inside you drives you on, although I really don't know what that something is.'

At 18, those solitary hours of toil were rewarded when McGregor was selected to compete in the 1962 British Empire & Commonwealth Games in Perth, Australia, where the teenager took the silver medal in the 110 yards freestyle behind Canadian Dick Pound, who would later become one of the major powers in the International Olympic Committee.

By the time of the 1964 Olympics in Tokyo, McGregor was world-record holder for the 110 yards freestyle; he was also captain of the GB swimming team that watched Yoshinoro Sakai, an athlete born in Hiroshima on 6 August 1945, the day on which the city was devastated by the atomic bomb that would bring about the end of the war, light the Olympic Flame in the most moving of Opening Ceremonies.

The Games were also memorable for a medley of sporting reasons: Joe Frazier won the heavyweight boxing gold; Ethiopian Abebe Bikila became the first man to win two successive Olympic marathon titles; and Bob Hayes won the 100 metres sprint on a slow, cinder track by equalling the world record of 10.00 seconds before entering the NFL, winning a Super Bowl title as a wide receiver for the Dallas Cowboys.

In the Olympic pool, all attention was centred upon the blue-riband event, the men's 100 metres, pitting the golden boy of American swimming, 18-year-old Don Schollander, against the Flying Scot, Bobby McGregor, who had been all but invincible for the past 24 months.

Whereas McGregor trained in Falkirk Public Baths – the GB Olympic selectors had shaken their heads in disbelief when they first surveyed his humble training facilities – Schollander prepared for Tokyo under the clear blue skies of Santa Clara, California, in an outdoor pool that could be heated should the air temperature inconveniently dip below 90 degrees.

The preliminaries only served to increase the excitement before their long-awaited showdown, with both McGregor and Schollander winning their first-round heats and semi-finals with ease. Schollander was joined in the final by two of his sprint relay teammates, Gary Ilman and Mike Austin, but only the lone Falkirk 'bairn' could stay with his blistering pace over the first length.

Over the final 50 metres, Schollander and McGregor matched each other stroke for stroke, the American finally touching ahead by one-tenth of a second, the blink of an eye being the difference between gold and silver.

Not that McGregor was seen as anything less than a champion back in Scotland, where the Lord Provost of Falkirk and the town council assembled to greet his arrival at Edinburgh's Turnhouse Airport. Schollander may have gone on to win four gold medals in Tokyo but McGregor's years of solitary confinement within Falkirk Baths had not gone unappreciated and a cheering crowd of over 2,000 filled the street outside the McGregor family home when the returning hero was reunited with his parents and sister.

McGregor was also invited to Buckingham Palace, along with Great Britain's four gold medallists – Lynn Davies (men's long jump), Mary Rand (women's long jump), Ann Packer (women's 800 metres) and Ken Matthews (men's 20 km walk) – during which the Queen sought him out for royal consolation. 'I watched your race on television and it was very exciting. If you'd had a longer finger, you would have won.'

Just as he had faced Schollander in Tokyo, so it was McGregor's misfortune to find himself in conflict with the latest wunderkind of the pool – Australian Mike Wenden – in the 110 yards freestyle final at the 1966 British Empire & Commonwealth Games in Kingston, Jamaica. But, after three silver medals in major competitions, McGregor finally struck gold in the 1966 European Championships in Utrecht.

If he had merely been 'involved' in swimming, it might have represented the ultimate achievement, but to someone as 'committed' as McGregor, victory in Holland could not compensate for the bitter disappointment of Tokyo. 'All I ever really wanted to do in the sport was win an Olympic gold medal,' he would recall. 'That was my target because that's what people remember you by. I knew Tokyo was my best chance to fulfil that ambition and I was always disappointed that I didn't do it. To win gold at the European Championships only made up for that a little bit.'

McGregor was being unnecessarily self-critical: at the age of 24, by which time his rivals affectionately referred to him as 'the old fella', the grand old man of swimming was only narrowly outside the medals in the 100 metres freestyle at the Mexico Olympics, where he finished fourth behind Wenden and American duo Ken Welsh and Mark Spitz, who would be the sensation of the Munich Games four years hence.

'Bobby McGregor was a true Olympian,' said Spitz. 'If he had been born in America or Australia, then he would undoubtedly have won a handful of gold medals. As it is, given the circumstances in which he was forced to train, then you have to say that his Olympic silver would translate into five gold medals in American currency.'

30. DAVE MACKAY
Football

Born: Edinburgh, 14 November 1934

CAREER (PLAYER):

Heart of Midlothian 1953–9: 135 appearances, 25 goals; Scottish League Championship 1957–58; Scottish Cup 1956; Scottish League Cup 1955, 1959

Tottenham Hotspur 1959–68: 318 appearances, 51 goals; English League Championship 1960–61; FA Cup 1961, 1962, 1967; European Cup-Winners' Cup 1963

Derby County 1968–71: 122 appearances, 5 goals; Footballer of the Year 1969 (shared with Tony Book of Manchester City)

Swindon Town 1971–2. 26 appearances, 1 goal

Scotland 1957–65: 22 appearances, 4 goals

CAREER (MANAGER):

Swindon Town 1971–2

Nottingham Forest 1972–3

Derby County 1973–6: English League Championship 1974–75

Walsall 1977–8

Al-Arabi (Kuwait) 1978–87: Premier League 1979–80, 1981–82, 1982–83, 1983–84, 1984–85

Doncaster Rovers 1987–9

Birmingham City 1989–91

El Zamalek (Egypt) 1991–3: Premier League 1991–92, 1992–93

Qatar national team 1994–7

Dave Mackay is popularly – and quite erroneously – portrayed as Desperate Dan in football boots: all barrel chest and jutting, stubbled chin demolishing a cow pie in the dressing-room before taking the pitch

145

to flatten everything that stood in his way. Even his photograph in the Scottish Football Hall of Fame at Hampden reflects this one-man wrecking-crew image. Instead of being pictured with a ball at his feet, Mackay is forever caught in time shaking Billy Bremner by the throat.

Aye, Mackay was a hard man. You could hear his tackles from the uppermost reaches of the terracing and who but Mackay could have recovered from two broken legs suffered within nine months of each other at a time when such injuries were frequently career ending?

But there was so much more to Mackay than the ability to rattle opponents' bones. Here was a player who was never once sent off in his entire career and whose party trick was to juggle an orange between both feet before flicking it into the air and catching said fruit on the back of his neck. When he got bored with oranges, Mackay would play keepie-uppie with a coin, ending this particular routine by lobbing it into the top pocket of his jacket. A player who, whenever he took the field with Tottenham at White Hart Lane, would boot a ball high into the sky then cushion it ever so gently on his instep in the final second of its descent; a player who could volley the ball off the stadium car park wall 20, 30, 40 or even 50 times from a distance of 15 yards without it once touching the ground, an exercise requiring strong legs and remarkable technical ability.

McCrae's Battalion

All too often, sportswriters feel sufficiently moved to litter their articles with words like 'tragedy' and 'disaster', 'bravery' and 'courage'. But such emotional descriptions should be reserved for true bravehearts like the Heart of Midlothian team of 1914.

When war was declared in August of that year, much of the country questioned why football continued to be played at a time when many young men were in uniform. This thorny question was the subject of a passionate Parliamentary debate which inspired Edinburgh textile merchant and former Liberal MP Sir George McCrae to announce that he would raise a battalion within seven days to be trained and sent to fight in France.

Although top of the league after starting the season with eight straight victories and, judging by the reports of the day, 'standing on the threshold of greatness', on 14 November, 16 Hearts players marched in formation from Tynecastle to Haymarket to enlist (a further five were later declared physically unfit for battle). Club staff, supporters, players from city rivals Hibernian, Raith Rovers and Falkirk, plus 150 Easter Road fans, were inspired to follow their path to the recruitment office, as McCrae's Battalion (officially known as the 16th Royal Scots) raised over 1,300 officers and men in a matter of days.

The combined effects of army training (mostly involving night manoeuvres) and football training began to take their toll on Tynecastle's soccer soldiers: having won 19 of their first 21 League games, Hearts went into decline in the early months of 1915, allowing Celtic to snatch the title. As the *Edinburgh Evening News* saw fit to comment: 'Between them the two leading Glasgow clubs have not sent a single prominent player to the Army.

According to Jimmy Greaves, who joined Spurs the season after their double-winning year of 1961: 'Yes, he went into battle like a warrior but he had just about everything: power, skill, stamina and enthusiasm. He was the best professional I ever played alongside. He should have been in the *Guinness Book of Records* for having the biggest heart in football. When Dave Mackay was missing from the team, we all had to work twice as hard. He was the greatest player in that great side.' Mackay also attracted admirers from beyond these shores. Eusébio, who pitted his wits against all the greats for Benfica and Portugal, described him as 'the finest wing-half I ever played against'.

Although he was revered at both Spurs and, latterly, Derby County, where he helped transform Brian Clough's side from Second Division anonymities into future League champions, Mackay's first and enduring love was Heart of Midlothian. 'I played in the Scottish Schools' Cup final at Tynecastle when I was 14 and just to get near the place was a dream. I was a Hearts fan all my life; I used to walk the three miles from our home to Tynecastle. I got there early so I could sneak in under the turnstile because I couldn't afford to pay. So when Hearts came along to sign me, I couldn't believe it. It was the original boyhood fantasy come true.'

Mackay was already a first-team regular when he was called up for National Service, spending two years with the Royal Engineers in Worcester while travelling north to play for his club on Saturdays, winning League Cup (1955) and Scottish Cup (1956) winner's medals and the first of his 22 international caps as an Army private. Demobbed in 1957, Mackay and Hearts would enjoy their finest season when he captained the side to the League Championship, setting a British record of 132 goals scored against 29 conceded.

Less than a year later – and somewhat reluctantly – he left his beloved Tynecastle bound for White Hart Lane, where Spurs manager Bill Nicholson needed a physical presence alongside the smooth skills of Northern Ireland's Danny Blanchflower in midfield. It was, as Nicholson

There is only one football champion in Scotland, and its colours are maroon and khaki.'

In April, all Edinburgh, so it seemed, turned out at Waverley Station to watch McCrae's Battalion board the train taking them south. As the last carriage disappeared, Hearts' kindly manager John McCartney commented: 'Gone. The finest men I ever knew.'

Seven Hearts first-team players were killed on the battlefields of Los, Ypres, Arras and the Somme, their names engraved on the club war memorial which stands outside Haymarket Station: Jimmy Speedie ... Thomas Gracie ... Ernie Ellis ... Henry Wattie ... Duncan Currie ... James Boyd ... John Allan. An eighth, Pat Crossan, died in 1933 as the direct consequence of being gassed.

would later observe, 'the shrewdest £32,000 any football manager in the world ever spent', not least because Mackay would recommend the signing of fellow international John White from Falkirk, who would form the final part of Spurs' golden triangle in midfield.

When Mackay arrived in London, Spurs were languishing in the lower regions of the First Division; within two years they had become the first club in the twentieth century to complete the coveted League and FA Cup double. Further glory beckoned when the Londoners brushed aside Gornik Zabrze of Poland (10–5), Feyenoord Rotterdam (4–2) and Dukla Prague (4–2, with Mackay scoring two priceless second-leg goals) to advance to the semi-finals of the 1962 European Cup.

Their 4–3 aggregate defeat to holders Benfica – Spurs had three goals controversially chalked off in the course of the two games – can still bring a wry smile to Mackay's features. The Portuguese club's Hungarian coach, Béla Guttmann, rated Tottenham the best team in Europe, and just as Benfica whipped an ageing Real Madrid 5–3 in the final, so Spurs would also have been clear favourites to overcome the Spanish side. 'We would have beaten the Real Madrid of '62, no question about it,' said Mackay. 'In fact, we were so confident, we could have beaten Real Madrid at their very best.'

There was further crushing disappointment for Mackay in Europe the following season when, after leading Spurs to the European Cup-Winners' Cup final with a series of inspirational displays, he was forced to miss the showdown against Atletico Madrid in Rotterdam with a leg injury. So shocked was Nicholson by Mackay's late withdrawal that he could not bring himself to break the news to the rest of the team in the dressing-room, leaving the task to skipper Blanchflower. Spurs trounced Atletico 5–1 and Mackay was awarded a medal by virtue of his previous performances in the competition.

Worse was to befall Mackay in the following season's Cup-Winners' Cup when Tottenham were drawn to play FA Cup holders Manchester United in the second round. Having scored one of the goals in Spurs' 2–0 first-leg victory at White Hart Lane, he recalled the subsequent events in the second leg on 10 December 1963 in his autobiography, *The Real Mackay*:

> The date is etched on my mind. We were only eight minutes into the game when the ball was in their box and I went charging in for it. Their defender Noel Cantwell was approaching with equal gusto. I got to the ball and Cantwell got to my shin. I heard the crack, and if what people tell me to this day is true, so did half the crowd. I did not feel any immediate pain, but felt panic when I looked down and my

foot had twisted 90 degrees. The surgeon told me it was a bad break
and it was possible I wouldn't play football again.

Without their spiritual leader, Spurs were beaten 4–1 – 'When Dave was
carried off, the heart of the double side went with him,' Jimmy Greaves
said. 'We were never the same again. Somehow the magic had gone' –
and it would be nine months before Mackay defied medical opinion
when he made his return in a reserve game against Shrewsbury Town at
White Hart Lane in September 1964. Cruelly, before the game was out he
was carried from the field on a stretcher, his left leg broken again.

In August 1965 and approaching his 30th birthday, Mackay confounded
the doctors yet again when, after almost two years out of the game, he
returned to the Spurs first team. He crowned his second comeback by
lifting the FA Cup as captain, and one of only two survivors of the double-
winning team, after a 2–1 victory over Chelsea in the first all-London
final at Wembley in 1967.

Twelve months later, he took Nicholson aside after the final game of
the season (a 3–1 loss to Manchester City) and sadly told him, 'I can't do
it any more, boss.'

'I had enjoyed a good season but after nine years I was finding it harder
and harder. During that match I just felt that the end of my career was
approaching and I knew it was time to go.'

Football's rumour mill suggested that Mackay might return home as
player-manager of Hearts but Brian Clough, who had visions of grandeur
at humble Second Division Derby County, saw him as the ideal leader to
inspire his talented but inexperienced squad of youngsters at the Baseball
Ground. He convinced the 33-year-old Mackay that he had an unexpected
future ahead of him as a sweeper (although he stood only 5 ft 8 in.)
alongside future England centre-half Roy McFarland, building attacks
from the back with his pinpoint passes. As an act of gratitude for his
endeavours at White Hart Lane, the Tottenham board accepted a token
transfer fee of £5,000. Some saw Mackay as an ageing, overweight crock
but Clough would subsequently describe his signing as 'the best day's
work I've ever done'.

At the first team talk following Mackay's arrival at Derby, Clough
informed the gathered players that 'you're lucky to be able to play with
this man'. 'I was monumentally embarrassed. He hadn't told me what he
was going to say but I have to admit I did rather enjoy it when it happened.
It was nice to be appreciated.

'As it turned out, that was the easiest season of my entire career. The
youngsters did all the running about and I picked up their work. We
walked the Second Division.' Mackay's role was recognised when he was

voted joint Footballer of the Year with Manchester City's 1969 championship-winning skipper, Tony Book.

'I cannot overstate the impact and influence Mackay had at Derby,' said Clough. 'Our self-confidence soared because of him. He was the consummate, complete professional, a man of immense talent. He was right up there with John Charles and Duncan Edwards. I know they had a bias against the Anglos of the day but the Scots must have been mad to play him only 20-odd times in internationals – if he'd been English, Dave Mackay would have won over 100 caps.'

Thus were Clough's Derby promoted to the First Division, finishing fourth and ninth before Mackay departed in 1971 (the season before County became League champions) to Swindon Town as player-manager only to return to the Baseball Ground as the gaffer two years later after 'Old Big Head' had been sacked. He arrived at a time when the players were threatening to strike unless Clough and assistant Peter Taylor were reinstated, yet the job held no fears for Mackay. 'There was a lot of hype but I never felt the player-power thing for one moment. They were just expressing their opinions about the Clough situation. They all kept having meetings and all I did was get on with the job,' explained Mackay, who put his own stamp on the team by signing Bruce Rioch, Francis Lee and Charlie George.

After a season's bedding in, Mackay led Derby to the championship in 1975 only to be sacked the following year, a victim of the 'Bring-Back-Cloughie' element in the boardroom; this, a few months after Derby had whipped Real Madrid 4–1 in the European Cup before being unluckily beaten in extra-time in the return in the Bernabéu.

He went on to coach with great success in Kuwait, Egypt and Qatar but, despite his managerial triumphs at home and abroad, it is as a player that Dave Mackay entered the book of legends. 'He was,' opined George Best, 'the hardest man I ever played against . . . and the bravest . . . and one of the greatest.'

31. KEN McKINLAY
Speedway

Born: Blantyre, 7 June 1928
Died: Leicester, 9 February 2003

CAREER:
Glasgow Tigers 1949–54
Leicester Lions 1954–61
Coventry Bees 1962–4, 1970
West Ham Hammers 1965–9: British League champions 1965;
    KO Cup winners 1965
Oxford Cheetahs 1971–2
Scunthorpe Saints 1973–5
World Finalist (9): 1956 – 5th; 1957 – 7th; 1958 – 5th; 1960
    – 9th; 1961 – 11th; 1962 – 7th; 1964 – 11th; 1965 – 13th;
    1969 – 8th

The first time I saw a speedway rider, he looked like a spaceman to my seven-year-old eyes: the shiny black suit, the curious helmet and ungainly moonwalk gait (just try looking elegant in a pair of heavy boots, one of which has a two-inch steel plate attached to the sole to protect the left foot when sliding round corners). By the time I reached my teens, I was completely hooked. American kids of the late '60s had Neil Armstrong to hero worship; I had the Glasgow Tigers.

In the good old days of the immediate post-war era, speedway attracted an aggregate 12.5 million spectators, making it the country's most popular summer sport and, so, when the 1949 World Final tickets at Wembley went on sale, over 500,000 frenzied fans applied for the 85,000 places available.

Such was speedway's popularity that they even made a movie about it, the 1948 less-than-epic *Once a Jolly Swagman* starring Dirk Bogarde as a young factory worker with dreams of cinders' glory and Sid James as the hard-bitten team manager. The action scenes were shot at the New Cross Stadium in London's Old Kent Road and when the New Cross Rangers' crowded schedule of home fixtures began to interfere with filming, the makers built an exact replica of the track, complete with pits, on a back-lot at Pinewood Studios. *Once a Jolly Swagman* did not win any Oscar nominations, but it did succeed in keeping speedway fans occupied through the long close-season break.

Ken McKinlay, who had been a grocer and farmer in Blantyre before receiving his National Service call-up papers, fell in love with the snarl of the bikes, the roar of the crowds and that intoxicating whiff of methanol fumes on the cinders – speedway's unique smell – while serving as a despatch rider in the Royal Signal Corps in Germany, where the British Army of the Rhine organised regular meetings involving the top riders from England by way of entertainment for the troops. The teenage McKinlay, something of a daredevil on two wheels in uniform, quickly persuaded his superiors that he might be allowed to swap khaki for leather.

Back on civvy street in 1949, McKinlay showed up unannounced and unheralded at the White City in Glasgow requesting a trial spin during which he so impressed the grizzled Tigers veterans in the pits that he made his league debut that same season. Over the next five years, 'Hurri-ken' established himself as one of the most exciting riders in the land,

Tony Hand

In terms of talent if not temperament, Tony Hand was the George Best of British ice hockey. The first of only two Britons ever to be drafted by a NHL club – the other being Glaswegian Colin Shields, who signed for the Philadelphia Flyers in 2000 – Hand joined the Edmonton Oilers in 1986.

A goal-scorer supreme, Hand's performances at the Oilers' training camp moved head coach Glen Sather to describe the 18-year-old wonder kid as 'the smartest player out there apart from Wayne Gretzky'. High praise when you consider that Gretzky is universally recognised as the greatest player to pull on a pair of skates.

But the Edinburgh teenager could not settle to life in Canada and quit the Oilers after a fortnight to return to the Murrayfield Racers, the team for which he had made his British League debut at the tender age of 14. 'I was homesick for my mum's cooking, my friends, my dog, that sort of thing,' he explained.

Sather did not give up easily, however, and 12 months later Hand was invited back to Edmonton, where he starred for the Oilers against Team Canada before turning his back on the NHL for a second and final time. 'It was a great pity,' admitted Sather. 'His intelligence on the ice stood out at our training camp. He was a real prospect.'

Now 44 and the recipient of an MBE for his services to ice hockey, Hand is currently coach of the Manchester Phoenix. The outstanding British player of all time, does he entertain any regrets that he did not seize his opportunity across the Atlantic? 'In some

becoming a regular in the 'England' team that competed in an annual Test series in Australia during the British winter. It was during one of these visits Down Under that he met and married his wife, Rena.

When Glasgow closed for business soon after the start of the 1954 season, one of speedway's many victims of televised sport and the Government's entertainment tax, McKinlay began his travels, which would take him to the Leicester Lions, Coventry Bees and the West Ham Hammers when the newly formed British League began operations in 1965. By now, McKinlay was one of the giants of speedway, as much a box-office attraction as serial world champions Barry Briggs of New Zealand and Sweden's Ove Fundin, or emerging superstars such as Glasgow Tigers' Australian Charlie Monk and Edinburgh Monarchs' Scottish sensation George Hunter.

Between 1956 and 1969 McKinlay rode in nine World Finals (and was on standby as a reserve in three others), twice finishing fifth, in an era when just reaching the showpiece climax to the season was considered a major achievement given the convoluted qualification system; Monk, in contrast, one of the best three riders in the sport for a spell in the mid-'60s, did not qualify on a single occasion due to a costly engine failure or an unfortunate fall at a crucial moment.

At Wembley in 1958, McKinlay finished the night tied for third place alongside Australian Aub Lawson and England's Peter Craven behind champion Briggs and runner-up Fundin after his five rides but lost his chance of a rostrum place by coming last by the length of a wheel in the resultant three-man run-off for third spot. Two years earlier on the same track, he had finished fourth in his fifth and final race when victory would have put him in a run-off against Fundin for the title.

Denied speedway's greatest individual honour, McKinlay had better fortune in the inaugural British League campaign of 1965, when he captained all-conquering West Ham to the championship and Cup double, a season in which, at the age of 37, he finished fourth-highest

---

ways. I've had a terrific career but I suppose it would be nice to know how good I could have been in the NHL.'

In the opinion of Alex Dampier, the Canadian-born coach of the Great Britain Olympic team from 1980–94, if Hand had not swapped Edmonton for his mum's steak pie then he could have been destined for greatness. 'A lot of inferior players to Tony made big money in Canada and the States. He was the best I've ever seen in this country, no question. He had it all, athleticism, strength, wonderful hands, vision. It may sound crazy, but he could also skate without thinking about it. Now that's an ability which comes naturally if you're born in Canada, Sweden or Russia. But you've no idea how difficult that is for a Briton.'

scorer behind Briggs, Englishman Nigel Boocock and Glasgow's favourite adopted son, Charlie Monk.

Renowned for having the most highly polished leathers and the most gleaming bikes in speedway, McKinlay was the ultimate team man, happy to spend hours passing on tactical advice and mechanical tips to youngsters just starting out in the sport. He continued racing until the age of 47 as rider-coach of Scunthorpe Saints, eventually and reluctantly retiring after suffering a serious shoulder injury in a crash during the Second Division Riders' Championship.

Actually christened John Robert Vickers – it was Glasgow promoter Johnny Hoskins who rebranded him as 'Hurri-ken' – Ken McKinlay died of heart problems at the age of 75 in 2003.

'Ken didn't need world titles to prove that he was a great champion,' recalled long-time rival and four times world champion Barry Briggs. 'He was the consummate gentleman on and off the track, a classicist of the old school. We had some mighty tussles but you always knew that no matter the importance of the race, Ken would always compete fair and square. He didn't have an unscrupulous bone in his body. Speedway was a huge sport in its heyday and Ken was always one of the most popular visitors at tracks the length and breadth of the country. You knew that if Ken McKinlay was riding, then you were in for one hell of a show.'

32. IAN McLAUCHLAN

Rugby Union

Born: Tarbolton, Ayrshire, 14 April 1942

CAREER:
Clubs: Jordanhill College and West of Scotland
Scotland 1969–79: 43 caps, 0 points
British Lions: 1971, New Zealand (won 2–1); 1974, South
    Africa (won 3–0)

The animated superhero Mighty Mouse, who came equipped with a
variety of superpowers including invulnerability and great strength,
made his cinematic debut for Twentieth Century Fox in 1942. The same
year, coincidentally, that his rugby playing counterpart was born in the
Ayrshire mining village of Tarbolton.

Like the cartoon rodent after whom he took his nickname, Ian
McLauchlan was blessed with powers beyond the human norm. As a
relatively tiny (5 ft 8½ in.) but muscular (14 st., although he would
subsequently bulk up to 17 st.) prop forward, McLauchlan was routinely
matched against giant-sized adversaries whether playing club rugby for
Jordanhill College or in the red shirt of the British Lions against the All
Blacks in New Zealand. That Scotland's 'Mighty Mouse' was still playing
international rugby at the age of 37 is testimony to the forcefield of
invincibility in which he appeared suffused.

In his *Complete Book of Rugby*, author Richard Bath wrote:

> McLauchlan was not the conventional size and shape for a loose-
> head prop in the 1970s, but in many ways it was precisely the
> combination of an amazing power-to-weight ratio plus his ability to
> get underneath the opposition that made him such an effective
> performer. As a larger than life character, he played best in the most
> intimidating circumstances . . . making him one of Scotland's most
> successful captains.

McLauchlan played for Scotland on forty-three occasions, nineteen as captain (winning ten) and also appeared in eight Tests on two Lions tours, finishing on the losing side only once.

Born into mining stock, from the age of 13 McLauchlan spent the school holidays working on a local farm, building muscles while the rest of his Ayr Academy classmates were scoffing ice creams on the beach. As he told Jeff Connor in *Giants of Scottish Rugby*: 'There was no shite about how old you were back then.'

Moving on to Jordanhill College to study physical education (he was a contemporary of future Scotland international football manager Craig Brown), McLauchlan came under the influence of Bill Dickinson, a visionary rugby union coach who made the students' XV into a major force in the game. It was Dickinson who encouraged McLauchlan to spend long hours in the gym lifting weights to add upper body strength while teaching his pupil the dark, satanic practices of the front row. Dickinson also devised specialist training programmes, reasoning that the needs of a prop forward were entirely different from those of a lithe stand-off or marauding full-back.

Although he was invited to play an international trial shortly after his 21st birthday, McLauchlan had to wait a further five years (some say Dickinson's sometimes uneasy relationship with the selectors was the root cause) before making his Five Nations debut in the 1969 Calcutta Cup match against England at Twickenham. Scotland lost 8–3 but the rampaging McLauchlan would remain a fixture in the team for the next decade, even captaining the side against the English in 1973 with a broken bone in his leg suffered two weeks earlier in the Five Nations contest with Ireland.

Selected for the British Lions as a member of arguably the finest squad ever to leave these shores for the visit to New Zealand in 1971, McLauchlan began the tour as understudy to Sandy Carmichael, but was summoned from the substitutes' bench by coach Carwyn James when his Scottish teammate suffered a damaged cheekbone courtesy of a heat-seeking Kiwi fist during the notoriously torrid encounter against Canterbury seven days before the First Test.

Retaining his place in a team containing J.P.R. Williams, Gerald Davies, John Dawes, Mike Gibson, David Duckham, Barry John, Gareth Edwards, Willie John McBride and Merv 'the Swerve' Davies, McLauchlan was instrumental in taming an All Black scrum led by the redoubtable Colin Meads as the Lions launched the Test series with a 9–3 victory in Dunedin. He highlighted a man-of-the-match performance by scoring the only try of the game in the opening minutes when he charged down Alan Sutherland's attempted clearance and charged through the New Zealanders' defences to touch down. 'Our very own Mighty Mouse,' muttered Lions manager Doug Smith. The moniker was to stick.

Although the All Blacks levelled the series in Christchurch, McLauchlan, now joined by international colleague Gordon Brown in the scrum, was again outstanding in the Third Test, which the Lions took 13–3 in Wellington before clinching a famous series victory (their first – and last – in New Zealand after almost three-quarters of a century of trying) with a 14–14 draw at Eden Park, Auckland.

'As a Welshman, I was obviously very proud of the part played by Barry John and the rest of the boys on that tour,' Carwyn James would recall. 'But it should never be forgotten that it was the dominance of Mighty Mouse and our front row that allowed us the attacking platform on which our victory depended.'

Kiwi skipper Colin Meads (now Sir Colin) was also unstinting in his praise. 'We thought Carwyn was having a laugh when this little fella trotted out onto the pitch. But we weren't laughing when we saw how he played rugby. He was Mighty Mouse all right, but a mouse with the heart of a Lion, British or otherwise.'

Three years later, McLauchlan reinforced his reputation as the best prop forward in the business when he reduced the fearsome Springboks' front row to tatters with a succession of performances in which he risked life and limb, continually driving back the massive South African pack with a tenacity bordering on the foolhardy. The British Lions emerged 3–0 winners from that series and, asked to pick one tourist that they would like to see in the green and gold of the Republic, the readers of the *Rand Daily Mail* voted overwhelmingly for Mighty Mouse despite Welsh winger J.J. Williams' four Test tries.

Now established as his nation's captain, McLauchlan presided over one of the most curious episodes in Scotland's Five Nations history, a spell in which they were nigh on unbeatable at Murrayfield but contrastingly fragile on foreign soil, sharing only one championship title in 1973, when all five teams finished on four points with two wins and two defeats apiece.

But as a skipper and inspiration he had no peers. 'The Mouse was the greatest prop forward with whom I ever shared a pitch,' said the late Gordon Brown. 'He was a ferocious trainer – unlike some I could mention. The heavier the rain, the icier the wind, the more slanting the sleet, the more he seemed to enjoy it. Then, of course, once the game started he went into overdrive. He was a terrific teammate in every way; on the pitch you could depend upon him never to shirk a challenge or, when the occasion arose, as it often did, particularly in South Africa, walk away from a scrap. Off the pitch, he enjoyed a laugh and a drink. What more could you ask?'

McLauchlan, now President of the Scottish Rugby Union, retired from international rugby on 10 November 1979 following the New Zealand All Blacks' 20–6 victory in Edinburgh. At thirty-seven years and seven months the mouse that roared was the oldest player ever to pull on the blue shirt of Scotland, a true giant in everything but stature.

33. G.P.S. (PHIL) MACPHERSON OBE
Rugby Union

Born: Newtonmore, Inverness-shire, 16 October 1903
Died: London, 2 March 1981

CAREER:
Clubs: Oxford University and Edinburgh Academicals
Scotland 1922–32: 26 caps, 12 points

It is the considered opinion of writer and broadcaster Norman Mair, the wise old owl of rugby union, that G.P.S. MacPherson was the greatest player ever to wear the white thistle of Scotland on his chest.

Everyone with a passion for the sport will have his or her own opinion on the subject but almost 80 years after his international debut, MacPherson was voted 'Scotland's greatest-ever attacking player' in a readers' poll conducted by *Scottish Rugby* magazine and *The Herald* newspaper.

And what is unarguable after reading the rugby scribes' accounts of the day is that given the number of dummies the Oxford University and Edinburgh Accies' centre sold opponents, he must have been a millionaire. MacPherson was possessed of a ghost-like presence, a spectre who could float through tackles, drifting here, there and everywhere to the bafflement of friend and foe alike.

Partnered by winger Ian Smith on his outside (the deadly duo scored twenty-nine of Scotland's forty-nine tries during their seventeen games in tandem over eight seasons), MacPherson touched new heights of sporting genius as captain of Scotland's 1925 Grand Slam-winning team, thereafter revered as 'the Immortals'.

Raised in India, where his father, Sir Colin, was a British government official, MacPherson attended Edinburgh Academy from the age of six before winning a scholarship to Fettes College, where he also excelled at athletics and cricket. It was as an 18-year-old Oxford University student that he was first selected for Scotland on the second day of 1922 in the 3–3 draw against France in the Stade Colombes, Paris, in the same XV as Eric Liddell.

After appearing in all four Five Nations matches that winter, his university studies (MacPherson would subsequently graduate from Oxford with a Double First in Classics and also spend a year at Yale) prevented him adding to his collection of international caps until 1924, when he marked his return with a try in the 35–10 rout of Wales at Inverleith in Edinburgh.

Appointed captain for the 1925 Five Nations Championship, MacPherson reacted to the honour in irresistible manner. Scotland began the campaign against France at Inverleith on 25 January – the 166th anniversary of the birth of Robert Burns – when even the heavens smiled upon the new skipper by supplying the 20,000 crowd with a partial eclipse of the sun during the second half.

Oh, how the French must have prayed for a complete blackout to hide the ritual slaughter, MacPherson creating all seven tries (four for his Oxford University colleague Ian Smith) in Scotland's emphatic 25–4 triumph. A fortnight later, it was Wales's turn to be left reeling by MacPherson's sorcery, the Scots' skipper producing another one-man master class at the St Helen's Rugby & Cricket Ground in Swansea, where Smith again scored four tries in the 24–14 defeat of the red dragon.

Without their injured captain, Scotland struggled to a 14–8 victory over Ireland at Lansdowne Road, leaving only an unbeaten England, who still harboured ambitions of winning the championship despite drawing in Dublin, standing in their way of a first-ever Grand Slam triumph; a showdown to be played out on 21 March in the suitably magnificent surroundings of the newly completed 70,000-capacity Murrayfield Stadium, which had been built to meet the rising demand for international tickets.

On a glorious spring afternoon, MacPherson led Scotland onto the Murrayfield turf for the first time to keep their appointment with destiny. It proved to be 80 minutes of unremitting, nail-biting intensity and excitement, with a possible treble of Calcutta Cup, Triple Crown and Grand Slam (although that term was unbeknownst to the players of that generation) riding on the outcome.

Both the sporting majesty of the setting and the historic import of the occasion might have been fashioned with MacPherson especially in mind. 'He was well known for his tactical sense and study of his opponents' weaknesses,' penned rugby writer Jack Dunn. 'His skills as a general allied to the inspiration he spread throughout the team were invaluable both in the international and in the club sphere. As a player he could find a way through an almost invisible gap by a variety of methods – a sudden burst of speed, a swerve, or a baffling "jink" of a kind of stop-start without actually stopping. On top of which, of course, he excelled in making openings for his wingers.'

England made a thunderous start when William Luddington, a prop forward with a kick like a mule who had clinched victory in the 1923 Calcutta Cup with an outrageous penalty from the touchline, put the visitors 3–0 ahead with another humungous effort. With MacPherson in will-o'-the-wisp mood, however, every Scotland attack threatened danger and he carved through the English rearguard yet again to set up J.B. Nelson for a try converted by Dan Drysdale to put Scotland 5–3 ahead (a try being worth three points – the same as a penalty – a conversion two and a drop goal a priceless four points in those far-off days).

Back came England with two rapid-fire tries from Richard Hamilton-Wickes (converted by the trusty boot of Luddington) and William Lavell Wakefield – later Baron Wakefield of Kendal – to earn the Auld Enemy an 11–5 half-time advantage. After the interval, MacPherson and Scotland launched wave upon wave of attacks and a swashbuckling passing exchange between skipper and winger Ian Smith allowed Johnny Wallace to touch down by the right-hand corner flag. There was not an Englishman, player, official or fan, inside Murrayfield who did not insist that Smith had put a foot in touch during the move but the Welsh referee was in no doubt as to the legality of the score. With the huge crowd hushed, Alexander Gillies landed a magnificent touchline conversion as Scotland moved to within one point of parity.

Despite having been run ragged by the dominant Scots, England found hidden reserves of energy to mount a stiff rearguard action and managed to hold out until, with just five minutes remaining, stand-off Herbert Waddell landed the drop-goal that secured a heroic 14–11 victory. MacPherson was carried from the pitch shoulder high by supporters amid scenes of celebration, so it was said, 'more reminiscent of Sauchiehall Street on Hogmanay than an international rugby football match'.

MacPherson went on to captain Scotland for a further seven years, leading his side to victory in the 1929 Five Nations Championship and a share of the title in 1926 and 1927 with Ireland. After retiring from the game, he devoted his energies to business and served as vice-president of Kleinwort Benson – merchant bank to the seriously rich. He also served with great distinction during the Second World War; the leadership qualities he had displayed on the field of play brought him renown on the field of battle, Brigadier George Philip Stewart MacPherson of the 7th/9th Battalion of the Royal Scots being awarded an OBE in 1943 for gallantry.

34. DICK McTAGGART MBE
Boxing

Born: Dundee, 15 October 1935

CAREER:
Olympic Games:
  Melbourne 1956: lightweight – Gold
  Rome 1960: lightweight – Bronze
European Championship:
  Belgrade 1961: lightweight – Gold
British Empire & Commonwealth Games:
  Cardiff 1958: lightweight – Gold
  Perth, Australia 1962: light-welterweight – Silver
Amateur Boxing Association (ABA) lightweight champion
  1956, 1958, 1960; light-welterweight champion 1963, 1965
Fight record: won 610, lost 24

Teofilo Stevenson could have demanded a king's ransom had he fled Havana to challenge Muhammad Ali for the world heavyweight title. But the 1972, 1976 and 1980 Olympic champion refused numerous offers to swap the amateur ring for untold riches. 'I don't believe in professionalism, only revolution,' Stevenson expounded. 'I tell these men from America, the promoters, that money means nothing to me. What is eight million dollars against the love of eight million Cubans?'

Dick McTaggart was no standard-bearer for Fidel Castro but with five million Scots – most notably his parents and a legion of seventeen siblings – taking pride in his every success, he, too, refused to throw a punch for money throughout his illustrious boxing career. McTaggart emerged triumphant from 610 of his 634 bouts (yes, 634 ring battles), winning Olympic, European and Commonwealth titles as a lightweight and becoming one of the few amateurs to be inducted into the sport's International Hall of Fame, a fitting tribute to the skilful southpaw who was the ultimate exponent of the so-called 'noble art'. 'He moves like a ballet dancer,' observed Frenchman Andre Vairolatto after being on the receiving end of a McTaggart master class. 'A ballet dancer with dynamite in his fists. It is a privilege to lose to such a boxer. He is unique. He is right there in front of you until the precise second that you prepare to unleash a punch, then – poof! – he has vanished. You only realise that he is still there in the ring with you when his fist lands on your chin.'

One of five boxing brothers, it was as an RAF corporal that McTaggart flew to Melbourne for the 1956 Olympics, a flamboyant figure with his trademark blond crew cut and white boots. Although the great Hungarian László Papp would win the light-middleweight gold by beating another future world champion, American José Torres, in the final (with Maryhill's John 'Cowboy' McCormack taking the bronze medal), the 21-year-old McTaggart also lifted the Val Barker Trophy as the 'outstanding and most stylish boxer of the Games'.

'Having beaten the German Harry Kurschat [who would subsequently lose only two of his thirty-four fights as a professional] clearly on points in the final, with two knockdowns in the first round, I was all ready to start celebrating – the champagne cork was being drawn, you could say,' recalled McTaggart. 'Then one of our team officials told me to hang about until the end of the night's finals because my name had been put forward "for something else". When the news of the award came, I was choked. It was an incredible compliment from the jury. Apart from any joyful tears of mine, the Val Barker cup was so big you needed two bottles of bubbly to fill it.'

The flight home from Australia via a stopover in Japan in the pleasurable company of 'Cowboy' McCormack and cheeky cockney Terry Spinks, winner of the featherweight gold medal, was an adventure of an entirely different kind on an epic scale. 'Terry went exploring soon after take-off at the start of our long journey. He disappeared up a little, half-hidden staircase and came back giggling. "Hey, guys," he whispered, "there's a little bar up there, and, guess what? It's free." Well, from then on that was our bar, me, Terry and John. Only trouble was, by the time we flew into London, I was in such a happy state that, for a few moments of panic, I couldn't find the Val Barker cup, big as it was.'

Although Dundee's ungrateful city fathers chose to ignore the nationwide clamour to mark McTaggart's homecoming by staging a civic reception, many thousands turned out to greet their returning hero's train when it pulled in from London. To the cheers of the huge crowd thronging the streets of Dundee, a body of local amateur boxers attached ropes to the front of a Morris Oxford car to pull McTaggart on the uphill journey from the old Tay Bridge railway station to the family's tenement home in Dens Road.

When he completed his National Service, during which he trained as a cook, McTaggart was inundated with 'name your own price' offers to turn professional – a bout against undisputed world champion Joe Brown in New York's Madison Square Garden was even suggested – instead of which he surprised all boxing by deciding to remain amateur while taking a job as a rat-catcher for Glasgow city council. 'I was never going to turn professional because I'd always had a wee bit o' trouble with my left eye ever since my days in the RAF,' he explained.

A comfortable winner of the Commonwealth Games' gold medal at Cardiff in 1958 – it was a good thing for rivals that he was not blessed with two good eyes – McTaggart was widely expected to retain his Olympic title at the 1960 Games in Rome. Selected to serve as the Great Britain flag-bearer at the Opening Ceremony in the team parade before Italian President Giovanni Gronchi, McTaggart was controversially adjudged the loser on points to eventual champion Kazimierz Pazdzior of Poland in the semi-finals and had to settle for bronze. Pazdzior, like the rest of the East Europeans of the Cold War era, was a full-time athlete funded by the Polish government and fought as a highly paid 'amateur' purely for cynical state propaganda purposes.

McTaggart exacted full revenge on the Communist bloc boxers at the 1961 European Championships in Belgrade, where he defeated Herbert Olesch of East Germany, Janos Kadji of Hungary and Yugoslav Peter Benedek (in front of a fiercely partisan audience) in successive bouts to win a piece of gold he regarded as even more precious than his Olympic medal.

By the time of the 1964 Olympics in Tokyo, where he became the first Briton to box in three Olympiads, a wearied McTaggart was no longer the irresistible force of his younger years. Although he would win his fifth ABA title the following year, having moved up a division to light-welterweight, he was beaten at the quarter-final stage by Poland's Josef Grudzien, who would go on to win the Olympic gold medal.

McTaggart retired at the age of 30 in 1965 – 'The greatest amateur boxer I ever saw,' according to BBC commentator Harry Carpenter – but such had been his impact worldwide that 23 years later Soviet television screened a 30-minute documentary in his honour while 'the world's greatest amateur' was in St Petersburg (Leningrad, as it was then known) as an official of the Scottish boxing team.

American Tyrell Biggs, who won the heavyweight gold medal at the 1984 Games in Los Angeles, described amateur boxing thus: 'It is the college of boxing. The kind of degree you receive depends upon how far you go in the tournament. If you win the Olympics, then you are awarded a doctorate.' Dick McTaggart is the professor emeritus of amateur boxing.

35. ROBERT MILLAR
Cycling

Born: Glasgow, 13 September 1958

CAREER:
Teams: Athletic Club Boulogne-Billancourt 1979–80; Peugeot
    1980–5; Panasonic 1986–7; Fagor 1988; Z-Peugot 1980–91;
    TVM 1992–4; Le Groupement 1995
Tour de France 1984: overall – 4th; King of the Mountains
Giro d'Italia (Tour of Italy) 1987: overall – 2nd; King of the
    Mountains
Vuelta a España (Tour of Spain) 1985: overall – 2nd; 1986:
    overall – 2nd

If you were to believe everything they say about Robert Millar, a
kaleidoscope identikit would begin to take shape: as private as Greta
Garbo . . . as irascible as Victor Meldrew . . . as enigmatic as the Sphinx
. . . as emotionless as Mr Spock . . . as acerbic as Dorothy Parker . . . as
eccentric as Basil Fawlty. And that is just his friends talking.

Born in the Gorbals, where most young boys dream of playing for
Rangers or Celtic, Millar found fame in the most foreign of sporting fields
for a Scot, the Tour de France; in 1984, he claimed the *maillot a pois rouge*
(the red polka dot jersey) as winner of the 'King of the Mountains', the
only English-speaking rider ever to emerge victorious from that gruelling
race within the most gruelling of races, and finished a remarkable fourth
overall behind victor Laurent Fignon, his fellow Frenchman Bernard
Hinault, a five-time champion, and American Greg LeMond. By being
the first Briton to step onto the podium after the final stage through the
streets of Paris to the Champs-Elysées, he won the respect of all continental
Europe.

Millar's odyssey from a high-rise block on the south side of Glasgow
to the oxygen starved peaks of the Alps and Pyrenees sitting astride a
narrow, leather saddle only marginally more comfortable than cheese
wire is as remarkable as any in sport; to the cycling-mad French, who

fully appreciated the magnitude of the pony-tailed Scot's achievement, a rider from a nation without any road cycling tradition was regarded as an exotic species; that he should be crowned 'King of the Mountains' was as unthinkable, say, as a Parisian pastry chef winning the caber tossing event at the Braemar Highland Games.

Educated at Shawlands Academy, where the unanimous sport of choice was football, Millar's fascination with cycling began when he joined the Glenmarnock Wheelers (he would later move to the Glasgow Wheelers), with schoolmate Willie Gibb. 'Even at school Robert had a total disregard for what people thought of him,' recalled Gibb. 'He was very obstinate; I knew him from when we were at primary school and at 15 you would have to say that he was a bit odd, something which didn't change all the time I knew him. He was a loner and he put off a lot of people with his attitude when he was younger. Part of the problem was that people just didn't know how to take him – but Robert didn't care, he was totally single-minded.'

Naturally shy and introverted yet articulate and wryly humorous when the mood was upon him, Millar showed no desire to be popular, merely to be successful. By the age of 17, he was Scottish junior champion, swiftly adding the national hill-climbing and British Amateur Road Race titles to his list of honours before celebrating his 21st birthday by joining Athletic Club Boulogne-Billancourt (ACBB), one of France's leading teams.

Fourth in the 1980 World Amateur Championship – following which he was presented with France's 'Amateur of the Year' award trophy – Millar turned professional as a mountain specialist, quickly establishing himself as a rider who could compete with the very best while continuing to baffle those around him with his weird and wonderful ways. When Mark Bell arrived from Liverpool to join the ACBB team, Millar was required to share the apartment of which he had previously enjoyed sole occupancy. On Bell's first night in his new bed, he heard strange noises emanating from the kitchen and padded off to investigate; he discovered Millar hovering over the cooker preparing his vegetarian dinner. As a fellow Brit in a foreign land, Bell might have expected some form of greeting or welcome instead of which a wordless Millar finished his task then disappeared into his room, closing the door firmly at his back.

Jamie McGahan, who also hailed from Glasgow and had regularly ridden with Millar in Scottish colours in team events at home and abroad, fared marginally better when he bumped into his former colleague in a supermarket on the outskirts of Paris. 'I asked him how life was treating him as a pro and we exchanged a few words and he left. That was it. Indifference is the word that springs to mind. There was no suggestion that we went for a ride together or even a coffee or a meal or anything. He was never a very warm character. Back then, at least. I was and am full of admiration for him as a bike rider, but as a human being he was a dead loss.'

Australian Allan Peiper, a colleague on three different teams during his racing days in France, was similarly unable to solve the enigma of Millar: 'I was on the same team as him almost half of my career but I never really knew him. We never had a heart-to-heart conversation. I never went to his house, and he never came to mine.'

This aloofness would cost Millar dearly on the 1985 Tour of Spain. Wearing the race leader's yellow jersey and holding a seemingly unassailable six-minute-plus lead on the penultimate stage, the Scot suffered a puncture, encouraging Spaniard Pedro Delgado to launch a sudden attack. What happened next was either a cynical conspiracy designed to thwart Millar or the combination of a series of unrelated episodes that secured Delgado an unlikely victory.

While Delgado was allowed to build up a seven-minute advantage – riding in the slipstream of a helpfully positioned car carrying a television camera to protect him from the head wind – for reasons that were never fully explained, Millar was allowed to continue in the belief that he was still in control of the race. Inexplicably, Millar's Peugeot team manager also delayed sending a message to his *domestiques* (literally 'servants'), informing them to work as a unit to ensure their number one regained the lead.

As Millar set off in lonely pursuit of Delgado the final puncture to his hopes of his first major victory came when the rest of the Peugeot team, who should have been assisting him, were reported to have been crucially held up at a level-crossing. As Delgado disappeared into the distance, there they sat, awaiting the passing of a train that would never arrive, as it transpired. And so – surprise, surprise – a Spaniard won the Tour of Spain.

Runner-up again the following year in the Vuelta a España and second in the 1987 Giro d'Italia in which he took the 'King of the Mountains' title, Millar retired in 1995 to pen insightful and highly entertaining articles for various cycling magazines, a curious career choice for someone who had always viewed most journalists with disdain. 'One interviewer asked me what I did when I wasn't riding,' he explained. 'He wanted to know what my full-time job was.'

In recent years, Millar's whereabouts and way of life have been shrouded in mystery. In 2002, he made a brief appearance at the Commonwealth Games in Manchester but was conspicuous by his absence when inducted into the Scottish Sports Hall of Fame, his former coach at the Glasgow Wheelers, Billy Bilsland, accepting the presentation scroll on his behalf. Millar has since been reported as having undergone a sex change operation to live as a woman in Dorset, as living as a recluse in the south of France, or as a wandering nomad in the outback of Australia.

Commonwealth Games cyclist turned author Richard Moore, whose biography *In Search of Robert Millar* makes riveting reading even if you have never climbed on a bike, managed to make contact with his elusive subject by email, seeking help with the project. After ignoring Moore's original enquiry, Millar finally replied via an exchange of computerised messages: 'There's a morbid attitude to privacy in this country. It's bizarre the need to diminish other people so that they can feel better about themselves. I've shared a part of my life as a professional cyclist, now that career is finished I have the same right to privacy and a quiet time as the next person.'

Millar's final email was brief and to the point: 'No more questions.'

36. COLIN MONTGOMERIE OBE
Golf

Born: Glasgow, 23 June 1963

CAREER:
European Tour victories: 31
Others: 9
European Tour Order of Merit winner 1993, 1994, 1995, 1996,
    1997, 1998, 1999, 2005
Ryder Cup: 1991, 1993, 1995 (winners), 1997 (winners),
    1999, 2002 (winners), 2004 (winners), 2006 (winners),
    2010, as non-playing captain (winners)

Who could have imagined that as a laddie the privately educated Colin
Montgomerie idolised wee Billy Bremner?

Although he was educated as a boarder at Glenalmond College,
nestling among 300 lush acres of rolling Perthshire countryside on the
banks of the River Almond, Monty was raised in Ilkley, Yorkshire, where
his father served as managing director of the Fox biscuit company in
nearby Leeds. And when not honing his golf skills at the local club
situated on the edge of Ilkley Moor, the youthful Montgomerie was a
regular at Elland Road, with eyes only for the red-haired enforcer of Don
Revie's win-at-all-costs Leeds United.

The title of Bremner's autobiography was *You Get Nowt for Being Second*,
a philosophy that must have repeatedly struck a chord with Monty over
the years. For despite his forty titles worldwide, his appearance on five
Ryder Cup-winning teams and his inspirational captaincy of the
victorious 2010 side, in the eyes of his fellow professionals, galleries and
the media, he remains The Greatest Player Never to Have Won a Major,
the most uncomfortable burden in golf.

You get nowt for coming second? Poor Monty has been second five
times – at the 2005 Open Championship, the 1994, 1997 and 2006 US
Opens and the 1995 US PGA – all the while insisting that he would not
swap one of his eight European Order of Merit titles for a single victory

in a major. His defiance is as understandable as it is commendable but the truly great figures in any sport are judged by the great championships they have won. Does anyone doubt that Ken Rosewall, Pancho Gonzales, Ilie Nastase and Ivan Lendl regret not having won Wimbledon, or that Stirling Moss will forever feel cheated by his failure to win the Formula One world drivers' title?

Despite Monty's protestations to the contrary, it is a criminal miscarriage of justice that he has been forced to witness a host of less worthy players – Ben Curtis, Todd Hamilton, Shaun Micheel, Rich Beem, Mark Brooks and Steve Jones, to list but a handful – steal off with the game's glittering prizes.

'People don't seem to realise how often you have to come in second in order to finish first,' observed Jack Nicklaus. 'I've never met a winner who hasn't learned how to be a loser.' The Golden Bear was a major runner-up 19 times but was a winner on 18 occasions, whereas the luckless Monty clearly never learned from his role of perennial runner-up. And so, before we turn to his many triumphs, let us look at the majors that eluded him, starting with the 1992 US Open, in which he did not even have the consolation of finishing second.

'Congratulations on winning your first major,' smiled Jack Nicklaus as Monty marched off the eighteenth green at Pebble Beach. Having shot a remarkable fourth round 70 in a ferocious wind that had ruined the hopes of Davis Love (83), Scott Simpson (88), Payne Stewart (83), Raymond Floyd (81), Paul Azinger (80), Mark Calcavecchia (80), Nick Faldo (77), Tom Lehman (77) and Ian Woosnam (79), Monty accepted Nicklaus's congratulatory handshake 'even though Tom Kite and Jeff Sluman were only on the 11th'. Minutes later, the Californian tempest was instantly transformed into a gentle summer breeze, allowing both Kite (72) and Sluman (71) to capitalise on the gentle conditions and relegate Monty to third place.

Two years later, Montgomerie came even closer to becoming the first British winner of the US Open since Tony Jacklin in 1971 only to bring up the rear in a three-man play-off against new champion South African Ernie Els and American Loren Roberts, known as the 'Boss of the Moss', the best putter on the US Tour. Monty's hopes were as good as over with sixteen holes of the eighteen-hole play-off remaining when he opened with a brace of error-strewn double-bogey sixes that led one commentator to mutter, 'I never knew the Keystone Kops played golf.' For his part, Monty regarded his collapse as part of his golf education. 'This is by far the most difficult course I've ever played, but I came here saying this was my best chance to win a major and I gave it my best. It's all part of the learning process – I'm always learning.'

Twelve months later in the 1995 US PGA Championship at the Riviera Country Club in Los Angeles (where the notorious O.J. Simpson used to play until declared *persona non grata* by the members), Montgomerie maintained his dubious record of never having won a play-off. After sinking birdie putts of sixteen, five and eighteen feet on the closing three holes to finish tied with Steve Elkington on 267, Monty was denied yet again when the Australian holed a massive thirty-five-foot putt at the first extra hole. 'My play-off record went through my mind on the buggy ride back to the 18th tee. But I thought by the law of averages it would be my turn today. I did nothing wrong but I've played enough golf to expect the unexpected. I don't feel I lost – it was a case of Steve winning.'

Montgomerie's opening 65 in the 1997 US Open at the Congressional Country Club in Bethesda, Washington, is still considered to be one of the finest rounds in the event's 116-year history; a level par-70 in the second round would have given Monty victory by a resounding five shots, instead of which he shot a ruinous 76 in perfect conditions and finished the tournament on 277, one stroke behind Ernie Els.

For once, it was not the fates that conspired against Monty at St Andrews in 2005 when, with Tiger Woods strolling home by five shots, the Scot won the 'other' Open by one stroke ahead of Fred Couples and José-Maria Olazábal. 'It's never a disgrace to lose to the best player of our generation by far,' said the ever-gracious runner-up. 'I was within one shot of Tiger at the turn but it wasn't to be.'

Most cruelly of all, it was not to be at the 2006 US Open at Winged Foot, New York, when Monty sank a humungous 60-foot birdie putt on the 17th green of his final round, then launched a fairway-splitting drive down the 18th, the distance between ball and hole and the holy grail of a long-awaited major victory was a mere 171 yards; a straightforward six-iron into the middle of the green, two putts and the US Open was most surely his. After a long delay while the pairing in front putted out – during which an indecisive Monty swapped the six for a seven-iron – he fluffed his second shot into the thick rough short and right of the green from where he took two ugly swishes to escape en route to a double-bogey six. Even a bogey five would have earned him a play-off against Australian Geoff Ogilvy, who unexpectedly found the trophy placed into his hands. 'Other chances I've had, other players have done very well,' he explained. 'This is the first time I've really messed up, which is OK. You're entitled to a couple of mess-ups along the way.'

The four majors apart, there have been precious few mess-ups along Monty's way. Aged 20 he returned to live in his native Scotland when his parents bought a sprawling red-sandstone villa on South Beach, Troon, one of Scotland's most desirable addresses, with its views of Arran and within a five-iron of the first tee of the championship course, where his father would later become club secretary.

After a highly successful amateur career, Monty turned professional in 1988, being named 'Rookie of the Year' before collecting the first of his 31 European Tour titles the following season with an 11-shot victory in the Portuguese Open. Although he would go on to win everything on offer – including the PGA Championship, Volvo Masters, World Match Play Championship, Dunhill Links, the 2007 World Cup in tandem with Marc Warren and seven successive Order of Merit triumphs between 1993 and 1999 – it was the Ryder Cup that was to cement his reputation as a true great of the game on both sides of the Atlantic.

After eight appearances as a player, Monty, who has played on five winning teams, is the second highest points-scorer in the history of the contest behind Sir Nick Faldo while remaining unbeaten in singles play with six wins and two halves.

All of which brought Monty universal admiration, but the affection of the public was rather harder to earn. Blessed with an ability to hear a child munch a crisp half a mile away, the click of a camera in the next county or the beat of a seagull's wings at 10,000 ft, he gained a reputation as a waspish character best avoided after a disappointing round. Oh, how the Americans chortled whenever a poor shot was accompanied by an immediate drooping of those broad shoulders. Even to those who play alongside him on a weekly basis, Montgomerie proved to be something of a mystery. Forget psychologists, you would have to be an expert potholer to tunnel into the recesses of his mind, for here is a dark place with many a twist and turn.

And yet the man could be both charming and amusing company. I recall sharing a drink with the then team captains John Parrott and Ally McCoist following an episode of *A Question of Sport* when I asked them to nominate their all-time favourite guest. 'Monty,' they chorused. 'He's absolutely hilarious after a couple of glasses of wine in the hospitality room.'

Monty's image as the grouch of the fairways was dispelled at Celtic Manor in Wales in 2010 when, after the dour Ryder Cup captaincy of Faldo two years earlier, he led Europe to an epic 14½–13½ victory over the United States in a manner that was as insightful as it was relaxed. The European players clearly revered him, the crowds adored him and the Americans appeared in awe of him. 'This is one of the greatest moments of my golf career . . . No, wait. This is the greatest moment of my golf career,' beamed Monty.

The newly crowned US Open champion Graeme McDowell, to whom went the honour of holing the Ryder Cup-winning putt, was fulsome in his praise of the European skipper. 'Monty's been amazing. For the last two years he's been right up for this. There is no one quite like Colin Montgomerie. He's everything there is in the Ryder Cup and to be able to do that for him was really special.' Vice-captain Darren Clarke added: 'Monty created a fantastic team atmosphere – he has been sensational.'

When it came his turn to air his thoughts, Monty's victory speech was an exercise in graciousness, at a moment in time when he could have been excused for reminding rival captain Corey Pavin 'You get nowt for being second.'

37. OLD TOM MORRIS/ YOUNG TOM MORRIS
Golf

Born: St Andrews, 16 June 1821 / St Andrews, 20 April 1851
Died: St Andrews, 24 May 1908 / St Andrews, 25 December 1875

CAREERS:
Open champion 1861, 1862, 1864, 1867 / 1868, 1869, 1870, 1872

Lying amidst the ruins of St Andrews Cathedral, near the grave of his father Old Tom, lies the last resting place of Young Tom Morris, golf's original superstar. Tiger Woods, Jack Nicklaus, Arnold Palmer and Seve Ballesteros are among the many thousands of golfers – from great champions to hopeless duffers – to have visited the site to pay homage and gaze upon the inscription carved on the headstone: 'Deeply regretted by numerous friends and all golfers, he thrice won the Championship Belt and held it without envy, his many amiable qualities being no less acknowledged than his golfing achievements.'

Dead at 24 under the most tragic of circumstances, Young Tom finished runner-up behind his dad as a 16 year old in the 1867 Open before winning the sport's most treasured prize the following year at the tender age of 17 years, 5 months and 8 days; the youngest player ever to do so and a record, one can safely presume, that will survive the sands of time. He triumphed again in 1869 – leaving his father with the runner-up's cash prize – and in 1870 by an imperious 11 and 12 strokes respectively, thereby winning the Championship Belt outright and posing Prestwick Golf Club with an unforeseen problem. Having held the exclusive rights to host the event throughout those early years, Prestwick suddenly found itself in the embarrassing position of being without a trophy to put on offer and the 1871 championship was cancelled while the members held a number of meetings to discuss what should be done.

It was eventually agreed to include St Andrews and Musselburgh in the Open rotation and a magnificent Claret Jug was commissioned from

Mackay Cunningham & Company silversmiths in Edinburgh at a cost of £30 to replace the Championship Belt now in Young Tom's permanent possession. New trophy, same result, with the fresh-faced master cruising to his fourth successive victory at Prestwick in 1872 to become the first name to be engraved on the Claret Jug. (To mark the 125th anniversary of the first Open, the Prestwick members presented 1985 Royal St George's champion Sandy Lyle with an exact replica of Young Tom's Championship Belt, which had been fashioned from red morocco leather and bore a golf scene on the silver buckle. The original Belt is on display in the Golf Museum in St Andrews across the road from the first tee of the Old Course clubhouse.)

Before being usurped by his son, Old Tom had reigned unchallenged as the king of the links with four Open Championship victories of his own. Born and raised near the Old Course, Morris Sr had been fascinated with golf since the age of ten when he routinely beat all-comers at sillybodkins, a popular children's game played in the streets of the town using a home-made club and wine bottle corks studded with nails as balls.

Apprenticed to club-maker Allan Robertson, Old Tom was summarily dismissed from his position when boss came across pupil playing with a new guttie ball when his business largely depended upon the sale of the traditional featherie version. Old Tom was not unemployed for long: an ambitious new golf project was being planned across the country in Prestwick and he was invited to design the course and serve as the club professional.

The visionary Old Tom realised that the public was eager to see all the best players competing against one another and he was one of the prime movers behind the first Open in 1860, launching the very first drive of the tournament. As Prestwick's reputation soared and St Andrews gradually fell into a state of disrepair, the Royal & Ancient offered Old Tom a salary of £50 per annum – an astronomical sum 150 years ago – to return to his home town in 1865 to oversee the redevelopment of the 'home of golf'.

After winning his fourth Open in 1867, Old Tom combined his roles as club pro, green-keeper, club-maker, ball-maker and instructor with that of course architect (he worked on Carnoustie and Muirfield among many), his most notable innovation being that of lowering the number of holes at St Andrews from 23 to 18, which swiftly became the accepted standard. He also placed bunkers and other hazards in the most inconvenient of places, requiring players to 'think' their way round any Old Tom Morris design.

His entry in the World Golf Hall of Fame reads: 'Old Tom Morris may not have invented the game of golf but he is recognised as the sport's founding father,' while in *The Book of Golf and Golfers*, published in 1899, Horace Hutchinson described him as:

> One of the most remarkable men – the best of men and the best of golfers – that ever missed a short putt . . . he has been written of as often as a Prime Minister, he has been photographed as often as a professional beauty, and yet he remains, through all the advertisement, exactly the same, simple and kindly.

In 1967, a later scribe, James K. Robertson, wrote of him in *St Andrews: Home of Golf*:

> As St Andrews became increasingly a Mecca for golfers, so, too, did the sturdy patriarchal figure and bearing of Old Tom come to symbolise all that was finest in the Scottish character and in the ancient Scottish game. His kindly, yet capable and gentle nature enshrined him a good many years before his death as the authentic Grand Old Man of Golf. To generations of people all over the world his name and picture came to epitomise the game.

Rich beyond his wildest dreams during his tenure at Prestwick, Old Tom could afford to send his son to the fee-paying Ayr Academy, where Young Tom was educated alongside the offspring of noblemen and wealthy merchants. But it was in golf rather than business that Young Tom's passion lay and the London newspapers regularly despatched their correspondents on an 800-mile round trip to report on his deeds, such as his 77 around St Andrews in 1869, a course record that would stand for 20 years.

Dashing, courteous and Hollywood handsome, Young Tom quickly became a national hero, attracting huge crowds north and south of the border, as he and his father travelled the land taking on – and beating – all the other leading professionals of the time in foursomes play. September 1875 found father and son in North Berwick, where they were engaged in a challenge match against brothers Willie and Mungo Park when play was interrupted by the arrival of a telegram requesting Young Tom to return home immediately. Margaret Drennan, his pregnant young wife of less than a year, had been taken desperately ill during a premature labour at their home in St Andrews. Rather than disappoint the huge gallery with only two holes remaining, the Morrises completed their customary victory before setting off to find a boatman to ferry them across the Firth of Forth and up the east coast to St Andrews. By the time they arrived back in town, Young Tom's wife and unborn son had died; four months later he, too, was dead, officially of a pulmonary haemorrhage on Christmas Day morning, but of a broken heart, according to friends, a notion discounted by his grief-stricken father. 'If that were the case,' he said sadly, 'then I wouldn't be here either.'

Old Tom survived his son by more than a quarter of a century, dying three weeks before his 87th birthday in 1908 after falling down a flight of stairs in the New Club in St Andrews. Among those who joined the sombre funeral procession that stretched the entire length of South Street in St Andrews, all the way from the port to the cathedral, was fellow professional Andrew Kirkaldy, who described the scene as 'a cloud of people'. 'There were many wet eyes among us,' he added, 'for Old Tom was beloved by everybody.'

38. ANDY MURRAY

Tennis

Born: Dunblane, Stirlingshire, 15 May 1987

CAREER TO DATE:
Singles titles (22):
  2012: Brisbane
  2011: London Queen's Club; Tokyo; Bangkok; Cincinnati Masters; Shanghai Masters
  2010: Shanghai Masters; Canadian Masters
  2009: Valencia; Canadian Masters; London Queen's Club; Miami Masters; Rotterdam; Doha
  2008: St Petersburg; Madrid Masters; Cincinnati Masters; Marseille; Doha
  2007: St Petersburg; San Jose
  2006: San Jose
Doubles titles (1):
  2010: Valencia (with Jamie Murray)
Grand Slam Record:
  Australian Open: 2010 – final; 2011 – final; 2012 – final. French Open: 2009 – quarter-final; 2011 – semi-final; 2012 – quarter-final. Wimbledon: 2008 – quarter-final; 2009 – semi-final; 2010 – semi-final; 2011 – semi-final; 2012 – final. US Open: 2008 – final; 2011 – semi-final
Olympic Games:
  London 2012: men's singles – Gold; mixed doubles (with Laura Robson) – Silver

When Fred Perry won the last of his three successive men's singles titles at Wimbledon in 1936, King Edward VIII was preparing to scandalise polite society by announcing his intention to abdicate in order to marry American divorcee (heaven forbid!) Wallis Simpson; Paul Robeson had them sobbing in the aisles of the Paramount Cinema (later renamed the Odeon) in Glasgow's Renfield Street with his classic rendition of 'Ol'

Man River' in the hit screen musical *Showboat*; and you could buy a sumptuous Georgian townhouse in Regent Terrace, Edinburgh, for around £1,000 against the £2 million-plus offers of the mid-2000s.

Three-quarters of a century on, Angela Mortimer, Virginia Wade and Ann Jones have achieved Centre Court glory in the women's singles, but for British men the manicured lawns of SW19 have been the scene of unremitting disappointment. Roger Taylor (1967, '70, '73), Mike Sangster (1961) and Tim Henman – on a heartbreaking four occasions – reached the semi-finals only to succumb and for the foreseeable future the hopes of the nation rest solely on Scottish shoulders.

When Andy Murray stood just five points away from victory against former Wimbledon runner-up David Nalbandian of Argentina in the third round of the 2005 championships, only to falter when his gangly teenage body started to suffer a variety of aches and pains, Jimmy Connors described that Saturday afternoon as 'Day One of the rest of his career'. Seven years have since passed and Murray is now firmly established as one of the best players in the world. Although he has yet to win a Grand Slam title, he has already gone further than his boyhood hero Henman by reaching the final of the 2008 US Open (losing to Roger Federer), the 2010 and 2011 Australian Open finals (bowing to Federer and Novak Djokovic in Melbourne) and, most memorably, the 2012 Wimbledon final, where he was again defeated by the Swiss maestro.

Having come through the toughest draw handed to any competitor in the 135-year history of the tournament – in successive rounds he had to defeat former world number three Nikolay Davydenko of Russia, Croatian Ivo Karlovic (he of the 156-mph serve), Cypriot Marcos Baghdatis, Marin Cilic of Croatia, Spaniard David Ferrer and French grass-court artist Jo-Wilfried Tsonga in the semi-finals – Murray had Federer reeling in the final and was poised on the brink of a two-set lead when the Swiss suddenly unleashed the tennis of the gods.

Murray's gracious and tearful loser's speech, delivered minutes after his heartbreaking defeat and under the gaze of 17 million TV viewers in Britain alone, earned him the affection of all – even those who had previously sneered at his so-called grumpiness and lack of emotion (more of which later). 'I'm getting closer,' he said, his voice breaking, when Sue Barker asked him to address a global audience in the immediate aftermath of his 4–6 7–5 6–3 6–4 defeat. After paying credit to his conqueror, who had won the title for a record-equalling seventh time, Murray reduced many in Centre Court to tears as he continued: 'Everybody talks about the pressure of playing at Wimbledon, how tough it is. But it's not you, the people watching; you make it so much easier to play. The support has been incredible. So thank you.'

Four weeks to the day later, Murray would face his serial tormentor across the same Centre Court net when the two players contested the gold-medal match of the London Olympics. Having beaten Djokovic 7–5 7–5 in the best-of-three-set semi-finals, the Scot was a man inspired in the garish colours of Great Britain, as designed by Stella McCartney, thrashing Federer 6–2 6–1 6–4 in under two hours, the Swiss's heaviest-ever defeat on the lawns of the All England Club.

The Olympic title (last won for Britain by Josiah Ritchie in 1908) may not carry the same cachet as the four Grand Slam championships, but the imperious manner of Murray's triumph finally silenced those detractors who suggested the Scot lacked the mental toughness to overcome the 'Big Three' of Federer, Djokovic and Nadal in a best-of-five-set final. Although he will probably have to win Wimbledon before joining Scotland's clan of sporting knights, Murray (who also teamed up with Laura Robson to win silver in a rare appearance in mixed doubles) had twin honours bestowed upon him by the Royal Mail: a postbox in his home town of Dunblane was repainted gold, while a stamp bearing his likeness was released.

Despite Murray's insistence that grass is his least favourite surface – a pronouncement somewhat diluted by his annihilation of Federer in their Olympic showdown – it is for two weeks every summer during the

---

Donald Budge

While most people would nominate Muhammad Ali as the greatest boxer of all time, Jack Nicklaus as the greatest golfer and Pelé as the greatest footballer, when it comes to the greatest male tennis player in history, the arguments start to rage. Old timers insisted that no one came close to challenging Bill Tilden; those who saw him remain convinced that Rod Laver reigned supreme; whereas a younger generation would no doubt promote the claims of Roger Federer or Rafael Nadal.

The one name that consistently appears in any All-Time Top Five list, however, is that of Donald Budge. Born in America but as Scottish as square sausage, Budge became the first of only two men to achieve the Grand Slam (Laver following in 1962 and 1968) when he won Wimbledon plus the US, French and Australian championships in 1938.

The son of John Budge, a printer by trade who played for Rangers in the 1890s before swapping Glasgow for sunny California, young Donald chased a fitba' in the streets of Oakland until he was introduced to tennis by his big brother, Lloyd.

According to Bobby Wilson, four times a Wimbledon quarter-finalist and one of this country's doughtiest Davis Cup stalwarts – winning 41 of his 61 matches in the competition – Budge should be recognised as the greatest. 'In my long tennis career, I had the honour of playing against or practising with 26 Wimbledon champions from Henri Cochet and Jean Borotra in a London versus Paris challenge in 1952 [the year the youthful Wilson won junior Wimbledon] to John McEnroe in the first round of the Wimbledon mixed doubles in 1977. I played Donald Budge in a couple of "friendly" sets in America in

Wimbledon Championships that he attracts the level of manic adoration normally reserved for Wayne Rooney, Jenson Button and English Ashes heroes by the great British sporting public. A nation expects and Murray would like nothing better than to deliver, even if he regards Wimbledon as no more important a venue than Roland Garros, Flushing Meadow or Melbourne Park. 'It goes without saying that I want to win a Grand Slam title but I'd happily settle for French, US or Australian championships. Any one of them. I have no preference.'

Although it was Andre Agassi who first attracted Murray to the All England Club as a wide-eyed seven year old clutching a bulging autograph book – his two-hour vigil outside the locker-room for the Great One's signature would ultimately be in vain – it was Henman who served as the Scot's youthful inspiration and his affection for 'the almost man' of British tennis is tangible.

'I know that some people will always regard Tim as a failure, yet he was undoubtedly one of our greatest-ever sportsmen. In his own era, I certainly can't think of anyone else who came close to matching his achievement for the best part of a decade. Everyone in the media used to go on and on about David Beckham but was he one of the best ten players in his chosen sport? No way. So, OK, Tim never won Wimbledon but the England football team never won anything at all with David Beckham in the side. It's plain stupid to call Tim a failure.'

With Henmania now superseded by Murraymania and Henman Hill, where the ticketless hordes assemble with their Tupperware lunches to follow the action on the Centre Court on the giant screen, renamed Murray Mount (or Murray Field, as I prefer to call it), how does our young hero relish the notion of being the focus of all eyes whenever he strolls through the Fred Perry gates to begin his latest adventure? 'It's cool,' he said. 'It goes with the job. I'm fortunate inasmuch that I'm only a wee bit famous for a fortnight then it tends to die down again. It's only during Wimbledon that I'm constantly under the microscope. I hate to think what it would be like to be really famous like Tiger Woods, whose every move is documented each and every day of his life.

'Yes, I do get recognised from time to time but I don't really go out that much. [Do not expect to see the home-loving Murray sashay down the red carpet in the company of the glitterati at a movie premiere in Leicester

1955 when he was aged 40. After giving me three games and a 40–0 start, I hardly won another point. No one, including Laver or Lew Hoad, ever beat me so easily. I felt completely outclassed. If Budge could do that at 40, then what must he have been like in his prime?'

Square.] I spend a lot of time walking my dog [a border terrier named Maggie in honour of Rod Stewart's 'Maggie May']. It's all pretty dull, actually.' For 'dull' read 'unassuming'. When asked why as Wimbledon champion he could shop in his local Sainsbury's in Fulham's King's Road without causing chaos in the aisles whereas Boris Becker generated mayhem where're he roamed, Stefan Edberg replied: 'Boris acts like he thinks a superstar should act. I'm just the son of a Swedish policeman.' And Murray will forever be the son of the endearingly down-to-earth Judy. 'I don't go out in disguise because I don't have to do that kind of thing. I don't wear a hat pulled down over my face. I dress in normal clothes and just try to fit in as unobtrusively as possible. People do stop me for photos or an autograph from time to time, but almost everyone's been very supportive.'

That is the inherent modesty of a decently brought up young man talking. Despite his protestations that he is 'only a wee bit famous', Murray has become an A-List celebrity in the British sporting firmament. Sir Sean Connery is wont to send him a 'good luck' text before important matches, Scottish band Rock Salt & Nails released 'Volley Highway' in his honour and Billy Connolly was seen in the VIP box at Melbourne sitting directly behind Judy.

As befits his status, Murray lives in the celebrity studded village of Oxshott in Surrey, where his neighbours include Cheryl Cole, Chelsea captain John Terry and publicist to the stars Max Clifford; home is a £5.45 million mock Tudor sprawl complete with indoor swimming pool, library, cinema, games room, jacuzzi, sauna, summer house but, curiously, no tennis court. He can well afford such little luxuries; over the course of his career, he is expected to earn something approaching £100 million in prize money and endorsements.

The great and the good tend to listen to what he has to say on any subject: at one meeting with the then Prime Minister Gordon Brown – 'I'm not too into politics but he was just so nice. Very polite, very clever, and he obviously worked incredibly hard. All you ever read about was how he did such a bad job. He couldn't win. Everyone just focused on the negative' – Murray happened to mention that his mother Judy's burning ambition was to open a tennis academy in Scotland. A few days later the telephone rang in Judy's home in Bridge of Allen requesting her presence at lunch with the Prime Minister at 10 Downing Street to discuss the logistics.

By now you may have formed the impression that if young master Murray were any more laid-back he would be reclining in a deckchair; he is also amusing, articulate, modest and gracious, although I have to admit to a level of bias as someone who has known him from boyhood. A genuinely likeble young man who, among those he knows and trusts, is happy to discuss any topic except the events of 13 March 1996, when Thomas

Hamilton shot dead 16 of his fellow pupils and their teacher in the gymnasium of Dunblane Primary School. 'I was very young so, fortunately, I don't remember too much about it now. It was very scary but I didn't fully understand what was happening. One of my best friend's brothers died but I didn't find out until about two or three days after it happened.'

In the past, his colourful on-court language and pithy Scots humour have led to misunderstandings among those of the English persuasion who, accustomed to Henman's clean-cut, boy-next-door image, regarded Murray as dour, unapproachable and downright rude on occasion, leading to several phone-ins on Radio 5 Live to discuss why he cannot conduct himself in the manner of Tim. Understandably, Judy Murray is fiercely protective of both her tennis playing sons. 'It goes without saying that I'm really proud of them – what mum isn't proud of her children? – but what I'm most chuffed about is that despite what they've achieved, they're exactly the same boys they always were; I love that about them both. I know that sometimes on court Andy's behaviour is not what I would choose but he is what he is. Off court he's great fun and so laid-back it's unbelievable. He's never in a foul mood – Jamie's much more likely to let rip than Andy – but people don't get to see that side of him. He's got no interest whatsoever in being a celebrity, he just wants to get out on court and do his job.'

Murray could not give two figs for the opinion of those for whom he has scant regard, even those who follow him around the world armed with reporters' notebooks. So deep rooted are his suspicions that there are certain members of the tennis writing fraternity who are just waiting for the opportunity to let fly with their slings and arrows that when it came time to pen his 'autobiography' four years ago it was no surprise that he looked outside their closed circle to appoint his 'ghost'. So why has he developed this intrinsic mistrust of those with whom he has to work on a daily basis?

'Oh, there are all sorts of reasons. Take the England–Scotland affair.' Aye, this is a young man with a long memory when it comes to being crossed. During the build-up to the 2006 Wimbledon championships and World Cup finals, Murray and Henman were conducting a light-hearted television interview when the Scot was asked to identify which country he would be supporting in Germany given Scotland's absence from the tournament. 'Whoever England are playing,' came the reply.

'I chuckled as I said it, I had a great big smile on my face. It should have been patently obvious to everyone that I was joking but it wasn't reported like that. They made up all sorts of stories about me buying a Paraguay shirt, the whole thing was absolute nonsense. Over the past year or two, it's started to finally die down but around the time it wasn't particularly nice. People tend not to mention it to me any more so much but I would guess there is someone out there who still thinks that I don't like the English.' Murray does not go quite as far as to plead, 'Honestly, some of my best friends are Sassenachs,' but surely the presence of his English rose girlfriend Kim Sears at his side says it all.

'Prior to his Wimbledon 2012, when he won over even his sternest critics with his racket and tears, it is fair to say that reaction in the south had been mixed, even while all Scotland rejoiced in their 'Super-Brat'. 'I'm very proud because I don't get home as much as I would like. Our national football and rugby teams have been struggling in recent years, so it's nice everyone is suddenly talking about a tennis player because Scotland has never been a hotbed of tennis before. If I can inspire other kids to take up the game, then that's brilliant.'

Victory on the hallowed greensward of Wimbledon's Centre Court would inspire a generation of kids – from the Home Counties to the Highlands – so can he ever win the damn thing? 'Obviously, I know I can win. It's equally obvious that I will have to play really, really well throughout the fortnight to do so. To return to what I said earlier, Wimbledon is one of four Grand Slam titles that I'd like to win but because this is my "home game", if you like, then the pressure and the attention from the public and the media are always going to be that little bit more intense. I'm not particularly comfortable with that but it's cool – it's the life I chose.'

Should Murray fail in his endeavours, will he (like Colin Montgomerie in golf) be remembered as 'the best player never to win a Grand Slam title'? That he has the talent is unarguable, yet the niggling thought persists that for all his skills, he might lack the mental stamina to win seven best-of-five-set matches over a fortnight.

But even greater talents than Murray have ended their careers without a single victory in one of the four major championships. Ecuadorean Pancho Segura was ranked world No. 1 by the Professional Lawn Tennis Association ahead of Pancho Gonzales, Jack Kramer and Donald Budge for a spell in the early 1950s. Although his amateur career was undistinguished – he never survived beyond the quarter-finals at any of the four 'slams' – the South American flourished in the professional ranks, winning the US Indoor title from 1950 to '52 and finishing runner-up on four occasions, three times to Gonzales and, at the age of forty-two, to American Butch Bucholz in the 1962 final.

Small of stature and bow-legged, Segura may not have looked like an athlete, but with his curious double-handed forehand – which Kramer described as 'the greatest single shot in tennis history' – he was the absolute master of every conceivable angle and spin.

Segura was the best in the world; as yet Andy Murray is merely the best Briton for three-quarters of a century.

39. GRAEME OBREE
Cycling

Born: Nuneaton, Warwickshire, 11 September 1965

CAREER:
World One-Hour Record: 1993 – 51.596 km; 1994 – 52.713 km
World Track Cycling Championships: 1993 (Hamar, Norway),
    individual 4,000 metres pursuit – Gold; 1995 (Bogotá,
    Colombia), individual 4,000 metres pursuit – Gold

As an actor, Jonny Lee Miller has been required to portray many diverse roles, including a computer genius in *Hackers*, following which he married (and was swiftly divorced from) his co-star Angelina Jolie, and a scheming con artist by the name of 'Sick Boy' in *Trainspotting*. Miller was widely tipped to become the new James Bond when Pierce Brosnan relinquished his licence to kill but lost out to Daniel Craig; perhaps the casting director forgot that he could boast a family connection, his maternal grandfather Bernard Lee having played M during Sean Connery's appearances as 007.

Surely no part, however, can have been quite as demanding as that of playing Graeme Obree in the 2007 movie *The Flying Scotsman*. As Sir Chris Hoy observed: 'I found Graeme to be an inspirational figure when I was just starting out in cycling. His life is like a Hollywood film – a film incidentally, that you would find unbelievable if you watched it in the cinema.'

And so Obree gained a global silver screen audience as the champion who only turned to cycling as an escape from the school bullies who made his childhood a continual misery. 'I had this idea that one day I would go out for a ride, cycle over the horizon and just disappear. The trouble was that the horizon never came. I liked trees more than I liked people.' A champion who made three attempts on his own life before being diagnosed as bipolar and who conquered the world riding a bike he put together in the garage of his home in Irvine using, among other things, a number of parts filched from his wife's washing machine.

Unbelievable? Whereas his great rival Chris Boardman had a team of experts – engineers, sports scientists, psychologists, nutritionists, trainers – at his disposal, Obree was an out of work one-man band who, like Paddington Bear, existed on a diet of marmalade sandwiches. Unbelievable? When his cycle shop went bust during the recession of the 1990s, Obree faced a court summons for a debt of £492, was drinking heavily and sniffing acetylene gas in a forlorn bid to conquer his manic depression.

When Boardman, whom Obree had beaten on many an occasion in domestic events, won the individual pursuit gold medal at the Barcelona Olympics in 1992, the Scotsman realised that he had not been making full use of his talent and concentrated mind and body on breaking the world one-hour record, traditionally regarded as the blue riband of track cycling.

The one-hour record had been cloaked in mystique ever since 1893, when Frenchman Henri Desgrange covered a distance of 35.325 km in the Paris velodrome. When Belgian Eddy Merckx, whom many regard as the greatest cyclist in history, took possession of the record in 1972 his immediate reaction was 'never again', such was the physical and mental torture of hurtling around a track at over 50 kph for a lung-bursting hour.

Intrigued by the challenge since 1984, when former world champion Francesco Moser set a new mark of 51.15 km at altitude in Mexico City, Obree saw an attempt on the Italian's nine-year-old record as a way to put his financial and emotional problems behind him. 'The record had fascinated me since Moser broke it. It was the ultimate test – no traffic, one man in a velodrome against the clock. I didn't tell myself that I will attempt the record, I said I would break it. When your back is against the wall, you can say it's bad or you can say: "I'll go for it." I decided, that's it, I've as good as broken the record.'

In between training runs, Obree began building the bike that he would ride to greatness from spare parts; it was fast but not fast enough. Lost in thought while gazing at the family wash through the glass porthole of the washing machine, Obree experienced a *'eureka!'* flash of genius. 'That drum spins at 1,200 revolutions a minute,' he thought to himself. 'I wonder what the bearings are like?' Armed with a metal saw and a hammer, Obree set about dismantling the machine, removing the bearings for use in his bike's crank housing to reduce friction, plus various struts to support the frame. He also dispensed with the familiar drop handlebars, fitting a straight pair more associated with an everyday pushbike.

Not content to set off in pursuit of Moser's record aboard a converted twin-tub (am I alone in thinking that if Obree had been around at the time of the Space Race then Scotland would have put a man on the moon long before the Americans?), which he affectionately dubbed 'Old Faithful', our wacky racer decided to 'reinvent the wheel' in cycling terms by adopting a unique riding style, as bizarre looking as it was excruciatingly uncomfortable.

Known as 'the tuck', Obree folded his bent arms tightly by his side (as might a diving bird with its wings in 'attack' position) with his shoulders pressed down against the backs of his hands and his head thrust forward; not a position any human would wish to adopt for 60 seconds let alone 60 minutes whilst pedalling like fury.

On 16 July 1993, Obree and 'Old Faithful' made their assault on Moser's record (which was considered unbreakable, having been set at high altitude) in the near empty Hamar velodrome in Norway watched by a small band of family friends, a solitary British journalist and a French television crew; they failed by 500 metres, whereupon Obree, brushing away the bouquet of flowers that accompanied his sea-level 'world record' – 'I don't want them for failing' – announced that he would make a second attempt the following day. 'My scalp went numb, my feet went numb,' he explained. 'I couldn't feel my lips – all simply through the lack of oxygen. I couldn't face the prospect of failure. It was more painful than any amount of physical suffering. Everything was tied up in that record. My entire life.'

In Italy, Moser was astounded. 'I'm surprised by what Obree achieved. To be frank, I had never heard of him before. The very least I ever left between attempts was a week. To go again the next day – that astonishes me.' Drinking pints of water to ensure that he had to wake up every couple of hours to visit the lavatory and stretch his aching limbs, after a fitful night's sleep Obree was on the track at eight o'clock the following morning, astonishing more than Moser by beating the Italian's world record by 445 metres.

Although the Tour de France was in full swing, the French daily sports paper L'Equipe devoted its front page to the unknown Scot. 'There are no words, in English or French, that can do justice to this true story; no phrases capable of capturing that hour in time; no clichéd superlatives worthy of this man's fight against all odds. Obree, we wanted you to carry on riding, always, forever, until an indelible furrow had been ploughed into that wooden track in the Hamar velodrome.'

Six days later, Boardman, riding a revolutionary Lotus engineered bike which cost £500,000 – approximately £499,950 more than 'Old Faithful' – broke Obree's record in Bordeaux, and so a Steve Ovett–Seb Coe style rivalry was formed. The following month, back on the Hamar track,

Obree defeated Boardman to win the individual pursuit title at the World Championships before regaining the world one hour-record in Bordeaux in April 1994.

The Flying Scot and 'Old Faithful' were denied a defence of the pursuit title at the 1994 World Championships in Palermo, Italy, where one hour before the start of the competition, officials decreed Obree's riding style illegal. It was to be a bleak year: in October, his brother, Gordon, was killed in a car accident, following which Graeme was found hanging from a tree on a farm near his Ayrshire home, the third time he had attempted to commit suicide.

With the unstinting love of his wife, Anne, Obree battled back from the twin diseases of alcoholism and depression to reappear with a new Superman riding style, his arms fully extended to the front. His satisfaction at regaining the pursuit gold medal at the 1995 World Championships was understandably intense, especially since Hein Verbruggen, the president of cycling's governing body and the man responsible for banning 'the tuck' was at the trackside in Bogotá. 'That Verbruggen was there to present the medals was undoubtedly an added incentive.'

Alas, for a number of reasons, Obree was never given the opportunity of following Boardman on to the Tour de France or the lucrative sponsorship deals enjoyed by many a lesser talent. 'I suppose the biggest regret of my career is ever mentioning to a journalist that there was a bit from a washing machine in my bike. I was forever remembered thereafter as "the washing machine guy". A good sponsor was not going to go with an athlete associated with a bike built from bric-a-brac.' Or perhaps it was his vehement opposition to the drug cheats who inhabited the tour; Obree was always vociferous in his condemnation of those who reached for a hypodermic or a pill box to pedal faster.

Whereas some rode for money or glory, Obree revealed that he was propelled by the fear of failure. 'Even when I was out training, I was driven by fear. Every day, I would really psyche myself up, then ride as though my life depended on it. It was all about fear. If I didn't train well, I wouldn't race well. If I didn't race well, I would never win anything. If I never won anything, nobody would think I was worthy.'

Graeme Obree was one of sport's worthiest champions.

40. RODNEY PATTISON MBE
Yachting

Born: Campbeltown, Argyll, 5 August 1943

CAREER:
Olympic Games:
  Mexico City 1968: Flying Dutchman – Gold
  Munich 1972: Flying Dutchman – Gold
  Montreal 1976: Flying Dutchman – Silver
World Championships:
  Burnham, England 1960: Cadet – Gold
  Acapulco, Mexico 1968: Flying Dutchman – Gold
  Naples, Italy 1969: Flying Dutchman – Gold; ¼ Ton – Gold
  Adelaide, Australia 1970: Flying Dutchman – Gold; Soling –
    Gold
  La Rochelle, France 1971: Flying Dutchman – Gold
European Championships:
  Balatonfured, Hungary 1968: Flying Dutchman – Gold
  La Rochelle, France 1971: Flying Dutchman – Gold
  Medemblik, Netherlands 1972: Flying Dutchman – Gold
  Travemunde, Germany 1975: Flying Dutchman – Gold

When Rodney Pattison won his second Olympic gold medal at the 1972 Munich Games, one Fleet Street tabloid hailed him as 'this nation's greatest sailor since Nelson'. Although he has never been honoured with a 169-ft column in Trafalgar Square to commemorate his great sea victories, Pattison towered over all others in the Flying Dutchman Class, in which he also won four world and four European championships.

Like the good admiral Horatio, Pattison was the master commander, blessed with a near mystical knack of persuading the elements to bow to his wishes. In yachting clubhouse bars the world over, sailors would sip their ales and exchange muttered tales of Pattison's fiendish powers. If one skipper could sniff out a race-winning puff of wind in the doldrums, then that man was the accursed Scotsman with the deceptively friendly grin.

Born into the salty air of Campbeltown, where the noisy cries of the seagulls accompany the arriving flotilla of fishing boats, Pattison moved away from this idyll at a young age to enrol at the Pangbourne Nautical College in Berkshire, which had been founded in 1917 to prepare boys for a career in the Royal or Merchant Navy. After receiving his commission, Lieutenant R.S. Pattison, who loved the sea breeze in his face, chose what most of us would regard as the very worst career opening the Navy had to offer: a dark and claustrophobic life spent under the ocean's waves as a submariner.

By then he was already a world champion, having won the Cadet Class event as a 17-year-old schoolboy at Burnham on the Essex coast, and the Navy actively encouraged his sporting ambitions, a debt he repaid by winning the 1968 World and European Flying Dutchman titles. Although endowed with abundant natural skill, Pattison knew he was at the mercy of the weather when under sail and utilised every trick in the nautical book to gain a human edge over his rivals.

Arriving in Acapulco for the 1968 Mexico City Olympic regatta with his crewman London solicitor Ian MacDonald-Smith two months early to prepare in the hot and humid conditions of the Pacific, Pattison made sure he was seen fitting a revolutionary shaped keel in the hull of his yacht (called *Supercalifragilisticexpialidocious* but shortened to *Superdocious*). As a what-is-he-up-to-now? debate swirled around the marina, away from prying eyes a smiling Pattison discreetly jettisoned the untested innovation before the opening race, reverting to a conventional centreboard. *Superdocious* also came equipped with an impressive-looking electronic wind indicator that drew many a covetous glance; Pattison did not have the heart to let anyone into the secret that this fabulous new gizmo was an utterly useless piece of gadgetry, having no battery.

Mexico City was the setting for one of the most memorable Summer Games in Olympic history: Tommie Smith made his iconic Civil Rights protest from atop the podium after winning the 200 metres sprint . . . Bob Beamon all but leapt out of the long-jump pit in the rarefied high-altitude air . . . Dick Fosbury won the high jump with a curious style that everyone agreed was a flop and would never catch on . . . and Tanzanian John Stephen Akhwari displayed the true Olympic spirit when he finished 57th and last in the marathon (over an hour behind gold medallist Mamo Wolde of Ethiopia) after falling and dislocating his knee joint; when asked why he had not quit, Akhwari replied: 'I don't think you understand. My country did not send me 5,000 miles to start the race. They sent me 5,000 miles to finish the race.'

And so Pattison's displays out in the Bay of Acapulco went largely unnoticed beyond the yachting community, but six victories and a second place from eight races (he was allowed to discount his worst result) earned him gold by the length of the Caledonian Canal over West German Ulli Libor. Pattison's total of three penalty points (Libor was second with 43.7) remains a record low for an Olympic regatta. 'Winning an Olympic gold medal is the ultimate in one's sport. Standing on the rostrum was special; it felt like being on top of the world.'

Widely acknowledged as the world's greatest sailor, Pattison resigned from the Navy to concentrate his efforts on competition and open a boat-building business in Poole before reaching the top of the world again at the 1972 Munich Olympics. Partnered by new crewman Christopher Davies, Pattison was again the dominant force; after winning four of the first six races held in the Baltic Sea port of Kiel, Pattison's lead over second-placed Frenchman Yves Pajot was unassailable, allowing the two Britons to skip the final race in order to begin the celebrations.

Seeking a third successive gold medal at Montreal in 1976, the Games started auspiciously for Pattison when his Great Britain teammates overwhelmingly chose him to act as the team's flag-bearer in the Opening Ceremony. The regatta also started well, with victory in the opening race, but technical problems saw Pattison slip behind West Germany's Jörg Diesch and he had to settle for a silver medal, a result he regarded as a personal failure.

Co-skipper of *Victory*, the British entry in the 1983 America's Cup that was defeated by eventual winner *Australia II* in the semi-finals, Pattison scored another triumph when he locked horns with an unknown figure in the establishment over the Government's continual refusal to grant 1972 fellow gold medallist Christopher Davies the MBE routinely awarded to all our Olympic champions since Prime Minister Harold Wilson established the practice after the 1968 Mexico City Games.

In between writing books and running his boat-building business, Pattison devoted untold time and effort into righting what he regarded as a monumental wrong. 'The system is unfair and unjust,' Pattison told the *Daily Telegraph*. 'Chris did as much as I did in 1972 but he is the only one among 50-plus Britons to have won an Olympic gold medal since 1968 and not been recognised. I am very proud of my MBE and I don't want to give it up but I am prepared to hand it back personally to the Queen. The whole thing stinks.'

Did the shy and seemingly unassuming Davies, who retired from competitive sailing to become a senior lecturer in yacht manufacture and marine technology at Southampton Institute, almost harbour a black and dastardly secret? 'I used to rack my brains,' he said, 'and the best – or worst – I could come up with was a speeding ticket I received many years ago. I just don't know, perhaps there was something I did in the past which I didn't think was important but they did.'

For his part, Pattison thought it had rather more to do with Edward Heath, the Prime Minster in 1972, who, as a keen sailor, paid a visit to Kiel at the end of the regatta during which an ever so slightly tipsy Chris Davies might have greeted him as 'Teddy'. He launched a withering broadside against Heath whom he accused of snubbing his fellow gold medallist in retribution for his light-hearted remark.

Not so, the former PM thundered in a letter to the *Daily Telegraph*. 'I am sorry to disappoint you, but there is no such case as far as I am concerned. Rodney Pattison approached me on this question by letter more than a quarter of a century after the event.

'I have no recollection of Chris being drunk, and I am used to being addressed by every variant of my Christian name, Edward. If, as described, I looked stern, it was because I had just flown up from Munich, where, together with the German Chancellor, I had been present at the Olympics when the ghastly catastrophe of the murder of some members of the Israeli team took place. This was a shattering experience and that was why I looked shaken and depressed.'

Ted Heath went on to name each and every Olympic gold medallist whom he claimed had been overlooked for a gong of some sort since 1968; a list that when scrutinised proved Pattison was right in his assertion that only his crewman had been snubbed. Thirty years after Munich, Tony Blair's government belatedly recognised Chris Davies' role in Britain's Olympic roll of honour when he was finally presented with the MBE that had long been his due.

The late Edward Heath chose the wrong man to battle on the high seas when he took on Rodney Pattison.

41. ST ANDREWS

Entering the hallowed recesses of the Royal & Ancient Golf Club clubhouse in St Andrews is like stepping inside a pyramid; an experience Arnold Palmer likened to 'being admitted to the Hall of the Gods'.

A hushed shrine where wondrous things are to be found: dark corridors lined with oil paintings depicting golfing kings . . . glass cabinets crammed with fabulous trophies fashioned from kangaroo paws and silver boomerangs . . . a hoard of ancient hickory putters, mashie-niblicks and brassies, lovingly sculpted by Willie Auchterlonie and his fellow nineteenth-century craftsmen. Chamber upon chamber of priceless antiquities.

Gazing down the first fairway with the seemingly unending stretch of golden sands to your right (where they filmed the opening scene of *Chariots of Fire*), the panorama is largely unaltered from the afternoon in 1873 when local professional Tom Kidd clutched the world's most precious claret jug on the first occasion the Open Championship was played on these links.

For St Andrews, where the eighteenth green nestles snugly in the corner of two narrow streets on the edge of the Auld Grey Toun – separated from the general public by a low, white fence and overlooked by a venerable red sandstone luxury apartment block and a quaint row of shops – is like no other golf course in the world. Critics will tell you it lacks the mighty challenge of Muirfield, the manicured glamour of Augusta, or the picture-postcard beauty of Cypress Point, but surely there can be no more starkly breathtaking or atmospheric spot on the golfing globe.

Not everyone is so besotted, however, particularly our pampered American cousins, who prefer their country clubs to be as carefully cultivated as a Californian cemetery, all rolling lawns, dyed blue ponds, banks of lilies and weeping willows. It is not an electric cart you need on this rugged coastline of Fife so much as a four-wheel-drive Land Rover. When Sam Snead first saw St Andrews spread out down below from the window of a light aircraft in 1946, he enquired of his pilot: 'Say, fella, there's an abandoned golf course down there. What did they call it back in the old days?'.

Snead's suspicions proved unfounded and he duly won the Open that year by four shots. Bobby Jones was so sceptical that he tore up his card after just six holes on his first visit and vowed never to come back. That was in 1921, yet return he did to win the Open six years later and the British Amateur title (then considered almost as important as any major) in 1930.

When he was awarded the freedom of the town at a ceremony held in front of the good citizens of St Andrews in 1958, Jones won the hearts of the entire Scottish nation with a suitably affectionate and gracious acceptance speech. 'You have to study the Old Course. And the more you study it, the more you learn. Of course the more you learn, the more you have to study it. If I could take everything out of my life except my experiences at St Andrews, I would still have enjoyed a rich and full life.'

Like so many who came before or followed after, Jones, who subsequently became one of golf's most accomplished course designers, gradually realised that St Andrews, where they have been playing golf since the 1400s, owed its subtle, deceptively uncluttered layout to the architect's pencil of God.

Former Open Championship and Masters champion Sandy Lyle, who has been treading its fairways for four decades and more, feels a sense of awe every time he returns to the place. 'I must have played over a hundred rounds, yet every time I come, St Andrews poses new problems. I am constantly finding bunkers I never knew existed before. It's unique in every way. Dripping in history but with a vibrancy you can almost touch. It doesn't matter who you are, Tiger Woods or a day visitor who has paid his green fee – don't forget, this is a public course – there is no greater thrill in golf than teeing off at St Andrews in front of the clubhouse windows.'

To the uneducated eye, it would appear God was some way short of his imaginative best on the morning he took up golf. The shared first and eighteenth fairway is really not a fairway at all, merely a giant polo field devoid of any geographical quirk save the Swilcan Burn and its tiny stone bridge which, on a frosty January morning, disappears into a curtain of mist like the path to Brigadoon.

From the third hole onwards, however, St Andrews becomes a rolling – sometimes cruel – sea of bumps and hillocks, gorse and heather, hollows and swales. And then there are the bunkers . . . a veritable desert of spiteful sand such as The Beardies, Hell Bunker, The Grave.

Although there are numerous 18-hole courses curved around St Andrews Bay – including the New Course (a mere 94 years old) – it is to the Old Course that worshippers flock from every golf-playing nation. Forty-five thousand rounds a year, which explains why the R&A deems it necessary to require 'strangers' (as they refer to visitors) to carry mats around with them at certain times of the year to protect the endangered fairways.

The day must come when departing tourists will be frisked at every Scottish airport to ensure they are not making off with a priceless divot. Perhaps the British and Greek governments might even meet to agree the exchange of the Elgin Marbles and the flagstick from the Road Hole, purloined from St Andrews by an Athenian 24-handicapper in Argyll plus-fours.

Special? Listen to the born-again Sam Snead: 'The only place in Britain that's holier is Westminster Abbey.' Or Jack Nicklaus: 'There are two British Opens. The one played at Muirfield, Lytham, Troon and the rest – and the one played at St Andrews. There is no place in the world I would rather have won a championship.' Or the late Tony Lema: 'What do I think of St Andrews? It's like going to Scotland to visit your sick grandmother. She's old and she's crotchety and she's eccentric. But look real close and my, isn't she dignified and elegant? I sincerely believe anyone who doesn't fall in love with her is totally lacking in imagination.'

Depending upon the weather, Grandma may be an elderly pussycat when the sun shines and the North Sea lies as blue and serene as the Mediterranean, but when the cauld wind blaws and she remembers to put in her teeth, St Andrews can bite your head off.

Take the infamous Road Hole, the most fiendish, the most difficult, the most round-wrecking hole on earth: the 461-yard par-four seventeenth. Asked the best way to approach the Road Hole, Arnold Palmer smiled wryly and replied: 'In an ambulance.' So what makes this stretch of coast along the North Sea, which Palmer once completed in ten ugly strokes, such a treacherous minefield?

According to the local caddies who gather in the nearby Jigger Inn of an evening to sup ale and swap Road Hole anecdotes amid much hilarity, the prescribed line of attack from the tee consists of a blind drive over the gold-lettered middle 'O' on the shed proclaiming 'St Andrews Old Course Hotel' to a narrow landing strip of fairway.

If you have avoided going out of bounds down the right and missed the jungle of rough that awaits to the left, your approach shot should be a low, controlled 'chaser' onto the obliquely angled and contoured green, hopefully avoiding the notorious ball-guzzling pot bunker that stands guard in front of the flag. Beyond the green lies further misery: a tarmac road bordered by an unforgiving stone wall behind which gather a legion of thrill seekers, folk like me who would also derive great delight in watching a nutty professor hurtling off a roof frantically flapping a set of wings fashioned from ostrich feathers in an attempt to master manned flight. You know the outcome could be catastrophic yet you cannot avert your eyes. Many are they who have crashed on the seventeenth at St Andrews.

The cruelty of the Road Hole is that danger lurks every inch of the way. During the 1978 Open Championship, tournament leader Tommy Nakajima of Japan arrived safely on the rolling green in two, only to send his putt off the green and into the sand, from where he needed four slashes to break free on his way to a traumatic nine. The bunker has henceforth been known as 'the Sands of Nakajima'.

He was neither the first nor last man to bid *sayonara* to the old Claret Jug at this spot. In 1885, local professional David Ayton led the Open by a seemingly impregnable five shots when he came to the seventeenth on the final afternoon. Short and right of the putting surface, Ayton's approach veered off into the bunker from where he sent his escape scuttling through the green and onto the road. His first chip ran up the bank, stopped and rolled back down . . . his second attempt flew the green back into the bunker which he had only recently vacated, this time taking three to get out. Ayton eventually signed for an 11, losing the Open to fellow Scot Bob Martin by two strokes.

But perhaps no golfer has been so bedevilled by the 'Curse of the Road Hole' than five times Open champion Tom Watson, who strode onto the tee on the final afternoon in 1984 tied for the lead with Severiano Ballesteros. A precision drive left him 183 yards from the pin whereupon he mystifyingly plucked a two-iron from his bag – you might as well try to land a ball on the bonnet of a Volkswagen Beetle – and duly sent his approach soaring over the green to within 18 inches of the wall.

Watson could but jab the ball onto the green some 40 ft from the flag and he holed out for a bogey at the very instant a thunderous roar of approval greeted Ballesteros's birdie on the last; it would be 25 long years before Watson would ever again be a contender in any major championship, finishing runner-up at the venerable age of 59 to compatriot Stewart Cink in the 2009 Open at Turnberry.

Armed with a handicap, it is entirely possible for anyone to play the Old Course. It is not so easy to achieve membership of the R&A, the game's ruling body (except in Mexico and the US) and just possibly the most exclusive club in the world, though it does not actually own the course on which it sits.

You need not send off for an application form – entry is strictly by invitation only – although it is possible to become an honorary member if you happen to have been born or married into the royal family like Prince Philip, the Duke of York and the Duke of Kent, or are a former US President such as George Bush Sr.

Occasionally the R&A will also see fit to admit a worthy commoner:Neil Armstrong, the first man on the moon, became a member this way, as did television's Voice of Golf, Peter Alliss, and a small band of former Open champions comprising Jack Nicklaus, Arnold Palmer, Gary Player, Tom Watson, Lee Trevino, Peter Thomson, Roberto De Vicenzo, Kel Nagle, Tony Jacklin and, most recently, Severiano Ballesteros.

Yet the R&A, for all its pomp and circumstance, is markedly less stuffy than the All England Club, say, or the Rugby Football Union, and blessed with a few quirks which suggest it also keeps a sense of humour stored among the invaluable artefacts. New captains, for instance, have to 'drive in' from the first tee and a silver replica of the ball they use is then attached to the cluster hanging on an ancient silver putter like a bunch of fruit. At the autumn dinner, new members are required to touch this ornament to their lips, a reverent ceremony Sean Connery irreverently called 'kissing the captains' balls'.

Just as Newmarket is given over to horse racing, so St Andrews is a golfing town. The Auchterlonie family still run a club-making business outside the R&A clubhouse, and another golfing equipment shop bears the name Tom Morris, though we will never know what the grand old man would have made of a cashmere sweater selling for £700 in the nearby woollen mill.

According to legend, however, that is nothing compared with the business transaction pulled off by Jock Anderson, a barman of 40 years ago at the Jigger Inn, which has stood beside the 17th tee since being converted from a railway station into a pub in the 1960s. As a sideline, Jock, so the story goes, sold off the pub's entire collection of stools and tables at the rate of one a week to visiting Americans, all nicely engraved: Tom Morris Drank Here. 26 June 1859.

42. BILL SHANKLY OBE
Football

Born: Glenbuck, Ayrshire, 2 September 1913
Died: Liverpool, 29 September 1981

CAREER (PLAYER):
Carlisle United 1932–3: 16 appearances, 0 goals
Preston North End 1933–49: 296 appearances, 13 goals; FA
    Cup 1938
Scotland 1938–9: 5 appearances, 0 goals

CAREER (MANAGER):
Carlisle United 1949–51
Grimsby Town 1951–4
Workington 1954–5
Huddersfield Town 1956–9
Liverpool 1959–74: English League Championship 1963–64,
    1965–66, 1972–73; FA Cup 1965, 1974; UEFA Cup 1973;
    Manager of the Year 1973

Merseyside: the mind reels with sights and sounds. 'She Loves You' . . .
'This Is Anfield', the intimidating plaque Bill Shankly erected above the
tunnel, 'to remind our lads who they're playing for, and to remind the
opposition who they're playing against' . . . 'All You Need Is Love' . . .
Shanks striding from the dugout, arms raised in triumph, to accept the
adulation of The Kop . . . and 'You'll Never Walk Alone' . . .

Just how did an ex-miner who began his football career in the South
Ayrshire Junior League with his local village team – the quaintly named
Glenbuck Cherrypickers – become as iconic a figure as John, Paul, George
and Ringo in his adopted city? Even the Goodison fans, who had to
suffer his mischievous jibes for many a long year – 'When I've nothing
better to do, I look down the League table to see how Everton are getting
along' – held Shanks in great affection. What they did not learn until

after his death was that before turning in every night, Shankly had made a point of taking the family dog across the road to the Everton training ground, where the obedient pooch was encouraged to leave a malodorous calling card. Bluff, gruff and armed with a devastatingly droll sense of humour – who else but Chic Murray could have been asked to portray him in a 1984 musical stage play? – Shanks was a man impossible to dislike.

As a skilful wing-half, he collected an FA Cup winner's medal with Preston North End at Wembley in 1938 and made five appearances for Scotland during a career interrupted by war. As the young manager of Carlisle United, Shankly's potential for greatness had first been spotted by Liverpool in 1951, when they interviewed him for the post recently relinquished by George Kay. It was not a happy meeting of minds: Shankly was informed that although he could select the team, the directors retained the right to make any changes they deemed appropriate.

'I was just over thirty-six [*sic*] years old then. I hadn't long finished playing and I was young and fit and ambitious. Liverpool were in the First Division but they were struggling. I could have started the job eight years earlier than I did. God Almighty, what I would have done for Liverpool then. But a manager must be a manager. He is in charge of the players and the training staff. He organises the training and the coaching, lays down the law – and picks the team. Without that he is nothing. So I just said, "If I don't pick the team, what am I manager of?" And that was that.'

While the Reds slid into decline, Shankly continued his managerial apprenticeship by moving to Grimsby, Workington and Huddersfield Town, where he exacted full revenge on the short-sighted Liverpool directors by guiding his team to a 5–0 victory over their guests at Leeds Road. When Liverpool came calling again in 1959 – by which time the club was flirting with the Third Division – the board were at pains not to repeat their crass error (although there would be conflict ahead nonetheless). 'How would you like to manage the best club in the country?' proposed chairman Tom Williams. 'Why?' came the Shanks response. 'Is Matt Busby packing it in?'

And so Bill Shankly descended upon Anfield harbouring a dream; an outrageous, fantastic, improbable dream. 'My dream is to build Liverpool into a bastion of invincibility. Napoleon had the same dream. He wanted to conquer the bloody world. I want Liverpool to be untouchable.'

As history now records, Shanks achieved just that, winning three League Championships, two FA Cups plus the UEFA Cup and, more importantly, laying the foundations that would transform a struggling

Liverpool into the greatest club side in the world 20 years into the future. Not that there was any indication of the glories to come when the new boss's first game resulted in a 4–0 humiliation against Cardiff City at Anfield in December 1959, convincing Shanks that he would have to embark on a major shopping spree.

The Liverpool board of directors did not share his spendthrift notions, however, and although a transfer bid was made for Leeds United centre-half Jack Charlton, the modest offer was swiftly rejected. Seeking new players in his own uncompromising image, Shanks then tried to sign Hearts' granite-hard Scottish international Dave Mackay, only for Tottenham to snatch the inspirational wing-half from under his nose. Less than a month after arriving at Anfield from Huddersfield Town, Shankly threatened to resign unless funds were made available.

Having successfully called Liverpool's bluff, Shanks set about assembling a team which he felt could not only win the Second Division championship but also become a force in the land. Shanks injected a vein of Scottish steel into the team with the signing of left-half Willie Stevenson from Rangers, centre-forward Ian St John from Motherwell and, the final part of his original jigsaw, centre-half Ron Yeats from Dundee United. 'Big Ron was a fantastic-looking man, with jet black hair,' recalled Shankly of the towering figure he would appoint captain. 'The first time I saw him he was wearing a light-grey suit and I said, "It should be Hollywood you're going to." He was better looking than all the film stars. When he came to Liverpool, I invited all the press boys into the dressing-room and told them, "Go on, walk around him. Take a good look. He's my Colossus!" With this man at centre-half we could play Jimmy Clitheroe [a popular 4 ft 3 in. comedian of the time] in goal.'

The memory can still bring a broad smile to Yeats' face. 'It's a bit embarrassing being called Colossus when you've just stepped out the shower and are standing there stark naked in front of a bunch of guys holding notebooks. But no manager has ever loved his club more than Shanks. Sir Alex Ferguson and Jock Stein might be the only ones who stand comparison. It was a wonderful honour to be Shanks' captain for ten years and I'm lucky that so many people continue to recognise me, probably because they've seen pictures of me receiving the FA Cup from the Queen.'

The master of mind-games, Shankly wrought other changes, discarding Liverpool's traditional white shorts and socks in favour of the all red strip now as familiar as Real Madrid's all white ensemble. 'Our game against Anderlecht at Anfield in November '64 was a milestone. That was the night we wore all scarlet for the first time. The players looked like giants. And we played like giants. The introduction of the new strip had a huge psychological effect. I went home that night and I said to my wife Ness: "You know something . . . tonight I went out onto Anfield and for the first time there was a glow like a fire was burning."'

Tales of Shankly's humour are legion but let us ask skipper Yeats for his fondest memories of the great man. 'Goalkeeper Tommy Lawrence – who we called the "Flying Pig" because of his less than svelte body shape – was scared to death of him. After our final tactic talk on Fridays – during which Shanks could talk for an hour and a half without pause – he would pick one of the first-team players to compete in a penalty challenge, with the loser donating a tenner to charity. Comes my turn: me, who had never taken a penalty in my life, and Shanks, who was a lovely kicker of the ball, slots home his first two against Tommy with all the players crowded around the back of the goal crying with laughter. Shanks scuffed his third attempt and Tommy managed to get a hand to it. Before Tommy could get to his feet Shanks, who hated losing at anything, was standing over him glaring down. "I was lucky there, boss." "Aye, you were lucky, you fat twat," came the reply.

'And now it's my turn; first one top corner, second one I close my eyes and the ball goes right as Tommy goes left. Number three I hit the best left-foot shot of my life, top corner just beyond Tommy's fingertips. Shanks, who hadn't lost in over a year, stood over Tommy's body. "Not so lucky that time, eh, Tommy? But I'll tell you what" – and Shanks never swore – "if it had been a fucking meat pie you'd have caught it"!'

And finally, to a confrontation with Tony Hateley, signed from Chelsea for £180,000 and shipped to Coventry less than two years later at a considerable loss after scoring but a handful of goals. 'Shanks didn't know he was a naturally funny man. "Big man, I don't know why I signed you: you can't kick a ball, you can't pass a ball, you can't shoot . . ." Big Tony lost the head at this point: "I'll give you that, boss, but you have to admit I'm great in the air."

"I'll grant you that, son, but so was Douglas Bader and he had two better legs than you'll ever have."'

What separated Shanks from most of his peers was his relationship with the Liverpool fans; they genuinely loved him and that devotion was reciprocated in full. 'The word "fantastic" has been used many times,' said Shankly, 'so I would have to invent another word to fully describe the Anfield spectators. It is more than fanaticism, it's a religion. To the many thousands who come here to worship, Anfield isn't a football ground, it's a sort of shrine. These people are not simply fans, they're more like members of one tremendous family.' On one occasion, Shankly erupted from the dugout to berate a Merseyside bobby for kicking a fan's scarf along the track: 'Don't ever do that – it's the lad's very life.'

To a man, the Liverpool players also adored their gaffer, who never failed to describe every one as a 'Superman in Red'. 'I don't believe everything Bill tells me about his players,' laughed his close friend, Jock Stein. 'If they're as good as he claims, they'd not only have won the European Cup, but the Ryder Cup, the Boat Race and even the Grand National.'

To the continentals, Shankly was a constant source of bafflement. On one European trip he was required to fill in a hotel registration form. Under 'Occupation' he wrote 'Football', and under 'Home Address' the single word 'Anfield'. 'But, sir, we need your full home address,' protested the woman at reception. 'Young lady,' came the reply, 'in Liverpool there is only one address which matters and that is where I live.'

But Shanks always insisted that his greatest signing was not Ian St John, Roger Hunt or even Kevin Keegan, but his loving and beloved wife, Ness. Although never as demonstrative as her husband, Ness, too, came blessed with a nice line in humour. Such as the time she was asked to confirm the rumour that Bill had taken her to a Tranmere Rovers game by way of a wedding anniversary present. 'Not true,' she said firmly. 'It was to see Accrington Stanley.'

43. JOCK STEIN CBE
Football

Born: Burnbank, Lanarkshire, 5 October 1922
Died: Cardiff, 10 September 1985

CAREER (PLAYER):
Albion Rovers 1942–50: 71 appearances, 4 goals
Llanelli Town 1950–1: unknown
Celtic 1951–6: 106 appearances, 2 goals; Scottish League Championship 1954; Scottish Cup 1954

CAREER (MANAGER):
Dunfermline Athletic 1960–4: Scottish Cup 1961
Hibernian 1964–5
Celtic 1965–78: Scottish League Championship 1965–66, 1966–67, 1967–68, 1968–69, 1969–70, 1970–71, 1971–72, 1972–73, 1973–74, 1976–77; Scottish Cup 1965, 1967, 1969, 1971, 1972, 1974, 1975, 1977; Scottish League Cup 1966, 1967, 1968, 1969, 1970, 1975; European Cup 1967
Leeds United 1978
Scotland 1978–85: World Cup finals 1982, 1986

'Gentlemen, I think I've found a manager.' So announced chairman Sir Robert Kelly on his return to the Celtic boardroom from a clandestine meeting with Jock Stein in March 1965. To be strictly accurate, Jock Stein, the master manipulator, had found himself a club.

Having guided Hibernian to third place in the League with a series of scintillating attacking displays during his few short months at Easter Road – highlighted by a 2–0 defeat of five times European Cup winners Real Madrid in a friendly – Stein was in demand. Wolverhampton Wanderers wanted him to replace Stan Cullis – surprisingly sacked after leading Wolves to three League titles and two FA Cup successes – but Stein had his heart set on a return to Celtic, who had not won the championship since 1954 under the benign but ineffective stewardship of Jimmy McGrory.

And so he engineered the discussion with Kelly, ostensibly to seek the older man's advice about the wisdom of moving to Molineux but, in reality, to force Celtic's hand. When the Parkhead godfather suggested he might like to serve as assistant to Sean Fallon, it was an offer that Stein found easy to turn down; so, too, the compromise proposal of a role as joint-manager. It has been claimed that Kelly was reluctant to appoint the first Protestant manager in the club's long history but, faced with the prospect of losing Stein to the Midlands, by the end of negotiations he discovered himself doing just that.

And what a manager he proved to be: under Stein, Celtic would win ten League Championships in twelve seasons (including the famous nine-in-a-row run from 1966–74), eight Scottish Cups, six League Cups and, towering above all other triumphs, the Lisbon Lions' European Cup victory of 1967.

Like the two other members of the great triumvirate – Matt Busby and Bill Shankly – Stein was born into an impoverished mining community during the Great Depression, combining his life at the coal face with donning the number 5 shirt for Albion Rovers on a Saturday while fired with the ambition of signing for Rangers, the club his entire family supported.

When Stein, a take-no-prisoners centre-half of the old school, did leave Rovers, his destination was not Ibrox Stadium but the rather less salubrious surroundings of Stebonheath Park, Llanelli, where the Welsh club were offering seasoned professionals £12 a week in a bid to gain entry to England's old Fourth Division. It was to be a brief stay in the valleys, Stein deciding on a return to Scotland after his home in Hamilton (where his wife, Jean, and young daughter, Rae, remained) had been broken into twice in a matter of weeks.

Celtic provided an unlikely lifeline, although the Parkhead supporters were less than enthused by the arrival of a 29-year-old former Albion Rovers defender who was deemed to be a 'Blue Nose'. It is safe to say that Stein's family and friends were equally unimpressed, especially when he captained Celtic to the League and Cup double in 1954.

When he retired two years later due to a chronic ankle injury, Celtic offered Stein the position of youth and reserve team coach, a position which introduced him to a number of Parkhead cubs who would develop into Lions. Celtic only realised the managerial genius they had in their midst, however, when they nonchalantly allowed him to assume control of relegation threatened Dunfermline in March 1960.

Stein's impact at East End Park was both sudden and dramatic, Athletic winning their last six games of the season to salvage their First Division status before winning the Scottish Cup for the first time by beating their boss's former employers at Hampden in 1961, thereby qualifying for the European Cup-Winners' Cup in which they reached the quarter-finals.

Dunfermline's next incursion into Europe, after finishing fourth in the League the following year, brought headlines across the continent. In the first round of the 1962–63 Inter-Cities Fairs Cup (the forerunner of the UEFA Cup), they were drawn to play Everton, nicknamed the 'Bank of England Club', owing to manager Harry Catterick's spend-spend-spend philosophy.

Catterick's money was no match for Stein's tactical guile, however, the Fifers winning both legs against an Everton side that would go on to win the English First Division by six points over Spurs a few months later with their gathering of international players such as Alec Young, Alex Parker and Jimmy Gabriel (Scotland), Brian Labone and Gordon West (England), Roy Vernon (Wales) and Billy Bingham (Northern Ireland).

From relegation candidates to conquerors of England's champions elect in their own citadel of Goodison, Stein then took his transformed team to Spain, where their European adventure appeared doomed after a 4–0 thumping against a classy Valencia side. The return on a frosty December night is still talked about in the pubs around East End Park on match days. To a man, the Spanish players wore gloves (oh, bless) but might have been better served by balaclavas to hide their humiliation as they were thrashed 6–2 by the rampant Fifers. Dunfermline lost the resultant play-off against Valencia (who would go on to beat Dinamo Zagreb in the final) by a single goal in front of a paltry crowd of just 2,500 in Lisbon; rather more would assemble when Stein returned to the city in triumph with his Lions less than five years later.

Their lost son's success at Dunfermline and subsequent revitalisation of Hibernian did not pass unnoticed at Parkhead and so, despite Sir Robert Kelly's misgivings over the thorny issue of religion, he also granted Stein unprecedented powers over team selection, transfer negotiations and the like to secure his signature on a contract.

In rapid time, Celtic became the most powerful team in the land but Stein's ambitions lay far beyond the shores of Scotland. However satisfying domestic success might be, it was in Europe that true glory lay; and so he visited Real Madrid and Barcelona, AC Milan and Inter Milan, to study Continental training techniques while spending hours on the phone discussing tactics with his close friend Bill Shankly.

By the time of Lisbon, Celtic were the best prepared team in European football, managed by the most astute coach in the game. What was astounding is that whereas Real Madrid conquered Europe with players drawn from Hungary, France, Brazil, Argentina and Uruguay, Stein did so with 11 men who were born within a one-gallon car journey of Parkhead.

'John, you're immortal,' pronounced Shanks, a stickler for using his friend's given Christian name and the first visitor into the Lions' dressing-room.

'There is not a prouder man on God's Earth than me at this moment,' said Stein in the immediate aftermath of the Lions' 2–1 dismantling of the Italian champions, Internazionale. 'Winning was important, aye, but it was the way that we have won that has filled me with satisfaction. We did it by playing football. Pure, beautiful, inventive football. There was not a negative thought in our heads. Inter played right into our hands; it's so sad to see such gifted players shackled by a system that restricts their freedom to think and to act. Our fans would never accept that sort of sterile approach. Our objective is always to try to win with style.'

As the manager of the first British club to win the European Cup, it seems inconceivable that Stein was not invited to Buckingham Palace to bend the knee before the Queen and arise as 'Sir Jock', or that Celtic did not see fit to promise him a job for life. Instead of which, he was denied a knighthood ostensibly for Celtic's role in the infamous 1967 World Club Championship match in Buenos Aires where four Parkhead players were sent off (he was awarded a CBE in 1970) while Celtic were equally miserly with their gratitude.

When Manchester United offered Stein the manager's office at Old Trafford following Sir Matt Busby's retirement in 1971, Celtic made no counter offer to the leading coach in world football and it was only Jean Stein's reluctance to leave her home in Glasgow that kept her husband at Parkhead. The parting of the ways had merely been postponed, however. After recovering from a near fatal car crash in 1975, Stein returned to lead the club to a League and Cup double in '77 but when the following season ended without a trophy, the Celtic directors moved to install Lisbon Lions skipper Billy McNeill as manager, offering Stein a humiliating position with the club's pools company.

A seat on the board, a role as a roving ambassador or the position of director of football might all have kept Stein at Parkhead. And so it was with an air of sadness that he almost reluctantly agreed to become manager of Leeds United, a position he held for just 45 days (24 hours more than Brian Clough before him) until accepting the position of Scottish national coach.

Under Stein's guidance, Scotland qualified for the 1982 World Cup in Spain and were about to secure their place in the 1986 tournament in Mexico when he collapsed and died of a heart attack near the end of the final group match against Wales in Cardiff.

His assistant, protégé and young friend Alex Ferguson would lead Scotland to Mexico in his stead. 'When wee Jim [McLean] gave up the job as Jock's assistant with the national team, I was praying the Big Man would phone me,' said Ferguson. 'I needed something extra as a manager and there was no one better qualified than Jock to provide that, so when he did ring up I grabbed the chance. Jock had a bigger intelligence network – he certainly had far more spies – than the CIA and the KGB put together. He knew everything that was happening before it happened. He used to phone me on a Friday night and casually ask, "So how are things going up in Aberdeen?" And by his tone of voice it was as though he was saying, "You might as well tell me because I know anyway." And I'd tell him the lot, I poured it out. "Well, I've made a bid for Billy Stark at St Mirren because it looks as though wee Strachan will be leaving in the summer." And Jock would reply, "Good, good, I was going to advise exactly the same thing."

'Like all great people, he was blessed with deep humility. I was young and eager to learn, so I'd quiz him about his various tactics in Europe. Jock, who'd out-thought everyone, was totally matter-of-fact. "Ach," he'd say, "wee Jimmy [Johnstone] was brilliant that night," or "[Bobby] Murdoch was fabulous," never, ever a word about his own role in making the Lisbon Lions champions of Europe. He never took any credit and that was a great example to me. I think I drove him crazy with all my questions but he was incredibly generous with his knowledge. Jock could be serious but he could also be great fun and we'd often sit up until two in the morning in a Scotland team hotel where he'd regale me with one hilarious tale after another – invariably involving wee Jimmy.'

Graeme Souness was another who stood in awe before the 'Big Man'. 'Bob Paisley was brilliant but he sometimes struggled to communicate with the players. Joe Fagan had the technical knowledge and could communicate but he got the Liverpool job when maybe he was too old for it. Jock had everything. He had the knowledge; he had that wee nasty bit that all great managers must have; and he could communicate. On top of all that, he was six feet tall and seemed to grow bigger as he was talking to you. He was the best.'

Not that Stein was convinced of his lasting stature in the game at home and abroad. 'Ach, we all end up yesterday's men in this business. In football, you're very quickly forgotten,' he was fond of saying. For once, the 'Big Man' was wrong, and Shanks was right: Jock Stein is a football immortal.

44. SIR JACKIE STEWART OBE
Motor Racing

Born: Dumbarton, 11 June 1939

CAREER:
Formula One world champion 1969, 1971, 1973
F1 Grands Prix (27 wins, 99 races):
  1965: Italian
  1966: Monaco
  1968: German, Dutch, United States
  1969: French, British, Dutch, Italian, South African, Spanish
  1970: Spanish
  1971: Canadian, French, German, British, Monaco, Spanish
  1972: Argentinian, Canadian, French, United States
  1973: Belgian, German, Dutch, Monaco, South African

'Not too long ago, I lay in bed and counted all the people I've known who died racing and after a while, maybe an hour, I'd reached fifty-seven.'

As a devoted husband and father, Jackie Stewart vowed to hand over the keys to his racing car before the time might come for one of his friends to number him among the dead. At the age of 34, therefore, he announced his intention to pursue a less perilous way of life at the end of the 1973 season, the climax of which, the United States Grand Prix at Watkins Glen, would mark his 100th appearance in Formula One.

Having previously taken the chequered flag in Belgium, Germany, Holland, Monaco and South Africa, Stewart had secured his third world title by the time the F1 travelling circus unhitched their trailers by the shores of Lake Seneca in upstate New York. He was in carefree mood, like a schoolboy contemplating the endless summer ahead on the last day of term.

Then on the final day of practice, Stewart's young friend and Tyrell teammate François Cevert was killed instantly when he crashed through the barriers on a fast bend, the supposed safety fence slicing the twenty-nine-year-old Frenchman's body in two between neck and hip. Among the first on the scene, Stewart took one glance – 'They had left François in the car because he was so clearly dead' – returned to the pits, withdrew from the race and walked away from motor racing at the height of his success and renown before his 100th race.

In his extraordinarily detailed autobiography, *Winning Is Not Enough* – at 170,000 words around twice the length of an average sporting memoir – Stewart wrote:

> Imagine an eleven-year window of time when you lose fifty-seven – I repeat, fifty-seven – friends and colleagues, often watching them die in horrific circumstances, doing exactly what you do, weekend after weekend. To be a racing driver between 1963 and 1973 was to accept the possibility, the probability of death, because the statistics suggested during that period that if an F1 driver was to race for five years or more, he would be more likely to lose his life on the track than to survive and retire.
>
> What these cold statistics don't record is the hush that used to descend over the pit lane when an ambulance appeared . . . the sense of foreboding that used to spread through this small community when a black plume of smoke rose on the other side of the circuit . . . the unimaginably brutal way people died . . . how it felt to be a driver continuing a race, speeding by and catching a glimpse of a crumpled car or the body of a friend . . . the agony of a devastated wife and the fear in the eyes of other wives as they wondered if it might be their turn next.

Seven years before Cevert's death, Stewart had brushed against his own mortality during his second season in F1 when, after winning in Monaco and being denied victory in the Indianapolis 500 by engine failure in the closing stages, having built up a lead of over a lap, he came to grief on the first lap of the Belgian Grand Prix at Spa Francorchamps. Driving in heavy rain, Stewart's BRM aquaplaned off the circuit at 165 mph on the Masta Kink S-bend, struck a telegraph pole, demolished a woodcutter's hut and flew over an eight-foot drop before coming to rest upside down in a farmer's barn.

His leg trapped by the steering column and driving suit soaked in leaking high octane fuel, Stewart lay there for 25 minutes while teammates Graham Hill and Bob Bondurant (both of whom had also slid off the track in the downpour) fought to free him with a box of basic tools borrowed from a spectator. Despite the imminent threat of an explosion, Hill and Bondurant maintained their heroic efforts until they finally lifted the Scot clear of the wreck.

'Graham and Bob got me out using the spanners from a spectator's toolkit. There were no doctors and there was nowhere to put me. In fact, they put me in the back of a van. Eventually an ambulance took me to a first aid spot near the control tower and I was left on a stretcher, on the floor, surrounded by cigarette ends. I was put into an ambulance with a police escort and the police escort lost the ambulance, and the ambulance didn't know how to get to Liège. At the time they thought I had a spinal injury. As it turned out, I wasn't seriously injured, but they didn't know that.

'I realised that if this was the best we had there was something sadly wrong: things wrong with the race track, the cars, the medical side, the fire-fighting and the emergency crews. There were also grass banks that were launch pads, trees that were unprotected and so on. Young people today just wouldn't understand it. It was ridiculous.'

And so, long before he became world champion, Stewart became the champion of his fellow drivers by mounting a personal crusade to improve safety standards throughout the sport. 'We were racing at circuits where there were no crash barriers in front of the pits and fuel was left lying about even though a car could have easily crashed in the pit lane at any time.'

With a spanner taped to the cockpit of his car and a private doctor standing by in readiness in the BRM pits, Stewart single-handedly challenged the might of the Formula One establishment, advocating the mandatory usage of full-face helmets, seat belts, fire-resistant race suits, thermal socks, gloves and underwear as a protection against burns, plus the introduction of crash barriers, chain-link fences, run-off areas, fire crews and improved medical facilities. Stewart regarded no venue as sacrosanct, not even the classic circuits of Spa and Nürburgring.

'Nothing gave me more satisfaction than to win at the Nürburgring and yet, I was always afraid. When I left home for the German Grand Prix, I always used to pause at the end of the driveway and take a long look back. I was never sure if I'd come home again.' Afraid, understandably, but no one could question Stewart's bravery around the 14 miles of 'the Ring' (each lap consisting of 147 arduous corners), where he won on three occasions, highlighted by his 1968 victory in a Ken Tyrell-designed Matra considered by many F1 experts to be among the greatest drives of all time.

Starting in sixth place on the grid, and with visibility drastically reduced by the rare combination of pouring rain and swirling fog, by the end of the first lap Stewart, driving with a cast to protect a broken wrist suffered in an earlier crash, had swept into a nine-second lead, after which all any of his rivals saw of him was the plume of spray disappearing ever further into the distance. By the end of the fifteen laps, he crossed the finishing line more than four minutes ahead of Graham Hill's Lotus.

The following season Stewart won six races to become world champion for the first time, even while continuing to irritate F1 officialdom, race organisers, sections of the media and even some of his fellow drivers – one of whom crassly dubbed him 'chicken' – with his incessant demands to make the sport increasingly safe. Many were they who thought the nagging Scot should stick to driving and leave safety matters to those who watched the action on television from a comfortable padded seat in the VIP grandstand with a gin and tonic or whatever to hand. 'I would have been a much more popular world champion if I had always said what people wanted to hear. I might have been dead, but definitely more popular.'

As someone who had once overheard his young son, Paul, come home from school to demand of his mother: 'When is Daddy going to get killed?' Stewart was happy to ruffle a few feathers to ensure that if he had any say in the matter then no child of the F1 family would ever ask such a question again. Thanks almost entirely to Stewart's untiring efforts, the last F1 driver to perish on the track was Ayrton Senna in 1994.

One of the half-dozen or so greatest drivers in history – up there with Fangio, Schumacher, Senna, Prost and his still mourned friend Jim Clark – long before he became Sir Jackie, Stewart had been adopted by the glitterati, partying with Prince Rainier and Princess Grace in Monte Carlo, schmoozing with Frank Sinatra backstage in Las Vegas, golfing with Sir Sean Connery and Jack Nicklaus in Marbella, clay pigeon shooting with the Princess Royal at Gleneagles. In retirement, his fame remained undimmed while he turned the fortune he had earned in F1 into a pension pot worth many, many millions through his shrewd head for business. He also returned to F1 as a team owner in the late '90s, Johnny Herbert winning the 1999 European Grand Prix at Nürburgring in a Stewart-Ford. Not bad going for a boy who had been the victim of mockery at school, where the teachers of the early 1950s freely dismissed him as stupid, blithely ignorant of the condition now known as dyslexia.

At his cheeriest manning the petrol pumps of the family's lucrative garage and car showroom in Dumbuck or stalking deer in the Dunbartonshire hills, Stewart's early sporting interests were football and shooting, becoming British Trap champion in 1959 but missing out on selection for the 1960 Rome Olympics when he was left shaking with nerves at the final trial. His life, and the history of motor racing, changed forever shortly after his Olympic disappointment when a regular customer at the pumps asked if he might like to race one of his Porsches at a sports car meeting in Ayrshire that weekend.

His meticulous drive through the ranks of sports cars, Formula Three, F2 and finally F1 – not to mention his astonishing attention to detail in all matters relating to safety – is typical of a man renowned for his fastidiousness, tidiness and punctuality. When Sir Jackie Stewart turns his mind to something, then he does so with obsessive application.

Consider this extract from *Winning Is Not Enough* concerning his role as a global ambassador for the Swiss watchmaker Rolex.

> For my part, I have sought to add value to Rolex by wearing the watch in a way that reflects positively on the company. This involves arranging for my shirts to be made with a slightly wider sleeve cuff on the left side than the right, to ensure the watch moves freely and is always visible.

And this was the man the grey suits of Formula One thought would simply go away and forget his demands if they ignored him long enough.

45. BOBBY THOMSON
Baseball

Born: Glasgow, 25 October 1923
Died: Skidaway Island, Georgia, 16 August 2010

CAREER:
New York Giants 1946–53
Milwaukee Braves 1954–7
New York Giants 1957
Chicago Cubs 1958–59
Boston Red Sox 1960
Baltimore Orioles 1960
Major League All-Star Games: 1948, 1949, 1953

Just as Wembley 1967 is a priceless treasure placed in our keeping for the wonderment of future generations, so all the fathers and all the grandfathers of America are charged with handing down the miracle of The Shot Heard Round the World.

This is the tale of Bobby Thomson, a young immigrant from Glasgow who became a baseball player in his adopted land and, with one swing of the bat, achieved sporting immortality. The Staten Island Scot, as he was known in ballparks across the States, conjured victory out of seemingly inevitable defeat by swatting the most momentous home run in baseball history. Six decades have passed, the old Polo Grounds up on 157th Street in the Bronx has long since fallen to the wrecker's ball, and even the deadly rivals involved – the New York Giants and the Brooklyn Dodgers – have decamped to San Francisco and Los Angeles, yet the echo from The Shot can be heard to this day.

When Thomson died in August 2010 at the age of 86, the *New York Times*, which is not known for delving into the realms of hyperbole, was moved to describe his home run as 'One of the greatest and most improbable moments in baseball history. Or maybe sports history. Or maybe all human history.'

Back in 1951, US President Dwight D. Eisenhower contented himself with the observation that 'In his own unique way, Bobby Thomson may have done as much to popularise baseball in this country as Babe Ruth or Joe DiMaggio. Whenever baseball people meet, he will be remembered as one of the great American heroes.'

Well, one of the great Scots-American heroes such as Alexander Graham Bell or Andrew Carnegie, to be strictly accurate. 'I came from Toonheid, as my mum called it,' recalled Thomson in an accent owing rather more to his upbringing in Noo Yoik than to the first three years of his life spent in a grim Glaswegian tenement of the 1920s. 'She was a real Scottish lady and very proud of her accent. We used to kid her all the time. "Come on, Mum, you're in America now, talk like an American." And she'd say "Ach, get awa' wi' ye. Ye ken fine whit ah'm sayin'."'

A heavily pregnant Lizzie Thomson was awaiting her sixth child when her husband, Jim, set sail on 20 October 1923 to forge a new life for his family. 'They'd waited years for the papers to come through, so, with my mum heavily pregnant, Dad decided to go on ahead, then send for us once he'd found a job and somewhere to live. We were poor and America was the land of opportunity. If Dad hadn't gone when the chance came up, then they'd have been put back to the end of the queue. He'd only

---

James Naismith

Just as it was a Scot who founded the US Navy – Captain John Paul Jones from Kirkcudbrightshire – so it was another man with Caledonian roots who invented one of America's most enduringly popular sports.

James Naismith, son of Ayrshire émigrés John and Margaret, was born in Ontario but it was while he was working as a PE teacher at the YMCA International Training School in Springfield, Massachusetts, in 1891 that he came up with the notion of basketball to keep his students active during the long New England winter. Bored with endless rounds of keep fit drills in the gym when forced to remain indoors, the young men under Naismith's care – most of whom came from troubled backgrounds – needed another sporting diversion to exercise body and mind. 'The invention of basketball was not an accident,' he explained. 'It was developed to meet a need. Those boys simply would not play "Drop the Handkerchief".'

Naismith could never have envisioned that one day far, far in the future basketball players such as Michael Jordan, Magic Johnson and Shaquille O'Neal would become global superstars when he went to work armed with a football, two peach baskets, a ladder to retrieve the ball and a few handwritten rules scrawled on a scrap of paper. Naismith decreed that there should be no tackling (this was a game to be played on unforgiving hardwood floors, after all) and no running with the ball in hand (only 'dribbling' would be allowed).

As news of 'basket ball' spread, schools and colleges across the United States rushed

been at sea five days when I was born and he didn't get to hold me until I was almost three.

'Even now, I marvel at the courage of my parents and the thousands of people like them. They were pioneers. Mum was seriously ill after I was born, but my granny moved in with us and we managed to survive – three or four to a bed – until Dad had saved enough to bring us all over in 1926.'

Young Robert, named after the youngest of four uncles killed in the First World War fighting alongside his father in the Scots' Guards, took as one of his few possessions on the long voyage across the Atlantic his scuffed leather football. 'One of my earliest memories as a bairn was of my dad and older brother, Jim junior, playing soccer – sorry, fitba'– in the street outside our home in New York. Dad was a fanatical Glasgow Rangers fan but he grew to love baseball, too. He'd walk miles to see a game, especially if the Dodgers were playing.'

Though it was in the uniform of the New York Giants that his younger son would find fame and undreamt-of riches, Jim Thomson was an impassioned follower of the Brooklyn Dodgers. 'I think Dad related to the Dodgers because they were known as "dem bums". They were always losing back in the '20s and he sympathised with them because he'd had a tough life himself. But me, I was a Giant through and through from about the age of seven.'

Bobby Thomson was just 14 when his father died after a long fight against heart disease. 'He was only in his early 40s. It was a constant regret that he didn't live to see me hit that home run. Even though it was against his beloved Dodgers, I feel he would have got a kick out of that.

'He was a proud man. A typical undemonstrative Scot but an incredibly loving father. He never failed to put me and my brother and four sisters before himself. We always went to Sunday school and even though he was often out of work during the Depression – invariably at Christmas, as I remember – every extra penny went on good clothes for us to wear to

---

to form teams but Naismith himself seldom played the game, preferring to watch quietly from the sidelines; when fans of the new sport started a campaign to rename it Naismith Ball, he refused to sanction the change. Naismith did, however, take quiet pride in the burgeoning popularity of what came to be known as basketball. 'I am sure that no man can derive more pleasure from money or power than I do from seeing a pair of basketball hoops in some out of the way place.'

Three years before his death, Naismith was a guest of honour in Berlin, where basketball made its Olympic debut in 1936, when he handed out the gold medal to the United States and silver to his native Canada. 'To watch basketball being played under the Olympic flame,' he said, 'was the proudest moment of my life.'

church. As usual, he neglected himself. Because he didn't feel his clothes were good enough to wear, he stayed home. That's the kind of man he was. Would he have been proud of me that afternoon in the Polo Grounds? Well, he used to clip me very gently on the jaw with his great fist when he was pleased with me. I guess he'd have done just that.'

The boy from Toonheid lived out his life after baseball in splendid luxury on Skidaway Island off Savannah, Georgia, where his basement was crammed with souvenirs of a glittering career in baseball, and the living quarters with treasured photographs of his late wife, Elaine (popularly known as 'Winkie'), who died suddenly in 1993, their three children and six grandchildren. 'If Mum and Dad had never come to America, if I'd never picked up a baseball bat, then I guess it's fair to say that my life would have been very different.'

Although he signed for the Giants on the day he graduated from high school in 1942 – 'A hundred dollars a month. Huge money back then for a school kid' – Thomson had to wait until he completed his military service as a bombardier in the US Air Corps before joining the club in '46. 'The Giants invited all returning servicemen to their training camp in Florida. It seemed like there was a million guys down there but I guess there was only three or four hundred of us.'

Even in an auditioning line of a million, however, Thomson's powerful hitting and speed around the bases – hence the Flying Scot nickname he also carried throughout his playing days – would have marked him down for greatness and he was sent to serve his apprenticeship with the club's nursery team in New Jersey. To a courteous young man raised in a Calvinistic Scottish household, his fellow ballplayers were a hard-drinking, tobacco-chewing band of brigands.

'I'd never been away from home before and because I was the youngest they called me "rookie". And, believe me, I was a rookie in every sense of the word. It was a whole new life, especially on road trips when we had to tour the country in an old bus for a week at a time. And, oh boy, did we have a bus. It had practically no tyres and the last three or four rows of seats at the back had no windows. Naturally, these were the seats reserved for the rookies. After a night game it was freezing cold at the back so I used to wrap myself in all the sweaty uniforms – remember there were no showers in any of the clubhouses way back then – just to keep warm.'

Blessedly, Thomson's stint at the back of the charabanc was a brief one and he graduated into the major league at the start of the 1947 season; for the next five years he was one of the nation's most popular players, as naturally talented as DiMaggio, in the opinion of many, but without Joltin' Joe's confidence or sense of destiny.

By 1951, DiMaggio's New York Yankees were the dominant force in the American League, while the Dodgers had emerged as the most powerful team in the National League. With but two months of the 154-game season remaining, the Dodgers led Thomson's Giants by 13½ wins and seemed certain to lift the league pennant and qualify to play the Yankees in the World Series.

'The Giants–Dodgers rivalry was like Rangers–Celtic times ten. We hated the Dodgers' players and they hated us, although it seems silly now. Anyway, we started winning. Game after game. Thirty-seven out of forty-four, including our last sixteen.' On the second-last day of the regular season, the Giants finally pulled level with the Dodgers and thus began the climactic three-game shoot-out for the National League pennant during which Thomson, the under-privileged 'wean' from the bleak streets of Glasgow, was to become an American icon.

Let us fast-forward through game one, which the Giants won 3–1 with a two-run homer from Thomson off ace pitcher Ralph Branca (of whom we will hear more) . . . past the Dodgers' runaway 10–0 victory in game two, which levelled the mini-series at 1–1 . . . to the ninth and last inning of the decider. 'Think about it. After 157 games we're still dead level. The last inning of the last game. Giants and Dodgers. The most bitter rivalry in sport. The whole of New York rooting for one or the other.'

By the time Thomson came up to bat for the last time, the Giants were trailing 4–2 but had two runners on base, while the tiring Dodgers' pitcher Don Newcombe, who had been in dynamic form, was in the shower, replaced by the hapless Branca.

Crack! The Shot Heard Round the World left Thomson's bat as though fired by a cannon. 'I hit it real well, heading straight for the upper deck of the stand. As I started running I was saying "home run, home run" but the ball had such tremendous topspin, it began to sink. Then just when I thought it wasn't going to clear the wall, it disappeared. We'd won 5–4 and my life changed forever.'

A generation on, it is possible to capture America's collective sense of disbelief by visiting the baseball Hall of Fame in Cooperstown, where Thomson's bat, glove and spiked shoes lie in a glass cabinet. Press the button by the side of the case and you can relive the original words of radio commentator Russ Hodges: 'Branca throws. There's a long drive : . . it's gonna be . . . I believe . . . the Giants win the pennant! The Giants win the pennant! The Giants win the pennant! Bobby Thomson hit that ball into the lower deck of the left-field stands. The Giants win the pennant and they're going crazy. They're going crazy. I don't believe it. I don't believe it. I WILL not believe it.'

In the *New York Herald Tribune*, Pulitzer Prize-winning sports journalist

Red Smith wrote, 'Now it is done. Now the story ends. And there is no way to tell it. The art of fiction is dead. Reality has strangled invention. Only the utterly impossible, the inexpressibly fantastic, can ever be plausible again.'

It was a sporting moment that touched the nation's heart like no other. American concert pianist Eugene Istomin remembers 'hearing' Thomson's shot from distant Europe. 'I was studying with Pablo Casals in the Pyrenees and listened to the game on the Armed Forces Network. When Bobby Thomson hit that home run, I jumped out of my chair and began to screech. I was a Dodgers' fan but I knew this was the most dramatic moment in sport history. Everybody in the room was stunned by my behaviour. I tried to explain it . . . but they never understood.'

Shortly before his death, Thomson received a letter from a former US Marine who had been fighting in the Korean War. 'I was in a bunker in the front line with my buddy listening to the radio. It was contrary to orders, but he was a Giants' fanatic. He never made it home and I promised him if I ever got back I'd write and tell you about the happiest moment of his life. It's taken me this long to put my feelings into words. On behalf of my buddy, thanks Bobby.'

To his dying day, Thomson was feted where're he roamed, though the Giants, drained by the emotion of the moment, lost the World Series, which began the following day, to the Yankees; he dined with presidents, played golf with Perry Como and became close friends with Branca, in whose company he made hundreds of appearances a year. 'I never thought I'd still be famous after such a passage of time but I guess baseball needs its heroes. The fans put men like DiMaggio, who had great dignity, on a pedestal. I never forgot what baseball did for me, a poor wee Scottish laddie. It's crazy, the attention I received. At first it bothered me because I didn't feel I had the right to be regarded as a hero. But it's the fans who kept alive the memory of The Shot Heard Round the World. But for that one incident, I'd have been forgotten years ago. I wasn't a washout but I could never live up to that moment. There's no excuse. Joe DiMaggio did it every day. I didn't.'

46. SAM TORRANCE MBE, OBE
Golf

Born: Largs, 24 August 1953

CAREER:
European Tour victories: 21
Others: 11
European Senior Tour victories: 11
Ryder Cup: 1981, 1983, 1985 (winners), 1987 (winners), 1989
    (winners), 1991, 1993, 1995 (winners), 2002, as non-
    playing captain (winners)

At the precise second Andy North's ball plummeted into the lake with a delicious plop, so the first tear trickled down Sam Torrance's cheek.

As he strode away from the 18th tee at The Belfry to be rejoined with his booming drive, one that seemed destined to secure the Ryder Cup for Europe, his eyes were already swimming. As he floated the gentlest of nine-irons to within twenty feet of the pin, his familiar Groucho Marx moustache was soaking. As that first unerring putt dropped into the cup for a birdie three, he was beyond caring.

And so, 26 autumns on, there stands our Sam forever frozen in time back in 1985: arms raised in ecstatic triumph, a great cheesy grin spread across that tear-stained face, a foul-smelling, half-smoked, roll-up fag jammed behind one ear. The Americans had been relieved of Sam Ryder's ancient trophy for the first time since 1957 and the honour of being the player to hole the winning putt could not have gone to a nicer man.

'Look at me . . .' blubbed Torrance, nerves a-jangle and lips a-tremble, into an out-thrust BBC microphone in a memorably unrehearsed victory speech, ' . . . and I don't give a shit.'

There never was a golfer from either side of the Atlantic who viewed the Ryder Cup more reverently than Torrance, enchanted by the contest since 1961 when he watched Arnold Palmer inspire yet another easy win for the Americans at Royal Lytham. The seven year old, who up to that weekend had desperately wanted to be a policeman patrolling the streets of Largs, where he was born and raised, sat by the television as his father, Bob, one of the modern game's pre-eminent gurus, offered a Ryder Cup history lesson by his side.

'Everyone thinks I made it up, but ask my dad if you don't believe me. Ever since watching that Ryder Cup I had two dreams. One was to win the Open at Muirfield – beating Jack Nicklaus on the last green – and the second, equally important to me, was to hole the putt that won the Ryder Cup. So I'd already sunk that putt at The Belfry a million times in my imagination.'

Torrance admits that a day seldom passes when he does not rewind the memory to that Sunday afternoon of 15 September 1985 when he stood on the eighteenth tee all square against twice US Open champion North and with Europe one point away from a historic victory. 'I'd hit a good drive myself and the moment Andy skied his, I knew it was headed straight for the water. Even as I walked up to my ball, I was aware that I'd only to get it onto the green to win.

'It was the sweetest, most emotional, single most nerve-racking moment of my sporting life. All I could think was: "Christ, I'm going to win the Ryder Cup. Me." Aye, we still get the video out every now and then, especially when my dad's down. And every time we stick it on, my eyes fill up. No matter how many times I see it, I come out in goosebumps the size of golf balls and the hairs on the back of my neck stand up. Just the thought of that moment makes me tingle all over. It's sheer magic.'

Having helped Europe retain the trophy in '87 and '89, Torrance can look back with wry amusement on his first appearance in the competition in 1981 as a naive 27-year-old tenderfoot. Drawn to meet the mighty Lee Trevino in his final-day singles, the nervous Scot was crouched over a putt on the practice green when SuperMex walked by with the whispered warning: 'Boy, I'm gonna wipe that moustache clean off your face.'

Torrance was beaten 4 and 2 but surrendered neither his dignity nor his humour and turned up for the official post-match banquet clean-shaven, having removed his beloved 'tash in Trevino's honour.

As single-minded as he was in his pursuit of precious Ryder Cup points, Torrance never forgot his roots. In the midst of a battle to win a place on the team in 1985, he skipped the Italian Open in order to contest the Scottish Professional Championship even though the event was not part of the European Tour. 'I'd learnt my golf in Scotland so I liked to support the local tournaments whenever I could. Anyway, it had always been a wee ambition of mine to get my name on the trophy alongside my first boyhood heroes, Eric Brown and John Panton. I don't suppose I can really explain why, when the Ryder Cup was so important to me, but I hadn't the slightest hesitation in playing Dalmahoy instead of Bologna that summer.'

The engaging Torrance, whose formal education ended at the age of 13, has never allowed success to change him. His first job was on the fruit'n'veg counter of his local Spar store in Largs, though he was rapidly moved on to another section of the supermarket 'when they twigged I was giving my granny bagfuls of potatoes and stuff for a few pence'. There followed stints as a van driver, cable television installations man and further consideration to joining the police before he followed his father into professional golf.

As winner of 43 tournaments worldwide, only his lifestyle has changed. He now owns a snarling cabriolet in the garage and a wardrobe cluttered with designer labels from Milan and Paris. Otherwise, he remains the Sam of old, who enjoys his Guinness, especially in the company of the opera-singing, wisecracking David Feherty, who is now a popular TV commentator on the US Tour. 'It's no secret that after I'd beaten Andy North that Sunday afternoon at The Belfry, David and I went out on a binge which lasted until four o'clock on the Wednesday morning.'

Nor has Torrance lost his liking for tobacco, though he has cut down dramatically from his peak of 60 a day since he began rolling his own in the early '80s. His present daily intake? 'Oh, I'm down to about . . . well, let's just say I've cut down, eh?' Torrance's puffing invariably intensified around Ryder Cup time, when the normal pressures 'increased tenfold'. 'It's obviously much worse when one mistake or one stroke of bad luck can rob the entire team of victory.'

Looking back over a glittering career, what stands out as his most precious memory? 'I have been blessed, truly blessed. I thought holing that putt in '85 was as special as it gets, then we won on American soil for the first time two years later at Muirfield Village, then we won perhaps the most exciting Ryder Cup contest of them all at Oak Hill in '95, when I played the best golf of my life. But the highlight of them all was the captaincy in 2002 by a mile . . . by a mile . . . by a mile . . . by a hundred miles.

'I never, ever dreamt I'd be awarded the captaincy. It just wasn't my vocation so I went through hell for those three years, fretting about the speeches. Night and day I was petrified because I knew I had to get each and every one just right. Thanks to the advice of my wife [former actress Suzanne Danielle] and my old pal David [Feherty] I like to think I didn't screw up once.'

Indeed, he did not; following on from the infamous Battle of Brookline, when passions and tempers ran high in 1999, the Torrance speeches even had the Americans dabbing their eyes. Play it again, Sam:

On greeting the American skipper and his team at the Opening Ceremony: 'Curtis [Strange], old friend, I bid you welcome to Europe, to England and to The Belfry. You are our invited guests and our worthy opponents and, as the old Scottish saying goes: "oor hoose is your hoose and you're mair than welcome here."'

Or, this, at the moment of triumph: 'Curtis, I accept the Ryder Cup into our safe keeping, and I accept it from an outstanding captain of a fine US team. We will cherish it for two years until we meet again. My last thank you is very special and it is to the winning team. I have got to say that only the birth of my children and my marriage to my wife have been more special. I will remember this forever. Thank you very much.'

When you consider all the great names to have been associated with the Ryder Cup – Nicklaus, Palmer and Trevino, Faldo, Ballesteros and Jacklin – none has been more beloved by the public than the ever-popular Slammin' Sam. But to remind him of that is to risk opening the tear ducts yet again. 'The Ryder Cup has been a part of my life since I was a tot. It's been a fairy tale and, yes, I suppose I am a legend of sorts, which is great, it's awesome. I'll be there forever now and that's a wonderful thing to think about. As I said at the time, I'd love to have bottled it and taken a wee sip every day.'

Torrance's relationship with the fans – founded at The Belfry in '85 – is joyous to behold. On the Sunday night at Muirfield Village in '87, it was Torrance who led a posse of players into the beer tent where the European spectators were celebrating. 'Jesse [Mark James], Woosie and me thought it would be nice to go along to register our thanks. The atmosphere was incredible, they greeted our arrival like the second coming. I gave away my shoes, my sweater, I'd have stripped naked for them if I thought I'd looked good. The players/fans get-together has now become a Ryder Cup tradition.'

There was a more recent but no less exuberant party in the bar of the Old Course Hotel, St Andrews, eight autumns ago when he and son Daniel emerged triumphant in the Dunhill Links team competition. 'When we went onto the practice ground before the final round, Samuel L. Jackson, the actor, looked up and called over to Daniel: "Hey, great play." Daniel was mightily chuffed the coolest of Mr Cools should recognise him.'

And there could yet be one more great celebration to come should Torrance win a major on either of the Seniors' Tours. 'It would have been lovely to win a real major, but that is a mild regret rather than a bitter disappointment because I gave it my best shot every time; sadly, I just wasn't good enough in the weeks it counted, so it would be nice to put that right among the golden oldies. I was incredibly lucky to start out on a new career when I turned 50 in 2003 – an opportunity unique to golfers – and sit around a table in the clubhouse listening to the likes of the Golden Bear spinning his yarns. Jack Nicklaus was, and remains, my ultimate golfing hero apart from my dad. Only recently I told him: "Jack, the greatest compliment I can pay you is that in the 400 majors I won in my imagination, you were runner-up every time." He absolutely loved that.'

The greatest compliment I can pay Sam Torrance is that from Routenburn Golf Club to Ryder Cup glory, the man has never changed.

47. ALLAN WELLS MBE

Athletics

Born: Edinburgh, 3 May 1952

CAREER:

Olympic Games:
  Moscow 1980: 100 metres – Gold; 200 metres – Silver
World Cup:
  Rome 1981: 100 metres – Gold; 200 metres – Silver
Commonwealth Games:
  Edmonton 1978: 200 metres – Gold; 4x100 metres relay –
    Gold; 100 metres – Silver
  Brisbane 1982: 100 metres – Gold; 200 metres – Gold;
    4x100 metres relay – Bronze
IAAF Golden Sprints:
  Zurich 1979 – Silver
  Berlin 1981 – Gold

In stark contrast to Usain Bolt, who is feted as a visiting monarch where'er he roams, Allan Wells swiftly became accustomed to being treated like a sporting pariah following his gold-medal-winning run in the 100 metres at the Moscow Olympics of 1980.

Like Britain's other Olympic champions that July – Daley Thompson, Steve Ovett, Sebastian Coe and swimmer Duncan Goodhew – Wells did not return home to a champagne reception at No. 10 Downing Street, followed by an open top bus ride through the streets of London to the cheers of a grateful nation, then on to a medal ceremony at Buckingham Palace. Indeed, it would be a further two years before Wells' 'treacherous' victory in front of Russian leader Leonid Brezhnev was pardoned when he was belatedly awarded an MBE.

To show her displeasure at the Soviet invasion of Afghanistan, Margaret Thatcher had tried everything in her Prime Ministerial powers to dissuade British athletes from competing in the Games. That only the hockey squad plus a few individuals should heed her counsel was tantamount to treason in the mind of the Iron Lady, who decreed that there should be no official recognition of the Olympic champions' efforts on the Communist side of the Iron Curtain.

'The pressure we were put under in the months leading up to Moscow was immoral,' recalled Wells. 'I received six personal letters from No. 10 Downing Street, the last of which included a picture of a wee girl sprawled dead on the ground with a doll lying a few inches from the tips of her fingers. It made me so angry that I became even more determined to compete. It was a very distasteful and underhand tactic; if at any time I had thought that by boycotting the Olympics one child was not going to be killed, then I wouldn't have hesitated in staying behind, but in my heart I couldn't see how my presence in Moscow was going to cause more deaths.'

From his Oval Office in the White House, Jimmy Carter was rather more successful than Mrs Thatcher in using questionable moral blackmail to bring about a blanket boycott of American sportsmen and women – plus those of sixty-one other nations – and so when Wells went to the starting blocks for the 100 metres final there were no nephews of Uncle Sam in the eight-man field. 'You can only beat those who show up,' he muttered darkly before settling into the starting blocks in lane eight, with local favourite Aleksandr Aksinin, Poland's Marian Woronin, Petar Petrov of Bulgaria and Cuba's Silvio Leonard, the third fastest man of all time, arrayed on his left.

By the 60-metre mark, the gold medal contest was a two-man duel between Wells and Leonard, the Scot timing his dip to perfection to defeat the Cuban by three inches – although they were both timed in 10.25 sec – to become the first Briton to win a sprint gold since Harold Abrahams in 1924 and the oldest 100 metres champion in Olympic history at the time. 'I didn't even get to hear "God Save the Queen" when I stood on the podium after receiving my gold medal. They played the Olympic anthem instead which, as it happened, was a tune I particularly liked.'

The 200 metres final was no less compelling, pitching Wells and Leonard against defending champion Don Quarrie of Jamaica and Italy's world record holder Pietro Mennea. Seeking the sprint double, Wells made an electrifying start and, coming out of the turn into the straight, he held a comfortable two-metre lead only to be overtaken by Mennea in the final strides to the line as the 103,000 spectators in the Lenin Stadium rose to their feet in acclamation of both athletes.

On returning to Britain, Wells realised the golden run for which he had trained so long and hard had not met with universal jubilation. 'I was enjoying a training run through the park when a woman stopped me to ask for my autograph. As I was signing the slip of paper, a chap walked past about 20 yards away and shouted over. "What did he say?" asked the young lady. "He was informing me that I only won because the Americans weren't there. And do you know what? He doesn't realise he's just done me the biggest favour possible; he's reminded me that I've still got something to do. I now know that Moscow isn't the end of anything, it's the beginning."'

Never one to shirk any challenge, a fortnight after being crowned Olympic champion, Wells dragged his wearied mind and body (he had run in the heats, semi-finals and final of the 100 metres, 200 metres and 4x100 metres relay in Moscow) to Koblenz in West Germany in order to put his reputation on the line against the two leading Americans, Stanley Floyd and Mel Lattany, both fresh and eager to take the shine off his gold medal.

'To be honest, I should never have run because I was shattered. There were two heats in Koblenz and I only qualified for the final as the eighth fastest. I still believe I didn't make the final on merit; I reckon the organisers let me in only because I was the Olympic gold medallist. Before the final, I went round the back of the stadium with my wife Margot and lay down on a bench. After a few minutes, I noticed I was bouncing around all over the place and said to Margot, "Will you stop shaking the bench?" I lay back down again and the same thing happened; but when I looked up, Margot was standing to one side. I was the one doing the involuntary shaking because of the state I was in.'

Unbeaten over 100 metres for 18 months – although he had never run against Wells – Floyd was particularly keen to reassert America's supremacy in the event. 'Even during the warm-up, he exuded arrogance, perhaps rightly so given his record. In my mind, I had no hope of doing well but crossed the line two one-hundredths of a second – about eight inches – in front. Floyd simply could not believe he'd been beaten and interrogated the chief timekeeper, the photo-finish official and the judges before accepting he was second. That race was something special to me; I'm convinced God was running for me – I'm a believer, though maybe not in the full sense of the word – and still believe someone was helping me – either God or the hopes of five million Scots.

'To his eternal credit, Lattany came straight over to me and said, "For what it's worth, Allan, you're the Olympic champion and you would have been the Olympic champion no matter who you ran against in Moscow." That meant as much to me as my gold medal because nobody will ever appreciate how big a win that was for me. I was the Olympic champion and I'd proved it in Koblenz.'

A decent but far from world-class triple-jumper and long-jumper until he decided to concentrate on sprinting, Wells was never the fastest man in the world but he made himself the most difficult to beat; by training mind and body with a ruthless intensity, Wells regularly trounced naturally quicker rivals by his sheer force of will. His training regime under the gaze of his wife and coach, Margot, drew curious glances from abroad, where his many hours of hill running, circuit training, punching a speed bag and hundred-metre hops on one foot and then the other were all regarded as a mighty strange way for a sprinter to behave.

But every avenue of possible advantage was explored, from enrolling in a Charles Atlas body-building course – even though he was already the well-developed son of a blacksmith – to refusing starting-blocks until forced to use them in Moscow because he thought an upright launch provided a fraction of a second advantage, and the all-in-one Lycra bodysuit that drew comparisons with the boys' comic book hero Wilson the Wonder Athlete.

Wells had announced himself as a sprinter of international standing at the 1978 Commonwealth Games in Edmonton, where he took the silver between gold medallist Don Quarrie and third-placed Hasley Crawford of Trinidad & Tobago (the Olympic champion in Montreal two years earlier), then struck gold in the 200 metres ahead of Guyana's James Gilkes. He won a second gold for Scotland in the 4x100 metres relay, spearheading the tartan quartet completed by Cameron Sharpe, David Jenkins and Drew McMaster.

Over the next four years, Wells enjoyed victories over each and every leading sprinter, including Floyd, Lattany, their fellow Americans Carl Lewis, Harvey Glance and Steve Williams, plus Canadian Ben Johnson at the 1981 IAAF Golden Sprint contest in Berlin. Johnson was left well beaten again in the 100 metres final at the 1982 Commonwealth Games in Brisbane, where Wells completed the sprint double by taking gold in the 200 metres, an event in which he finished in a rare dead-heat with England's Mike McFarlane.

'The 100 metres is unlike anything else in sport; it's different from scoring a try, from Formula One, from knocking a ball in a pocket on a snooker table. No disrespect to the marathon, the hurdles, the high jump or all the rest of them, but there's nothing to compare with an Olympic 100 metres final. You've got to be like a boxer before the first bell in a world title fight by being aggressive while remaining in control; you've got to be like a footballer preparing to take a penalty in the World Cup final by entering a trance-like state. It's the purest form of sport.'

To Allan Wells went an honoured place in the Olympic Hall of Fame; to Margaret Thatcher went a personal spot in sport's Hall of Shame.

48. THE WEMBLEY WIZARDS, 1928

England 1, Scotland 5

Beaten by Northern Ireland at Hampden, held to a draw by Wales in Wrexham, few gave Scotland any chance against the mighty English, especially when the selectors chose a forward line of titches in which Alex Jackson towered above all others at 5 ft 7 in.

'It's not a great side,' admitted one *Daily Record* scribe, ruing the surprise exclusion of Celtic goal machine Jimmy McGrory at centre-forward and Rangers' prolific striker Bob McPhail, plus both Old Firm skippers Davie Meiklejohn and Willie McStay from a defence that had to cope with the great Dixie Dean.

In the lounge of London's Regent Palace Hotel in The Strand at around ten o'clock on the night before the game, SFA President Robert Campbell took captain Jimmy McMullan aside to suggest that it might be an appropriate time to coax his players from the bar and deliver the kind of inspirational team talk that would raise their Caledonian passions and pride.

McMullan kept his address brief. 'The President wants us to discuss football but you all know what's expected of you tomorrow. All I've got to say is, go to your bed, put your head on your pillow and pray for rain.'

Someone, somewhere must have been listening to Scottish prayers: London awoke to a downpour and the Scots fans set off in the direction of Wembley – where the King and Queen of Afghanistan were among the crowd of 80,000 – displaying a new-found confidence that their tiny tartan terrors would glide across the heavy pitch while the lumbering English defenders would become stuck in the mud.

And so it proved. Alex Jackson struck a hat-trick, Alex James scored twice and Bob Kelly's 89th-minute counter was a trivial irritant on an otherwise perfect afternoon. 'England were not merely beaten,' wrote Ivan Sharpe in *Athletic News*. 'They were bewildered – run to a standstill, made to appear utterly inferior by a team whose play was as cultured and beautiful as I ever expect to see.'

Introducing the Wembley Wizards:

THE WEMBLEY WIZARDS, 1928

JACK HARKNESS (QUEEN'S PARK, GOALKEEPER)

Two months after Wembley, Harkness would turn professional when he signed for Hearts but it was as an amateur Corinthian that he played his most famous game.

He gained twelve international caps (winning on eight occasions) before retiring at the premature age of twenty-nine in 1937 to pursue a career in newspapers on the *Sunday Post* where, as a young trainee, it was my task to dictate his pithy reports on many a big match from Hampden while he puffed away contentedly on his pipe.

Jack Harkness's middle name was 'Diamond' and that is exactly what this gentleman was – a gem. He was awarded an MBE for his services to journalism in 1971.

JAMES NELSON (CARDIFF CITY, RIGHT-BACK)

Born in Greenock but raised in County Antrim from childhood, Nelson was originally selected to play in the Home International Championship by Northern Ireland until he revealed that he was Scottish.

Wembley was the scene of Nelson's three greatest triumphs: twelve months before starring for the Wizards, he had won an FA Cup winner's medal with Cardiff, an achievement he repeated with Newcastle United in 1932, the beaten finalists on both occasions being Arsenal.

TOMMY LAW (CHELSEA, LEFT-BACK)

Surprisingly preferred to Parkhead skipper Willie McStay, debutant Law won only two caps but was renowned for his dependability at Chelsea, where he made 318 appearances for the club.

His second appearance for Scotland proved to be less memorable than his debut, when he returned to Wembley in 1930 on a day on which England gained a measure of revenge for their humiliation two years earlier with a resounding 5–2 victory.

JIMMY GIBSON (ASTON VILLA, RIGHT-HALF)

Reputed to be the highest paid player in Scotland, Jimmy Gibson had been the subject of protracted interest from a clutch of English clubs ever since earning his first cap in the 1–0 defeat of England at Old Trafford in 1926.

Knowing that Partick Thistle desperately needed cash to complete the construction of the main stand at Firhill, Everton tabled a cheeky offer of just £4,000. 'That,' sniffed club chairman Tom Reid, 'wouldn't pay for the big fellow's boots.' Eventually, it took a world record transfer bid of £8,000 from Aston Villa to persuade the Jags to sell. Thistle got a new grandstand and Villa bought themselves a legend.

TOM 'TINY' BRADSHAW (BURY, CENTRE-HALF)

The giant-sized 'Tiny' was the last surviving Wizard when he died at the age of 82 in 1986. Curiously, although he had an outstanding game, completely nullifying Dixie Dean – who would score 60 goals for Everton that season – Bradshaw was never invited to represent his country again.

JIMMY McMULLAN (MANCHESTER CITY, LEFT-HALF)

Like Jimmy Gibson, McMullan was first capped while a Partick Thistle player in 1920, developing into the greatest half-back of his day. He was 30 before he took his silky skills to the English First Division when Manchester City finally succeeded in prising him away from the Jags, who were understandably reluctant to part with their inspirational skipper.

A keen student of the game, who would subsequently go into management, McMullan was happy to explain to the English exactly why their defence had been torn asunder by the fleet-footed Wizards. 'I want to emphasise that all our forwards are inherently clever. But I wish to say that the English tactics were wrong. The Saxon wing-halves paid more attention to our wingers than the inside-forwards – therefore the latter were given a lot of space. It is a common thing in England to let wing-halves, and not full-backs, mark the wingers. It doesn't pay and I don't know why they pursue it.'

ALEX JACKSON (HUDDERSFIELD TOWN, OUTSIDE-RIGHT)

Always a prolific goal-scorer and one of the main reasons that Huddersfield became the pre-eminent team in England, Jackson netted three goals, all from crosses supplied by Alan Morton on the other wing.

Despite his heroics, Jackson's international career was over at the age of 25 when, in one of their periodic flashes of madness, the SFA decided to ban Anglos from the national team. In Jackson's seventeen games in dark blue, Scotland won fifteen, drew one and lost one.

Jackson went on to play for Chelsea, for whom he scored 31 goals; he played in 78 games for them despite his appearances being restricted by injury. At the end of the 1933 season, Jackson was offered a fortune in wages by French club Nîmes and when Chelsea refused to release him, select him or improve his contract, he was forced to turn out for non-League outfits such as Ashton National and Margate before finishing his career across the Channel with Le Touquet. Jackson was killed in a road accident in 1946 while serving with the British Army in Egypt.

JIMMY DUNN (HIBERNIAN, INSIDE-RIGHT)

Known as the 'Clown Prince' at Easter Road because of his circus tricks with a ball at his feet, Dunn was one of football's great entertainers.

The pocket dynamo in the Wizards' midfield, Dunn covered every single one of Wembley's many blades of grass, inspiring a fabulous £5,000 transfer bid from Everton that Hibs could not afford to reject. It was a shrewd investment on Everton's behalf, the gifted playmaker inspiring the Toffees to the Second Division, First Division and FA Cup in successive seasons between 1931 and 1933.

HUGHIE GALLACHER (NEWCASTLE UNITED, CENTRE-FORWARD)

Football's original troubled genius, Gallacher stood only 5 ft 5 in. but scored a remarkable 406 goals from 554 games in his career, plus 23 in his 20 international appearances. Even so, he was a controversial selection given that he had not kicked a ball for over two months owing to injury.

A mazy dribbler who relied on guile and instinct, he was an obvious target for unscrupulous defenders and one St James' Park teammate described seeing Gallacher sitting in the dressing-room 'with pieces of flesh hanging from his legs and his socks and boots soaked in blood'. When referees refused to come to his rescue, Gallacher was wont to seek retribution on his own behalf and served numerous suspensions.

He became a hero on Tyneside when he captained Newcastle to the First Division championship in 1927 but was later declared bankrupt after his first marriage ended in a financially ruinous divorce. When his second wife died at an early age of a heart attack, Gallacher tried to fight depression with alcohol, and following a family dispute he committed suicide at the age of 54 in 1957 when he walked in front of the London–Edinburgh express on the line near his home in Gateshead.

ALEX JAMES (PRESTON NORTH END, INSIDE-LEFT)

On the six occasions that James and Gallacher appeared in the same team, Scotland won every game. That he won a meagre eight caps was due entirely to Preston's reluctance to release him for internationals, hastening his move to Arsenal, where he inspired the club to four championship titles and two FA Cup successes.

James' trademark baggy shorts (later adopted by Tom Finney in his honour) were worn to hide the 'long johns' he favoured in his constant battle against rheumatism, a complaint that hampered neither his ball control nor the quality of his passing.

According to the official club history: 'It is impossible to underestimate James' contribution to the successful Arsenal side of the 1930s. He was simply the key man.' Or as Arsenal manager George Allison put it: 'No one like him ever kicked a ball. He left the opposition looking on his departing figure with amazement.'

ALAN MORTON (RANGERS, OUTSIDE-LEFT)

The 'Wee Blue Devil', as the 5 ft 4 in. Morton was known at Ibrox, was a qualified mining engineer whose style of dress was as immaculate as his wing play, turning up for training in the bowler hat and rolled umbrella of the city gent.

Morton played 495 games for Rangers, scoring 115 goals and winning six Scottish championships. He also gained thirty-one international caps, an extraordinary total in an era when Scotland traditionally played only three matches a year.

Such is the abiding affection in which Morton is held at Rangers that one of the first things visitors to the stadium notice is his oil painting hanging at the top of the marble staircase in the main stand.

49. THE WEMBLEY WIZARDS, 1967

England 2, Scotland 3

It had been a particularly traumatic 18 months for Scottish football. In October 1965 we surrendered any chance of qualifying for the 1966 World Cup finals in Sassenachland by allowing an unremarkable Poland to score twice in the last five minutes to condemn us to a 2–1 defeat in front of 107,540 incredulous spectators at Hampden.

Our anguish was far from over. The following summer, we were required to endure the sight of England's players cavorting around Wembley with the Jules Rimet trophy that, so we still like to imagine, might have been ours had we secured an invitation to the shindig south of the border.

Come the 1967 Home International championship (which also served as a qualifying group for the 1968 European Championships in Italy), England had put together an unbeaten run stretching back 19 games to October '65. Roger Hunt was missing from their World Cup-winning line-up but with Jimmy Greaves replacing the Liverpool striker in attack, England were arguably stronger than they had been nine months earlier when they beat West Germany in the final.

Scotland crossed Hadrian's Wall under the command of a new manager in former Queen's Park and Rangers goalkeeper Bobby Brown, who surprised many by giving an international debut to Ronnie Simpson at the advanced age of 36. Unnecessarily, perhaps, the *Glasgow Herald* voiced the concern that the last Celtic keeper to face England at Wembley had been the hapless Frank Haffey in 1961, when we were routed 9–3.

With Bobby Murdoch and Jimmy Johnstone missing through injury, Brown sprang two further surprises by selecting the 20-year-old Sheffield Wednesday centre-forward Jim McCalliog for his first cap in midfield and by naming Celtic centre-forward Willie Wallace on the right wing.

In the *Daily Express*, the acerbic columnist Desmond Hackett was moved to opine: 'The Jocks don't deserve to be on the same pitch as Sir Alf Ramsey's world champions, seeing as they aren't much better than Luxembourg.' Although four of the side – Simpson, Wallace, Tommy Gemmell and Bobby Lennox – would become Lisbon Lions the following month, Ronnie McKinnon and John Greig would reach the European Cup-Winners' Cup final with Rangers, and Denis Law, Billy Bremner and Jim Baxter would feature in any all-time Tartan XI, even the Glasgow bookmakers rated England at 4-7 on, with Scotland 4-1 outsiders. 'On the face of it, we'd no reason to feel confident,' said skipper Greig. 'But we'd considered ourselves unfortunate not to qualify for the 1966 World Cup finals and felt we had a point to prove.'

The only survivor of the team humiliated six years earlier, Law was fired up as never before. He had not been able to bring himself to watch the World Cup final, preferring to play golf that afternoon. When he walked off the 18th green, he threw his clubs in the boot of his car and drove home rather than join the scenes of jubilation he could see through the clubhouse windows. When he returned to Old Trafford to meet up with Bobby Charlton and Nobby Stiles after the summer break, he studiously made no mention of his Manchester United teammates' roles in England's World Cup triumph.

Baxter was another with a personal score to settle. Slim Jim's career had been in inexorable decline since 1965, when he left Rangers for Sunderland, where he was viewed as a serial party animal who was living on his past reputation; could he produce one last performance of true majesty before the ravages of drink would reduce him to a cruel caricature of his former self? In the dressing-room before the game, Baxter had been at his gallus best as he listened to Brown deliver his final team talk. 'See this English lot?' interjected a Fife voice. 'They can play nane.'

From the moment Law scored with a typically intuitive finish in the 27th minute, Scotland were a class above the world champions to the gleeful delight of the 30,000-strong Tartan Army. Full-backs Tommy Gemmell and Eddie McCreadie joined Wallace and Lennox on their rampages down the touchline, reducing Ramsey's 'wingless wonders' to headless chickens.

By the time Lennox added a second in the 78th minute and Law went agonisingly close to a third goal with a sumptuous chip that inspired a wonder save from England keeper Gordon Banks, Baxter was in his pomp. With his shirt flapping outside his shorts and socks rolled down to his ankles, Slim Jim teased and tormented the World Cup holders by playing keepie-uppie underneath the twin towers.

'Who are you, son?' he enquired breezily as Nobby Stiles became the next English player to step forward in a vain attempt to deprive the King of Scots of the ball bobbing back and forth twixt instep and knee. 'Jimmy Clitheroe?' (See Bill Shankly entry.) 'I shall cherish for a long time the memory of Baxter slowing down the game to almost walking pace, insouciantly juggling the ball with instep, forehead and knees, while

Stiles, no more than a couple of yards away, bobbed up and down, unsure whether to make his challenge at knee or head level,' wrote Glyn Edwards in the *Glasgow Herald*.

At one stage, Baxter, Bremner and Gemmell played 'piggy-in-the-middle' with Alan Ball, exchanging upwards of 20 passes as the little midfielder scurried between the trio in a vain attempt to snaffle possession and end the torment. 'A myth grew up that I sat on the ball on one occasion, waiting for Stiles to make his tackle,' recalled Baxter. 'But I did no such thing. I didn't mind taking the mickey but that would have been a step too far, even for me. And anyway, that would have made us the same height and the wee man might have been tempted to bestow a Glesca kiss upon yours truly and I wanted to keep things friendly like.'

The game ended in a mini goal rush, with Jackie Charlton netting in the 84th minute, McCalliog restoring Scotland's two-goal advantage with a splendid strike three minutes later and Geoff Hurst grabbing a second for England in the last minute, but there was no disputing the Wembley Wizards' overwhelming supremacy. 'Only Scotland could hump someone 3–2,' bemoaned The Lawman. 'But Jim wanted to play to the crowd at 3–1 when we might have scored five or six. When I screamed, "Let's give them a doing," Jim would smile that infuriating smile of his and reply, "Naw, let's just take the piss out of them." But he was magnificent that day, just magnificent, and you could never stay angry with Jim for long.'

Enraged at the manner in which his world champions were utterly outclassed, come the final whistle Sir Alf mumbled a grudging 'well done' to Bobby Brown, then scurried off down the tunnel never again to raise the subject of Wembley '67 in public. 'Oh, it hurt, all right,' explained Bobby Charlton. 'We knew it had to happen, that we had to lose to someone after winning the World Cup. But the fact it was Scotland made it all the more painful. When I returned to Old Trafford for pre-season training after the 1966 World Cup, Denis could barely bring himself to look at me. He muttered something about hoping I'd had a nice holiday and turned away. Which is why to this day Denis will tell you how that victory in '67 made the Scots world champions.'

On Fleet Street, much was made of the fact that England had been hampered by an early injury to Jackie Charlton, who made a goal-scoring switch to centre-forward, this being in the days before substitutes. What the English hacks chose to ignore was that four years earlier at Wembley, Rangers' left-back Eric Caldow had been carried off with a broken leg after only six minutes, requiring outside-left Davie Wilson to move into defence and leaving Scotland with just ten men. Result: England 1 (Bryan Douglas), Scotland 2 (Jim Baxter 2).

And so it came to pass that on the golden-rayed evening of Scotland's most famous football triumph, Baxter sashayed into the Café Royal in Piccadilly in the beaming company of The Lawman. 'Walking into the Café Royal was almost as much fun as playing England off the park,' Baxter would recall of that night. 'There was this big, round table in the middle of the floor with 12 hairy-legged Highlanders sitting round it in kilts. Instead of a tablecloth, however, the table was covered in this huge swatch of lush Wembley turf. They had the kitty in the middle and all their drinks lined up on top of their precious cutting from Wembley.'

ENGLAND / SCOTLAND

Gordon Banks (Leicester City) / Ronnie Simpson (Celtic)
George Cohen (Fulham) / Tommy Gemmell (Celtic)
Ray Wilson (Everton) / Eddie McCreadie (Chelsea)
Nobby Stiles (Manchester United) / John Greig (Rangers)
Jackie Charlton (Leeds United) / Ronnie McKinnon (Rangers)
Bobby Moore (West Ham United) / Jim Baxter (Sunderland)
Alan Ball (Everton) / Willie Wallace (Celtic)
Jimmy Greaves (Tottenham Hotspur) / Billy Bremner (Leeds United)
Bobby Charlton (Manchester United) / Jim McCalliog (Sheffield Wednesday)
Geoff Hurst (West Ham United) / Denis Law (Manchester United)
Martin Peters (West Ham United) / Bobby Lennox (Celtic)

50. DAVID WILKIE MBE

Swimming

Born: Colombo, Sri Lanka, 8 March 1954

CAREER:
Olympic Games:
  Munich 1972: 200 metres breaststroke – Silver
  Montreal 1976: 200 metres breaststroke – Gold; 100 metres
    breaststroke – Silver
World Championships:
  1973 Belgrade: 200 metres breaststroke – Gold; 200 metres
    individual medley – Bronze
  1975 Cali, Colombia: 100 metres breaststroke – Gold; 200
    metres breaststroke – Gold; 4x100 metres medley relay –
    Bronze
European Championships:
  1974 Vienna: 200 metres breaststroke – Gold; 200 metres
    individual medley – Gold; 4x100 metres medley relay –
    Silver
Commonwealth Games:
  1970 Edinburgh: 200 metres breaststroke – Bronze
  1974 Christchurch: 200 metres breaststroke – Gold; 200
    metres individual medley – Gold; 100 metres breaststroke
    – Silver

Was it any wonder that David Wilkie came to find training an irksome chore during Edinburgh's bleak midwinter? Raised in Sri Lanka, where his Aberdeen-born father was an executive on a tea plantation, Wilkie had learned to swim in the pool of the Colombo Swimming Club, where even in January the afternoon temperature hovered around 90 degrees Fahrenheit and a cooling drink awaited in the colonial clubhouse. A few yards away stood the golden sands and swaying palm trees fringing the warm waters of the Indian Ocean.

It was a paradise lost when the eleven-year-old Wilkie, who had been competing in galas from the age of eight, arrived in the Scottish capital to be enrolled as a boarder at Daniel Stewart's College, where he joined the Warrender Park Swimming Club. Now a twenty-first-century facility to rank with any in the country, in 1965 the Warrender had not changed much since it opened in the Victorian age, with its cold tiled walls and choking chlorine. 'It was like swimming in the Forth,' recalled Wilkie, who missed many an early-morning training session when he could not bring himself to climb out of bed. 'It was choppy; it was freezing cold. I just didn't get swimming. I couldn't understand why people went up and down doing laps.'

Despite its austere aspect, the Warrender had a reputation for producing champions and Wilkie, a natural talent but notorious slacker renowned for spending the minimum possible hours in the pool with coach Frank Thomas, swiftly joined the club's roll of honour. He celebrated turning 16 by winning the bronze medal in the 200 metres breaststroke at the 1970 Commonwealth Games in his home city, shearing a remarkable 30 seconds off his previous personal best time. 'I hardly trained. I didn't know what to expect – I really didn't know what swimming was all about, competing at that level. I was really totally unprepared and unready. And therefore to get a bronze was a freak in many respects, both in my eyes and in the eyes of my coach.'

Always a free spirit, Wilkie had entered the Commonwealth Games pool in Edinburgh resplendent in a cap, the first swimmer to do so in competition, and the capped crusader would later introduce another innovation when he appeared in goggles, a fashion statement that everyone would follow. Not that Wilkie suggested the cap – worn to keep his flowing locks under control, while the goggles were to combat a lifelong allergy to chlorinated water – was the reason behind his unexpected success. 'The home support made a hell of a difference. Because I was a lazy little devil, I didn't go training; I hated training. If you don't do the work, no matter how talented you are, you don't get any rewards. And swimming being a hard sport, you really have to put in the hours and get in that water. I just didn't do that. I couldn't be bothered. I was 16. Not that I had anything else to do with my time; I just didn't like swimming.'

Even when Wilkie returned from the 1972 Olympics in Munich, where he finished second in the 200 metres breaststroke to the Californian John Hencken – who would become his greatest rival – British team coach Dave Haller described him as 'the most unfit athlete at the Games and yet he still won a silver medal'.

Prior to the Olympics, Wilkie had been ranked 25th in the world; if he could reach the final as second fastest qualifier and then push Hencken all the way without pushing himself in training, then just what could he achieve were he to adopt the lifestyle of the elite athlete? Intrigued by that conundrum, the leading universities in America rushed to offer him a scholarship in his chosen field of Marine Biology (he would subsequently switch to English & Mass Communication); even Harvard, the original Ivy League seat of learning which numbers Franklin D. Roosevelt, John F. Kennedy and Barack Obama among its alumni, came a-wooing.

Still a beach boy at heart despite his many years away from Sri Lanka, Wilkie was fully aware that the climate of Massachusetts in the winter months was even harsher than that of Auld Reekie. So, in January 1973 he began his freshman year at the University of Miami, where he was introduced to the spartan regime of swimming coach Charlie Hodgson.

To the previously work-shy Wilkie, life in Miami proved to be something of a culture shock. Hodgson's training schedule consisted of a gruelling four hours a day, Monday to Saturday, in the magnificent open air pool, covering anything up to 20,000 metres a day. But there was method in this apparent madness: in September that year, Wilkie defeated Hencken to win the 200 metres breaststroke title at the World Championships in Belgrade (he also won a bronze medal in the 200 metres individual medley), setting a world record in the process.

Proud Scot that he was, against all perceived wisdom Wilkie insisted upon competing for his country at the 1974 Commonwealth Games in Christchurch, even though they were staged just seven months prior to the vastly more important European Championships in Vienna. Jet-lagged and exhausted by his selection in three events, he won the 200 metres breaststroke and 200 metres individual medley but was bitterly disappointed to have to settle for a silver medal in the 100 metres breaststroke.

Wilkie was also denied his golden treble in Vienna when, as the finalists in the 100 metres breaststroke dived into the pool, he was distracted by a cow horn sounded by a spectator (ah, the famous Austrian sense of humour) and stopped swimming in the belief that the noise signalled a false start.

Cali in Colombia, the venue for the 1975 World Championships, proved equally inhospitable for entirely different reasons. The hotel accommodation was distinctly one star and most of the British team suffered food poisoning before the competition began. Even given these hardships, Wilkie was at his imperious best in winning both the 100 metres and 200 metres breaststroke events and only being deprived of twin world records by the powerful crosswinds that blew over the outdoor pool.

By the 1976 Montreal Olympics, Wilkie had acquired a transatlantic accent and the long hair and moustache of a West Coast rock star but remained Scottish to the core. 'I will always remain Scottish, no matter what happens,' he told the BBC in an interview before the Games. 'Even though my accent changes, even though I live in the United States, I still maintain that I am Scottish. And I always will do, even though I have only lived half my life in Scotland.'

To Hencken, the sprint specialist, went gold in the 100 metres breaststroke by 0.32 seconds but it was over the longer distance that Wilkie had focused his preparation. Bidding to become the first British male swimmer to win an Olympic title since Henry Taylor at London in 1908 (and become the only non-American to win one of the 13 gold medals on offer in Montreal), Wilkie allowed Hencken, swimming alongside him in the next lane, to lead for the first 100 metres before launching his attack.

By the third turn, the race as a contest was over as Wilkie pulled away to smash Hencken's world record by over three seconds, with the American trailing in his wash in what was unanimously voted by swimming journalists 'the Race of the Games'. As Haller saw it: 'David was absolutely phenomenal. That swim in Montreal is still probably the greatest individual performance I have ever witnessed. The most beautiful fluid technique, powered by the strongest legs in swimming. It was like watching a periscope cut through the water when he charged up the third or fourth lap of a 200 metres. Of course these days you are allowed to duck your head under the surface and can go even quicker, but David is still comfortably the best the event has ever seen.

'And he was such a gentleman, possibly the nicest bloke I have met. We never exchanged a cross word at training, we just worked away together quietly. But he was a man of steel in the pool. Once he started taking the sport and his event seriously, it was always a matter of who would finish second.'

Wilkie retired after Montreal at the tender age of 22 but the memory lingers on. 'The emotion of winning an Olympic gold medal is like getting all your Christmas presents wrapped up in one. You feel every emotion: joy, happiness, relief and pride – pride in being Scottish, pride in being British, pride in winning for the country, pride in winning for yourself and your parents.'

REFERENCES AND BIBLIOGRAPHY

TOMMY ARMOUR:
And Then Arnie Told Chi Chi, by Don Wade, published by Contemporary
    Books, 1993
Inside Golf, by Bob Chieger and Pat Sullivan, published by Atheneum, 1985
World Golf Hall of Fame website profile

JIM BAXTER:
Daily Telegraph, author's interview notes
Slim Jim Baxter, by Ken Gallacher, published by Virgin Books, 2003
The Guardian, obituary

IAN BLACK:
The Scotsman
BBC Sports Personality of the Year website profile
Scottish Sports Hall of Fame

JAMES BRAID:
World Golf Hall of Fame website profile
Elie Golf Club website profile
Golf Legends website profile

BILLY BREMNER:
Scottish Football Hall of Fame website profile
The Book of Football Quotations, by Peter Ball and Phil Shaw, published by
    Stanley Paul, 1984
The Independent, obituary
'Still Greatly Missed', LeedsUnited.com

GORDON BROWN:
Rugby-Heroes.net website profile
Giants of Scottish Rugby, by Jeff Connor, published by Mainstream
    Publishing, 2003

Daily Telegraph, author's interview notes
United States Soccer Hall of Fame website
British Lions website

KEN BUCHANAN:
Daily Telegraph, author's interview notes
Sports Illustrated
World Boxing Hall of Fame profile

SIR MATT BUSBY:
Official Illustrated History of Manchester United, published by Simon & Schuster, 2008
The Munich Air Disaster, by Stephen R. Morrin, published by Gill & Macmillan, 2007
Sir Matt Busby: A Tribute, by Rick Glanville, published by Manchester United, 1998

FINLAY CALDER:
Giants of Scottish Rugby, by Jeff Connor, published by Mainstream Publishing, 2003
Rugby-Heroes.net website profile
British Lions website

WILLIE CARSON:
Daily Telegraph, author's interview notes
The Book of Racing Quotations, by Nick Robinson and David Llewellyn, published by Stanley Paul, 1988
BBC: A Sporting Nation website

JIM CLARK:
Grand Prix Hall of Fame website profile
The Greatest, by Daley Thompson, Stewart Binns and Tom Lewis, published by Boxtree, 1996
Jim Clark: The Legend Lives On, by Graham Gauld, published by Motorbooks International, 1989

KENNY DALGLISH:
Liverpool FC website
English Football Hall of Fame website
The Book of Football Quotations, by Peter Ball and Phil Shaw, published by Stanley Paul, 1984

REFERENCES AND BIBLIOGRAPHY

The Greatest, by Daley Thompson, Stewart Binns and Tom Lewis, published by Boxtree, 1996

SIR ALEX FERGUSON:
Managing My Life, by Sir Alex Ferguson with Hugh McIlvanney, published by Hodder & Stoughton, 1999
The National, author's interview notes

ELENOR GORDON:
Daily Mail, John Greechan interview
The Herald, Doug Gillon interview
British Olympic Association website

HAMPDEN PARK:
Queen's Park website
Hampden: Scotland's National Stadium website

GAVIN HASTINGS:
Daily Telegraph, author's interview notes
Giants of Scottish Rugby, by Jeff Connor, published by Mainstream Publishing, 2003
Rugby-Heroes.net website profile
British Lions website profile

STEPHEN HENDRY:
The Book of Snooker and Billiards Quotations, by Eugene Weber and Clive Everton, published by Stanley Paul, 1993
The Greatest, by Daley Thompson, Stewart Binns and Tom Lewis, published by Boxtree, 1996
South Wales Echo, Sarah Bunney interview

SIR CHRIS HOY:
Chris Hoy: The Autobiography, by Chris Hoy, published by HarperSport, 2009
Sunday Herald, author's interview notes
Heroes, Villains and Velodromes, by Richard Moore, published by HarperSport, 2008

CAROLINE INNES:
Daily Telegraph, author's interview notes

ANDY IRVINE:

Giants of Scottish Rugby, by Jeff Connor, published by Mainstream Publishing, 2003
Rugby-Heroes.net website profile
British Lions website profile
The Scotland Rugby Miscellany, by Richard Bath, published by Vision Sports Publishing, 2007

DOUGLAS JARDINE:

Daily Telegraph, author's interview notes
Wisden Cricketers' Almanack
As I Said at the Time: A Lifetime in Cricket, by E.W. Swanton, published by HarperCollins, 1983

JIMMY JOHNSTONE:

Jinky, by Jim Black, published by Sphere, 2010
Daily Telegraph, author's interview notes
The Guardian, obituary
Scottish Football Quotations, by Kenny MacDonald, published by Mainstream Publishing, 1994

DENIS LAW:

Daily Telegraph, author's interview notes
English Football Hall of Fame profile

ERIC LIDDELL:

The Greatest, by Daley Thompson, Stewart Binns and Tom Lewis, published by Boxtree, 1996
Reuters
Scottish Sports Hall of Fame profile

THE LISBON LIONS:

Only a Game?, by Eamon Dunphy, published by Penguin, 1985
European Cup 1955–80, by John Motson and John Rawlinson, published by Queen Anne Press, 1980
The Lisbon Lions: The Real Inside Story of Celtic's Triumph, by Billy McNeill et al., published by Black & White, 2007

SANDY LYLE:

To the Fairway Born, by Sandy Lyle with Robert Philip, published by Headline, 2006

REFERENCES AND BIBLIOGRAPHY

European Tour website profile
PGA Tour website profile

BENNY LYNCH:
Benny: The Life and Times of a Fighting Legend, by John Burrowes, published
    by Fontana Press, 1984
World Boxing Hall of Fame profile
www.bennylynch.co.uk

LIZ McCOLGAN:
Daily Telegraph, author's interview notes
BBC profile
The Herald, Doug Gillon interview
Scottish Sports Hall of Fame profile

BOBBY McGREGOR:
BBC: A Sporting Nation website profile
Falkirk Wheel website profile
Scottish Sports Hall of Fame profile
British Olympic Association profile

DAVE MACKAY:
The Real Mackay, by Martin Knight, published by Mainstream Publishing,
    2005
National Football Museum Hall of Fame profile by Robert Galvin
FourFourTwo magazine
www.derbycounty-mad.com

KEN McKINLAY:
Leicester Lions website
Blantyre's Hall of Fame profile
Barry Briggs, author's interview notes

IAN McLAUCHLAN:
Giants of Scottish Rugby, by Jeff Connor, published by Mainstream
    Publishing, 2003
Rugby-Heroes.net website profile
British Lions website
The Scotland Rugby Miscellany, by Richard Bath, published by Vision
    Sports Publishing, 2007

SCOTTISH SPORTING LEGENDS

G.P.S. MACPHERSON

The Scotland Rugby Miscellany, by Richard Bath, published by Vision Sports Publishing, 2007
BBC.co.uk
Scottish Sports Hall of Fame profile
International Rugby Union: A Compendium of Scotland's Matches, by John McL. Davidson, published by Polygon, 1994

DICK McTAGGART:

BBC: A Sporting Nation website profile
Daily Mail, Neil Allen interview
The Courier

ROBERT MILLAR:

Cycle Sport, article by Kenny Pryde
A Peiper's Tale, by Allan Peiper, published by Mousehold Press, 2005
In Search of Robert Millar, by Richard Moore, published by HarperCollins, 2007
Daily Mail

COLIN MONTGOMERIE:

The Real Monty, by Colin Montgomerie with Lewine Mair, published by Orion, 2003
Sunday Times, Lynne Greenwood interview
Press Association
Life Swings, by Nick Faldo with Robert Philip, published by Headline, 2004
European Tour profile
PGA Tour profile
Sports Illustrated

OLD TOM MORRIS/YOUNG TOM MORRIS:

To the Fairway Born, by Sandy Lyle with Robert Philip, published by Headline, 2006
World Golf Hall of Fame website profile

ANDY MURRAY:

The National, author's interview notes
ATP Tour profile

GRAEME OBREE:

The Independent, Alastair Campbell interview

The Flying Scotsman, by Graeme Obree, published by Birlinn, 2004
BBC: A Sporting Nation website

RODNEY PATTISON:
Daily Telegraph, author's interview notes
The Greatest, by Daley Thompson, Stewart Binns and Tom Lewis, published by Boxtree, 1996

ST ANDREWS:
The World Atlas of Golf Courses, by Bob Ferrier, published by Bantam Books, 1991
Inside Golf, by Bob Chieger and Pat Sullivan, published by Atheneum, 1985
Life Swings, by Nick Faldo with Robert Philip, published by Headline, 2004
The Guinness Dictionary of Sports Quotations, by Colin Jarman, published by Guinness Publishing, 1990

BILL SHANKLY:
The Book of Football Quotations, by Peter Ball and Phil Shaw, published by Stanley Paul, 1984
Liverpool Echo, Chris Bascombe article
Shankly, by Bill Shankly, published by Arthur Barker Ltd, 1976
It's Much More Important Than That, by Stephen F. Kelly, published by Virgin Books, 1997

JOCK STEIN:
BBC: A Sporting Nation website
Jock Stein: The Celtic Years, by Tom Campbell and David Potter, published by Mainstream Publishing, 1999
Scottish Football Quotations, by Kenny MacDonald, published by Mainstream Publishing, 1994
Reuters obituary

SIR JACKIE STEWART:
The Greatest, by Daley Thompson, Stewart Binns and Tom Lewis, published by Boxtree, 1996
The Guinness Dictionary of Sports Quotations, by Colin Jarman, published by Guinness Publishing, 1990
Winning Is Not Enough: The Autobiography, by Sir Jackie Stewart, published by Headline, 2009

Grand Prix Hall of Fame biography
BOBBY THOMSON:
Daily Telegraph, author's interview notes
Baseball Hall of Fame profile

SAM TORRANCE:
Sunday Times, author's interview notes
Sam: The Autobiography, by Sam Torrance with Alan Fraser, published by
    BBC Books, 2003

ALLAN WELLS:
The Greatest, by Daley Thompson, Stewart Binns and Tom Lewis,
    published by Boxtree, 1996
Daily Telegraph, author's interview notes

THE WEMBLEY WIZARDS, 1928:
Sunday Post
Wikipedia

THE WEMBLEY WIZARDS, 1967:
The King, by Denis Law with Bob Harris, published by Bantam Press,
    2003
BBC: A Sporting Nation website
Scottish Football Quotations, by Kenny MacDonald, published by
    Mainstream Publishing, 1994

DAVID WILKIE:
Daily Telegraph, Brendan Gallagher interview
The Greatest, by Daley Thompson, Stewart Binns and Tom Lewis,
    published by Boxtree, 1996
Scottish Sports Hall of Fame website profile

Also:
Joe Baker: Arsenal FC official website
McCrae's Battalion: *McCrae's Battalion: The Story of the 16th Royal Scots*, by
    Jack Alexander, published by Mainstream Publishing, 2003
Murray Rose: ABC.net, Olympic Legends
James Naismith: BBC, The Canadian Who Invented Basketball
Rose Reilly: Scotsman Publications
Rubstic: Grand National website
Sir Arthur Conan Doyle: *Wisden Cricketer's Almanack*

REFERENCES AND BIBLIOGRAPHY

Donald Budge: *100 Wimbledon Championships,* by John Barrett, published
by Willow Books, 1986
Tony Hand: author's interview notes
Ed McIlvenny: US Soccer Hall of Fame profile

ACKNOWLEDGEMENTS

I would like to thank Sir Alex Ferguson, who never forgets a promise, even though he probably has more pressing duties than penning forewords for books and sharing his reminiscences of Jock Stein, among many others. The man truly is a legend.

My thanks, too, to those friends and acquaintances such as Denis Law, Sandy Lyle, Caroline Innes, Sam Torrance and Andy Murray who have given their time on numerous occasions – usually with a bottle of red wine to hand. I will also raise a glass to those whom I had the privilege of knowing but who are no longer around to share their wit and mischief: Jimmy Johnstone, Jim Baxter, Gordon Brown and Bobby Thomson.

To Bill Campbell, Graeme Blaikie, Kate McLelland and Ailsa Bathgate at Mainstream, and my editor Chris Stone, my heartfelt gratitude for their encouragement, advice and untiring work. Thanks to my agent Danny Phillips and researcher Ian Garside for their efforts on my behalf; the drinks are on you.

I am also indebted to the many writers and journalists – a list of whom appears at the back of this book – whose work proved so invaluable in our research.

And, finally, thank you to my wife, Yvonne, who watched me lying in a hammock on a beach on the Thai island of Koh Samui for three months before interrupting my reverie with the suggestion: *Why don't you write a book about . . .?*